Global Jihadism

D0223578

"Jarret Brachman's brilliant analysis of the ideology that inspires and sustains al-Qaida and other violent Jihadist movements will greatly enhance understanding of the threat they pose to peace and security. It is an invaluable aid for those engaged in combating the recruitment of future generations of Jihadist suicide terrorists."

Paul Wilkinson, Emeritus Professor of International Relations,
University of St Andrews

"*Global Jihadism* is an important contribution to the literature on al-Qaida and Salafist Jihadism specifically and terrorism in general. Brachman masterfully dissects the ideology and strategy as well as the information operations and actual plots and attacks that have sustained this movement since 9/11. The book provides a timely and incisive analysis of the most pressing security challenge of our time."

Bruce Hoffman, School of Foreign Service, Georgetown University

"*Global Jihadism* is an erudite, well-organized, and interesting tour through the world of transnational Jihadist terrorism that will be of interest to specialists, students, and interested readers alike. Jarret Brachman has written an authoritative account of this complex subject."

Peter Bergen, author of *Holy War, Inc.* and *The Osama bin Laden I Know*

Global Jihadism: Theory and Practice exposes the core doctrine and strategy of today's global Jihadist movement.

The first half of the book explores the ideas upon which groups such as al-Qaida are built, including the concepts of *Jihad*, *al-Wala wal-Bara*, *Takfir*, and *Tawhid*. Jarret Brachman exposes a genre of Jihadist strategic scholarship that has been virtually ignored in the West and helps to situate it within the broader Salafist religious movement. The second half explores the thinking and activities of al-Qaida's propaganda machine, explaining its intricacies and idiosyncrasies. It includes case studies on the rise and fall of global Jihadist terrorism in Saudi Arabia post-9/11, and highlights the explosive results of bringing theory to bear on practice in the United Kingdom over the past twenty years. The book concludes by providing innovative strategies for combating the global Jihadist ideology.

This book will be of much interest to students of terrorism studies, al-Qaida, international security, and Middle Eastern politics, as well as to professionals in the field of counter-terrorism.

Jarret M. Brachman is Director of Research in the Combating Terrorism Center at the United States Military Academy, West Point, and an Adjunct Professor at New York University's Center for Global Affairs.

Series: Political Violence

Series Editors: Paul Wilkinson and David C. Rapoport

This book series contains sober, thoughtful and authoritative academic accounts of terrorism and political violence. Its aim is to produce a useful taxonomy of terror and violence through comparative and historical analysis in both national and international spheres. Each book discusses origins, organizational dynamics, and outcomes of particular forms and expressions of political violence.

Aviation Terrorism and Security
Paul Wilkinson and Brian M. Jenkins (eds)

Counter-Terrorist Law and Emergency Powers in the United Kingdom, 1922–2000
Laura K. Donohue

The Democratic Experience and Political Violence
David C. Rapoport and Leonard Weinberg (eds)

Inside Terrorist Organizations
David C. Rapoport (ed.)

The Future of Terrorism
Max Taylor and John Horgan (eds)

The IRA, 1968–2000
An analysis of a secret army
J. Bowyer Bell

Millennial Violence
Past, present and future
Jeffrey Kaplan (ed.)

Right-Wing Extremism in the Twenty-First Century
Peter H. Merkl and Leonard Weinberg (eds)

Terrorism Today
Christopher C. Harmon

The Psychology of Terrorism
John Horgan

Research on Terrorism
Trends, achievements and failures
Andrew Silke (ed.)

A War of Words
Political violence and public debate in Israel
Gerald Cromer

Root Causes of Suicide Terrorism
Globalization of martyrdom
Ami Pedahzur (ed.)

Terrorism versus Democracy (Second Edition)
The Liberal state response
Paul Wilkinson

Countering Terrorism and WMD
Creating a global counter-terrorism network
Peter Katona, Michael Intriligator and John Sullivan (eds)

Mapping Terrorism Research
State of the art, gaps and future direction
Magnus Ranstorp (ed.)

The Ideological War on Terror
World-wide strategies for counter-terrorism
Anne Aldis and Graeme P. Herd (eds)

The IRA and Armed Struggle
Rogelio Alonso

Homeland Security in the UK
Future preparedness for terrorist attack since 9/11
Paul Wilkinson

Terrorism Today (Second Edition)
Christopher C. Harmon

Understanding Terrorism and Political Violence
The life cycle of birth, growth, transformation, and demise
Dipak K. Gupta

Global Jihadism
Theory and practice
Jarret M. Brachman

Global Jihadism

Theory and practice

Jarret M. Brachman

LONDON AND NEW YORK

First published 2009
by Routledge
2 Park Square, Milton Park, Abingdon, Oxon, OX14 4RN

Simultaneously published in the USA and Canada
by Routledge
270 Madison Avenue, New York, NY 10016

Routledge is an imprint of the Taylor & Francis Group, an informa business

Typeset in Times by
Keystroke, 28 High Street, Tettenhall, Wolverhampton
Printed and bound in Great Britain by
TJ International Ltd, Padstow, Cornwall

British Library Cataloguing in Publication Data
A catalogue record for this book is available from the British Library

Library of Congress Cataloging in Publication Data
Brachman, Jarret.
Global jihadism : theory and practice / Jarret M. Brachman.
p. cm. – (Cass series on political violence)
Includes bibliographical references and index.
ISBN 978–0–415–45242–7 (pbk.) – ISBN 978–0–415–45241–0 (hardback) – ISBN
978–0–203–89505–4 (e book) 1. Jihad. 2. Qaida (Organization) 3. Islamic fundamentalism.
4. Terrorism–Religious aspects–Islam. I. Title.
BP182.B73 2008
320.5'57–dc22
2007051286

ISBN10: 0–415–45241–4 (hbk)
ISBN10: 0–415–45242–2 (pbk)
ISBN10: 0–203–89505–3 (ebk)

ISBN13: 978–0–415–45241–0 (hbk)
ISBN13: 978–0–415–45242–7 (pbk)
ISBN13: 978–0–203–89505–4 (ebk)

For my Dad,
Daniel F. Brachman

Contents

Acknowledgments

The brave men and women who selflessly dedicate their lives to public service in the professions of arms, law enforcement, intelligence, first response and emergency management are the quiet heroes of this war. It is my sincere hope that this book serves as a resource for them and those seeking to serve the greater good.

This book would not have been possible without the constant love, support and indulgence that I received from my best friend and loving wife, Erin, my little hammy, Adam, and my little princess, Kayla. I also thank my parents, my little sister, Bryn, other members of my family, my mentors and my friends for their encouragement and advice throughout this process.

I especially want to acknowledge the recent passing of an American hero, General Wayne A. Downing. In the three years that I had the honor to serve under him at West Point's Combating Terrorism Center, I gained a lifetime of lessons about being a professional, a leader, a scholar and a man.

Part I
Theory

1 Introduction

We are the lions of war who do not scare . . . We are the soldiers who sleep on the backs of horses and if someone calls for jihad . . . we will answer that call.

Abu_Uqla, Jihadist internet user

Few Saudi boys coming of age during the 1980s could resist the desire to fight against invading Soviet forces in Afghanistan, former al-Qaida commander Abd al-Aziz al-Muqrin recalled during a 2003 interview with al-Qaida's media arm in Saudi Arabia.[1] How could they? Kids across the peninsula came to view these *mujahidin* (those who struggle for Islam) as heroes. In Saudi Arabia, as was the case through much of the Islamic world at the time, regularly updated news about the campaign could be heard in official government statements, in school classrooms, in the daily newspapers, in mosques, and on local television stations. The Saudi regime even began subsidizing airline tickets in order to facilitate the movement of fighters to Afghanistan. The multifaceted Islamic concept of Jihad assumed a single meaning for most children across the Arab world at this time: violent struggle against an enemy occupier.

By 1980, the Afghan Jihad had become a funding priority for many countries, some of which were seeking to suppress the military expansion of the Soviet Union, while others were looking to deny Iran's attempts to bolster the influence of their Shia brethren in Pakistan and Afghanistan.[2] The wealth of resources pouring into the country, combined with the emotionally rousing call to resist the occupation of infidel invaders in Muslim lands, helped to make the Afghan Jihad experience a banner under which thousands of Jihadist-minded Muslims would fight for decades to follow.

The Saudi regime, in particular, began saturating the Afghan battlefield with money, weaponry, and young fighters by way of Pakistan. These armed cadres of Islamic youth traveling from around the Islamic world, or "Afghan Arabs," and their Pakistani and Afghan brothers in arms, became known to the world as the *mujahidin*. The only obstacles for Muslim boys seeking to wage Jihad in Afghanistan, carped Muqrin in his al-Qaida interview, were the Saudi religious scholars who believed that parental permission was a prerequisite for any such Jihadist venture to Afghanistan.

Because most of the *ulama*, or religious authorities—the revered community of scholars in the Sunni Islamic world—defined the Islamic concept of Jihad (struggling for the sake of God) as a community-wide responsibility, parents were able to impede their children's journey knowing that others had heeded the call on behalf of the *ummah*, or the global community of Muslims. Given that most of these young boys, raised in Saudi Arabia's staunchly puritanical interpretation of Islam known as *Wahabism*, wanted to be right with God, they grudgingly complied with their parents' prohibitions on fighting in Afghanistan until they were of age. This is not to say that the Saudi youth movement simply accepted the ruling of the Saudi *ulama*, however. To the contrary, Saudi kids like Muqrin pressed their local scholars hard, hoping that they would revise their interpretation of Jihad as a community responsibility.

At long last, the 17-year-old Muqrin received a *fatwa*, or religious edict, from one Islamic scholar who interpreted the concept of Jihad not as a community responsibility but as an individual responsibility. For Muqrin, the implication of this was clear: he would be religiously justified in violating the sacred Islamic tenet of filial piety for the greater good of fulfilling God's call to each Muslim to wage Jihad. Muqrin dropped out of secondary school and went to Afghanistan. He went on to have a career in Jihadist insurgency and terrorism operations. His life as a *mujahid* would culminate with his death in 2004 while serving as the director of al-Qaida operations in Saudi Arabia.

Abd al-Aziz al-Muqrin, or Abu Hajar as he became affectionately known within the global Jihadist community, was just one of thousands of Muslim boys who have come of age believing that violent Jihad is a religiously mandated venture. He saw himself as the vanguard of a quickly diminishing group without which Islam, as God intended it, would dissapear into oblivion. As such, he and his Jihadist brothers were uniquely qualified to wage holy warfare, to judge the religiosity of other Muslims, and to establish God's kingdom on Earth in the form of the Islamic Caliphate, a state ruled entirely by Islamic law.

The al-Qaida terrorist organization published its 16-question interview with Muqrin in the debut, October 2003 issue of its internet magazine, *Sawt al-Jihad* (*Voice of the Jihad*). The article's recounting of Muqrin's life story reflects exactly what one might expect from a career *mujahid*: radically puritanical views on Islam, deep hatred for American and Jewish influence over Arab governments and societies, unwavering deference to al-Qaida's high command, and a desire above all else to fight and die for the Jihadist cause. The life of Abd al-Aziz al-Muqrin, like so many others of his generation and the next, sheds profound light on the mindset of the modern Jihadist.

Jihadism

"Jihadism" is a clumsy and controversial term. It refers to the peripheral current of extremist Islamic thought whose adherents demand the use of violence in order to oust non-Islamic influence from traditionally Muslim lands en route to establishing true Islamic governance in accordance with *Sharia*, or God's law. The expression's most significant limitation is that it contains the word *Jihad*, which is an important religious concept in Islam. For much of the Islamic world, *Jihad* simply refers to the internal spiritual campaign that one wages with oneself. Although not one of the five key "pillars of Islam," it is considered by most Muslims to be a critical element of living a pious life. It can also refer to the act of physically waging warfare, most commonly in defence of Islam. (The meaning and application of the Jihad concept is one of the most vigorously contested topics among counter-terrorism researchers. An excellent book on the concept is David Cook's *Understanding Jihad* (Berkeley: University of California Press, 2005).)

The word *Jihadism*, on the other hand, is a modern neologism: it is not native to Islamic history and, therefore, its use has little religious significance to Muslims. Those who employ the term do so out of convenience because, despite its inherent problems, the word communicates a vital point: namely, that al-Qaida and groups like it are distinguished from other Muslims by their singular focus on the violent side of the Jihad concept. In recent years, the "Jihadism" label has been validated as the least worst option across the Arabic-speaking world, appearing throughout Arab television and print media. It has also grown in appeal across the world's counter-terrorism community, if only because it is a quick, albeit problematic, way to refer to Sunni Muslims who use violence in order to pursue their universalistic political agendas.

Jihadists believe themselves to be the tip of the Islamic spear. In their eyes, they are the last remaining vestige of an Islam that was practiced and preached by the Prophet Muhammad and the generation that immediately followed him (*Sunnah*). The religion of Islam, they argue, has deviated from the true path, and Muslims will continue to face humiliation, oppression, and persecution so long as they passively sit, waiting for situations to self-correct. The solution, they argue, has always been, and can only ever be, Islam. But it is not any Islam. It is an Islam willing to fight and die by the sword. It is an Islam that seeks to reinvigorate the spirit of monotheism. It is an Islam that seeks to purge itself of everything that is not fully in line with God's teachings or the Prophet's life. It is an Islam that rejects religious innovation or interpretation. It is an Islam where every believer is a warrior.

The Jihadist movement is far from a homogeneous entity, however. On the contrary, even a quick glance behind its public face reveals a highly variegated and fractured Jihadist community. Internal debates are almost always rooted in one of two issues: religious doctrine and pragmatic necessity. Often these issues are almost impossible to disentangle. Questions such as whether it is ever appropriate to overthrow an Islamic regime, whether it is ever acceptable to kill other Muslims, and what to do about the Shia, all have religious precedents and doctrinal prescriptions and proscriptions, but they also involve contemporary power calculations.

Jihadist praxis

In a posting that appeared on a number of Jihadist websites in 2007, an English-speaking al-Qaida supporter reflected:

a)   Imagine if Shaykh 'Abdullah Yusuf 'Azzam (rahimahullah) never spoke a word or picked up his pen when it came to matters related to Jihaad?

b)   Imagine if Shaykh Yusuf bin Saalih al-'Uyayree (rahimahullah) never gave his guidance to the Mujaahideen in practice and knowledge and kept silent on matters related to Martyrdom Operations?

c)   Imagine if Shaykh Abu Muhammad al-Maqdisi (fakkAllahu Asrah) never wrote his harsh criticisms of the Tawaagheet and never commented on al-Walaa' wal Baraa'ah?

d)   Imagine if Shaykh Naasir bin Hamaad al-Fahd (fakkAllahu Asrah) never raised his pen against the misconceptions that the Scholars of the Ummah were passing regarding Jihaad?

e)   Imagine if Shaykh Abu Yahya al-Libbi (hafidhullah) chose to sit back with the woman of his household, and never brought glad tidings to the Muslim Ummah regarding the successes of the global Jihaad?

f)   Imagine if Shaykh Husayn bin Mahmood (hafidhullah) kept silent on the current events of the Jihaad and the tongue lashing of the palace Scholars?

g)   Imagine if Shaykh Abu 'Umar al-Husaynee al-Qurayshee al-Baghdadi (hafidhullah) didn't lead the Ummah in 'Iraaq to victory upon victory, and guidance upon guidance, from the will of Allah Ta'aala?

h)   Imagine if Mullah Muhammad 'Umar Mujaahid (hafidhullah) chose to be like every other traitorous Afghan that sold themselves to the Apostates and Crusaders?

i)   Imagine if Shaykh 'Umar 'Abdur Rahmaan (fakkAllahu Asrah) told the men to sit back whilst the Ummah was being raped to death and robbed of its resources?

j)   Imagine if Shaykh 'Abdil Qaadir ibn 'Abdil 'Azeez (fakkAllahu Asrah) never laid out the in-depth analysis of Jihaad fe Sabeelillaah?

k)   Imagine if Imaam Anwar al-'Awlaki (fakkAllahu Asrah) never gave his excellent series of lectures of the masterpiece works on Jihaad and his analysis of the current global Jihaad?

l)   Imagine if Shaykh Usaamah bin Laadin (hafidhullah) lived in the Arabian Peninsula, received a fixed salary from the Taaghoot, and told men to abandon the Jihaad and its leadership?[3]

Few outside of the Jihadist movement can identify many of the people or concepts that he discusses. This is largely because existing literature on the global Jihadist movement tends to focus on the high-profile personalities, like Usama Bin Laden and Abu Musab al-Zarqawi. Little has been written, at least outside of the Islamic world, that covers these thinking men of global Jihadism.

This book is an explanation of global Jihadist praxis, or the ways in which theories are translated into practice. It is an attempt to make a body of complex thought and previously obscure personalities accessible to a Western audience. It is, above all else, an effort to show that big ideas can have big consequences. Understanding the political, economic and social phenomena at play in a given context helps analysts to characterize the nature of the threat that they are facing.

The classic example is the vast difference between America's experience with home-grown terrorist cells and that of the United Kingdom. In order to paint an accurate threat portrait, one must recognize the dramatic differences in Muslim demographics and levels of immigrant integration in the UK and America. One must understand the existence of decades-old roots that the Jihadist movement has grown in the UK. One must understand the various law enforcement and domestic intelligence capabilities and cultures.

Consider the experiences of Jihadism in Egypt during the 1960s, in Syria during the 1980s or in Saudi Arabia during the 1990s. Each of these social contexts is unique and telling with regard to the nature of the Jihadist threats that were faced. Contextual background provides key cues about the types of incentives and constraints that operate on a given individual or group. Without a nuanced understanding of the social actor, however, it is difficult to acquire a comprehensive picture of a situation. Without a deep cultural, historical and social picture for the context in which global Jihadist thought emerges and festers, it is impossible to develop sophisticated counter-strategies for exposing and defeating that movement. What complicates everything is that this picture constantly changes. With every interaction, people change, group dynamics change, and social contexts change.

The ways in which one understands their world both constrains and encourages certain types of behavior. Understanding the nature of the interplay between people and their environments is a key part of being able to forecast threats, assess future risks or discuss possible evolutionary trajectories of a movement. To put this framework in perspective, consider the example of Abd al-Aziz al-Muqrin. On an individual level, Muqrin looks no different than most youth in his generation. Like most young Saudi men, he was seeking autonomy from his parents and the religious establishment that constrained his actions. He was slightly rebellious, concerned with peer pressure, but not too doctrinally motivated. But even recognizing that he was a typically angry teenager who had something to prove to himself, his family, his friends and his God still fails to explain his path to becoming one of the world's most prominent Jihadist commanders.

Muqrin cannot be understood as a man or as a Jihadist without being situated in the proper context, particularly in the political, religious and social environment of 1979. Three cataclysmic events occurred during this time that would profoundly affect him and his generation: the Iranian revolution, the Soviet Union's invasion of Afghanistan and the storming of the Grand Mosque in Mecca by Saudi Islamic dissidents. Each of these would impact upon young Sunni Muslim men, including Muqrin, in a profound way.

The Iranian Shah, a man hated by the Shia hardliners in that country, and widely viewed as a secular puppet of the West, represented all that was wrong with Islam to young Shia revolutionaries. His overthrow empowered them, with backing from the senior Iranian mullahs, or religious men, providing an international stage upon which to broadcast their Islam. Sunni hardliners in Saudi Arabia, Syria, and Egypt viewed this event as a model of what was possible, in terms of establishing a theocratic state and using it to advance a revolutionary religious ideology. It was also seen as catastrophic for Sunni Islam as their arch-rivals, the Shia, now had made exporting *their* Islam a top priority. The Shia minorities in a host of Sunni-majority countries needed to be kept down, many Sunnis argued, before they began revolting across the Middle East. Sunni hardliners knew that it was time to begin thinking seriously about dealing with the Shia.

It was also during this time that the Sunni world would develop its own internal discord. When the ragtag followers of the Juhayman al-Utaibi stormed the Grand Mosque in Mecca in 1979, the Sunni world faced an existential crisis. Utaibi had drawn a line in the sand with the Saudi state, which few had been willing to do, at least with such bravado. Although his revolution would be short-lived, he provided future Sunni revolutionaries with a hero, a doctrine and an enemy for decades to come. The near enemy—the Saudi state as well as other Arab regimes—was forced on to the back-burner, however, when the Soviet Union began its military incursion into Afghanistan. This desolate, remote land became the birthplace for thousands of young revolutionary fighters. These men learned guerrilla tactics, they shared the common bond of having gone to war together, and those who survived came to believe that Afghanistan was only one small battle in a much larger war.

As Muqrin learned more about Jihadism, fought harder against his enemies and disseminated his writings more prolifically, the nature of the Jihadist movement and his social context changed around him. The Saudi government cracked down even harder because of the threat that he seemed to pose, but more young Saudi kids joined al-Qaida's activities in the peninsula because of his writings. Muqrin grew only angrier with the Saudi regime and more hopeful about the future of the Jihadist movement in the kingdom. The cycle continued with his death as eulogies were written about him.

Afghanistan in the 1990s

Beginning in the mid-1990s, in concert with the rise of the Taliban movement in Afghanistan, a second wave of migration into that country began. The first wave (1979–89) had included young men who were seeking to support a fuzzy notion of Jihad against a world superpower. They had little more than a dream and a plane ticket. This second wave, however, looked quite different. The Jihadist movement had been percolating for over a decade by the mid-1990s. Droves of Afghan veterans became peripatetic recruiters, fighters, fundraisers, propagandists, and troublemakers wherever they went. Others remained in places like Peshawar, Pakistan. Some had gone to fight in Somalia or Bosnia. Others were arrested stirring up trouble in their Arab homelands. With the rise of the Taliban in the early 1990s, Muslims began making their way back toward Afghanistan in order to support this new Jihadist campaign. Some of those who returned included:

- *Trainers*: Professional military instructors came for short periods of time in order to provide tactical training to the Jihadists. These men, most of them veterans of previous Jihadist campaigns in Afghanistan and Bosnia, usually stayed for the duration of a given course, which could last from a few months to a year.

- *Resettlers*: Numerous Muslim families journeyed to Afghanistan in order to establish a new life under the rule of Islamic law, rebuild Afghanistan, and fight in the name of God.
- *Jihadist organizations*: These organizations came from various Arab and Islamic countries. They had well-defined Jihadist goals against their respective home countries and came to Afghanistan in order to rebuild their organizations from abroad before returning to strike those countries with a vengeance. To that end, the organizations were to be ethnically based, secretive and hierarchically structured. They included:

1   The Libyan Islamic Fighting Group (LIFG), which worked under the direction of Abu Abdallah Al-Sadeq. Its immediate goals were to overthrow the Qadafi government in Libya, support the establishment of the Taliban and help advance the global Jihadist movement.

2   The Moroccan Islamic Fighting Group (GICM), which worked under the direction of Abu Abdullah al-Sharif. GICM's goal was to train Libyan and Moroccan Jihadists in order one day to depose the Moroccan government.

3   The Egyptian Islamic Jihad (EIJ), which worked under the direction of Ayman al-Zawahiri and Abd al-Qadir ibn Abd al-Aziz. EIJ sought to reconstitute the Egyptian Jihadist movement in order finally to oust the Egyptian government and seize control of the country.

4   The Islamic Group (IG) of Egypt, which worked under the direction of the 'Blind Shaikh', Umar Abd al-Rahman, and other exiled Egyptian radicals. Its stated goal was also to overthrow the Egyptian regime.

5   The Armed Islamic Group (GIA), which was established by Algerian combat veterans of Afghanistan who would recruit other Algerians and train them for warfare against the Algerian government. They would be aided in Afghanistan, Pakistan, Algeria and London by a variety of senior Jihadist leaders, including Abu Hamza al-Masri, Abu Musab al-Suri and Abu Qatada.

6   Tunisian fighters, who came to Afghanistan in order to recruit young Tunisians and train them for warfare against the Tunisian government. They established a number of training camps inside Afghanistan and some of their members had participated in the Bosnian Jihadist campaign.

7   Jordanian and Palestinian fighters, who travelled to Afghanistan in order to train for a war that they hoped to wage against the Jordanian government. Under the guidance of Abu Musab al-Zarqawi and Abu Muhammad al-Maqdisi, they would return to Jordan in the early 1990s and launch their revolution (albeit unsuccessfully).

8   Al-Qaida, which under the leadership of Usama Bin Laden and Ayman al-Zawahiri sought to use Afghanistan much like they had used Sudan previously: as an HQ from which to organize a global war against the United States and her hand-maidens around the world. Their protectors would be the new government of Afghanistan, the Taliban, and their leader, Mullah Muhammad Umar.

9   Central Asian groups, who had different aims and goals from al-Qaida. Some wanted to reside permanently in Afghanistan. Others wanted to use the country, like al-Qaida, as a base of operations for waging strikes against their own home countries. The two largest groups in this category included Uzbek fighters (well funded by the Uzbek diaspora community) and East Turkistan fighters (fighting the Chinese, whom they argued were occupying their territory).

10 Pakistani fighters, comprising individuals who had been students at religious schools (madrassas) in Pakistan. Many had also been members of Jihadist organizations that had previously fought in Kashmir.

11 Turkish and Kurdish fighters, comprising a small group who operated and organized in closed, secretive factions and mainly focused on conducting military training.

Taken together, this hodgepodge of ethnicities, worldviews and competing organizational agendas made for an explosive environment. Afghanistan quickly became the global Jihadist movement's launching pad.

Global Jihadism

The al-Qaida organization, the most well-known practitioners of the Jihadist ideology, shook the world on September 11, 2001 when it deployed 19 suicide hijackers against the United States. Under the direction of Usama Bin Laden, al-Qaida became a household name. In response, the American counter-terrorism community, in cooperation with governments around the world, initiated its global war on terrorism. In the years following the 9/11 attacks, Jihadist terrorists conducted devastating assaults on Afghanistan, Great Britain, Egypt, India, Iraq, Israel, Indonesia, Jordan, Lebanon, Morocco, Pakistan, Russia, Saudi Arabia, Somalia, Spain, Tunisia, Turkey, Uzbekistan, Kenya, Kuwait, and Yemen.

Now the question is: how can the Jihadist movement continue to conduct massive terrorist attacks worldwide in the midst of a global war against it and in an era when billions of dollars are being poured into homeland security, intelligence and law enforcement efforts that are meant to defend against such atrocities? There are three interrelated reasons for the Jihadist movement's endurance in the face of what seems like overwhelming global pressure to defeat them: first, the Jihadist message provides a universal rallying cry that resonates locally but applies globally; second, Jihadists are continuously empowering one another with the new skills and knowledge that they need to counter the security efforts that are being launched against them; and third, America's invasion and subsequent destabilization of Iraq have provided a proving-ground for the perfection of insurgency and terrorist operations.

Message resonance

A core group of global Jihadist thinkers have forged an intellectually coherent, emotionally compelling and globally accessible ideology. Over the past few decades, these highly erudite scholars have outlined the basic parameters of that ideology. Their messages are now available on a variety of media, including cassette tapes, pamphlets, large books, compact discs and DVDs, as well as the internet. Their writings are translated into multiple languages by the Jihadists' own translation bureaus. Indeed, information written by Jihadists for Jihadists has never been more accessible or prolific than it is today.

In general, ideologies tend to share several basic features. They articulate a set of grievances by one population against another. These grievances tend to deal with themes of oppression, alienation and victimization, allowing ideologues to simplify complex situations into binary oppositions with visceral impact. Reality, for ideological adherents, becomes nothing more than a reductionist Manichean dualism, a struggle between good and evil, between the light and the darkness. In almost all ideologies, such diametric opposites will remain in constant conflict until one triumphs over the other. It is for this reason that ideologies need to present their followers with an alternative vision for the future. In order for someone to turn themselves over to an ideology, they must be convinced that their grievances will be redressed. The only way to arrive at that end-state, for most ideologies, is by demanding immediate and unquestioning action. It is only through action that an ideology can grow. And process is edifying. Movement purifies the spirit, while stagnation allows the status quo to prevail. These elements—oversimplification, presentation of an alternative goal-culture, and a demand for action—form the skeleton of every modern ideology, including anarchism, fascism, communism and liberalism. Their manifestations may differ, but if present in a ripe social context, one where there is a pervasive sense of humiliation, inadequacy, anger and emasculation, ideologies can move millions of people to action. Since the defeat of fascism and the collapse of communism, Jihadism has arguably become the world's next great ideological opponent of Western-style liberalism.

The teachings of this broad array of global Jihadist thinkers, most of whom are unknown names in the West, have convinced countless young, angry Muslim men to commit, or at least support, violent acts of terrorism by intertwining the call for action with a puritanical interpretation of Islam. By tapping into existing religious concepts, histories and beliefs, the most influential Jihadist ideologues, such as Abu Qatada al-Filistini, Abd al-Qadir ibn abd al-Aziz, Abu Muhammad al-Maqdisi and Nasr Bin al-Fahd have had enormous success building their version of God's army on Earth.

As an ideology, Jihadism relies on several basic assumptions that adherents find useful for framing their personal sets of grievances, articulating their hopes, and identifying the means for achieving their objectives. The first premise of Jihadism is that there is a global conspiracy working to destroy Islam. The central conspirators, Jihadists argue, are the Christian Crusader countries of the West and their Jewish Zionist allies in Israel. The Jihadist intelligentsia, which consists of a core group of radical thinkers writing in various places around the world— most of them unknown in the West—has exhaustively detailed the nature and implications of this conspiracy. Usama Bin Laden, the symbol and leader of the al-Qaida organization, popularized this grievance through his recorded statements and actions. In his oft-cited 1996 statement, for instance, he stated, "It should not be hidden from you that the people of Islam had suffered from aggression, iniquity and injustice imposed on them by the Zionist–Crusaders alliance and their collaborators; to the extent that the Muslims' blood became the cheapest and their wealth as loot in the hands of the enemies."[4] This theme of global victimization forms the backbone of a global Jihadist movement: it is an indisputable fact for adherents to this ideology. Take, for instance, a statement published on the internet in January 2007 by the Kuwaiti Jihadist thinker Hamid al-Ali, who has emerged of late as a rising star among the movement's intellectual hierarchy. In his 34-page statement, "Accord of the Supreme Council of the Groups of Jihad," he identifies two primary enemies facing the movement around the world: Shia Muslims, who seek "to demolish Islam's civilization and slaughter the Muslims under false religious slogans," and the Zionist–Crusader–apostate Arab alliance, who "oppress the Muslims . . . tarnishing its religion, seeking to extinguish the light of Islam." Global Jihadists believe that the only way to stop this unending cycle of economic, military and cultural colonization imposed upon the Islamic world by the West in collaboration with Israel and phony Muslim regimes in the Middle East is to unite the world under the banner of their version of Islamic rule.

Transforming consumers into producers

The second major reason why the Jihadist movement has been able to sustain its momentum in the face of global counter-terrorism efforts is because it has mastered the art of the social movement: transforming consumers of its ideas into producers of them. The term "social movement" refers to a specific type of group action in the fields of sociology and political science. It is a large, informal conglomerate of individuals, groups and organizations all focused on making political and social change. Social movements in their contemporary form are particular to a global-izing world, wherein information, money, resources, people and nearly anything else can be transferred almost instantaneously.

For the more strategically minded Jihadists, of whom there are many, al-Qaida has been an important, but not sufficient, step along the path of establishing Islamic rule throughout the world. The al-Qaida organization has been more successful in calling attention to the victimization of Muslims, Jihadists argue, than previous groups because it learned from and applied the lessons of earlier Jihadist resistance efforts. The symbiotic relationship that Jihadists have crafted between their violence and their use of media to publicize that violence has served to popularize the notion of Islamic resistance in a way never seen before. The next step, Jihadist thinkers argue, is to cultivate generations of intellectual, cultural and military insurgents around the world. By building organizations, elaborating ideologies, mobilizing constituencies and shaping collective identities, the global Jihadist movement has positioned itself as the catalyst for social change. The change that today's global Jihadism promises to deliver is the ousting of foreign occupiers in Muslim lands, the removal of all vestiges of cultural pollution that violate the laws of Allah, and the application of laws that are informed solely by the Quran, selective *Hadith* and the model established by the Prophet Muhammad and his companions.

Social movements, like global Jihadism, are situated in a broader social context characterized by fluid configurations of incentives and constraints—or political opportunity structures. The more that a given social movement can localize these incentive and constraint structures, the more success they tend to have fostering broad-based participation. A key element of this localization process is the creation of a unified identity on which collective action can occur. The innovative ways in which Jihadists now use the internet and other new media technologies have helped open Jihadist participation to anyone, anywhere.

With guidance from Jihadist curriculum designers like Abu Musab al-Suri, a young Muslim seeking a more hardline version of Islam than the one practiced by his parents, teachers, or peers now has a wide range of resources at his disposal. A vibrant community exists on the internet where Jihadist-minded individuals from all walks of life meet to share recent writings, exchange personal stories of discrimination or alienation with their home country, and provide one another with technical resources to help in preparation for waging violence. Web forum sites like Al-Hesbah, Al-Boraq, Al-Ehklaas, Al-Faloja and a variety of others serve as initial entry points from which interested viewers from around the world can read about the breaking news from Iraq, follow links to attack videos from active Jihad campaigns, view motivational imagery of martyr operatives in heaven, and download debates about the religious justification for waging violent Jihad. Some of these forums even post Jihadist job openings.[5] To access the latest news and current events from a Jihadist perspective, interested viewers have a number of options. They can follow the links on web discussion forums to a series of al-Qaida-friendly news broadcasts (called the "Voice of the Caliphate") highlighting recent attacks, criticizing Arab governments for collaborating with Jews and Christians, or discussing future goals of the Jihadist movement.[6] Those searching for Jihadist-oriented updates can easily sign up for daily email feeds from one of the number of Jihadist news groups, or they can visit the Jihadist news repository site, the World News Network.

Individuals interested in setting up their own terrorist cells—like those responsible for the Madrid train bombing—can find more than news updates online. Jihadist web forums provide links to several al-Qaida magazines which outline step-by-step instructions for communicating with cell members, defining tactics and procedures, and constructing explosives, among other topics. With little trouble, they can find the Jihadist webpage that hosts the *Encyclopedia of Preparation*, a voluminous training manual for everything from kidnapping officials to building nuclear devices.[7] Increasingly, Jihadist technology specialists are making publicly available detailed instructional documents and videos that explain how to use specific software packages or access certain types of file online. These tutorials are accompanied by a "Jihadist-approved" version of the software to download, which often includes computer programs for video editing or webpage design. To this end, Jihadist computer programmers have launched new web-browsing software, similar to Microsoft's Internet Explorer, which searches only particular sites. By structurally constraining web traffic, the software discourages the freedom to navigate to other online destinations, thus facilitating the intellectual separation of Jihadists from the general chaos of cyberspace. These efforts to define and bound Jihadist ideological space, which is critical for Jihadist success in light of the multiplicity of alternative viewpoints that can be accessed online, will almost certainly accelerate as ideologues seek dominance over this technology.

Perhaps the most important resources of the Jihadist movement, though, are the ideological and strategic texts available from such websites as the main al-Qaida library website, which contains over three thousand books and monographs from respected Jihadist thinkers. These scholarly texts provide Jihadists with the core doctrines, rationale and religious legitimation for their violent approach. They serve to sustain Jihadists' momentum, deepen their investment and expand their understanding of why the world as it is can no longer be ignored. The internet has made it easier for Jihadists to distribute and read the writings that they hold most important to the future of the movement. It is becoming increasingly clear that, in the process of consuming and producing these writings, individuals become more deeply knowledgeable of and invested in the Jihadist interpretation of Islam.

Jihadist-minded individuals and organizations are increasingly looking to extend the discussion into more mainstream Salafist web forums as well as into the broader Sunni community. By embedding Jihadist writings on mainstream Islamic sites, and posting Jihadist arguments on non-Jihadist web forums, proponents of this hostile ideology are providing new avenues for Muslims to engage with the ideology whereas previously they might not have had the opportunity to do so.

Regional inflammation

The third reason why the Jihadist movement has been able to persist in the face of a global war against it is that America's military venture into Iraq in 2003 has resulted in the destabilization of the country's security situation to such an extent that it has become the new proving-ground for Jihadist insurgent and terrorist operations. Each day, Jihadist militants learn and implement new combat tactics, techniques and procedures against the US military. They learn from their successes and failures and adapt almost instantaneously. Most importantly, they communicate this knowledge by means of the internet to Jihadists both inside Iraq and beyond.

Even more significant, however, is that the Iraqi Jihad campaign serves the Jihadist ideology as a proof-of-concept. Crusader forces storming Baghdad, historically one of the holiest places within Islam, and occupying it through the use of force adds tremendous credence to the Jihadist claim of global victimization. Jihadist willingness to fight against an overwhelmingly superior military force, regardless of outcome, adds important legitimacy to the Jihadist claim of being the vanguard of Islam, willing to die to defend Muslim lands against the occupation of infidels while the majority of other Muslims remain passive observers, if not tacit collaborators.

The question of whither Bin Laden, therefore, whither al-Qaida—and, therefore, whither Jihadism—is first on the mind of most Western policy-makers. But the more one studies the Jihadist movement, the more one sees that it has come to transcend one man and even one organization. It is now a social phenomenon, in large part because the ideology has helped to diversify its participants functionally.

Inside global Jihadism

There is no easy way to classify the various dimensions of today's global Jihadist movement. Some use a tiered framework in order to highlight the fact that there is no single "al-Qaida." In it are the al-Qaida high command (Bin Laden, Zawahiri); al-Qaida affiliate groups and individuals (Jemaah Islammiyyah, Lashkar-i-Taiba, al-Qaida in the peninsula, al-Qaida in the Islamic Maghreb) and those individuals and groups who are supported by al-Qaida (Istanbul bombers, London 7/7 bombers); and those individuals and groups who are inspired by al-Qaida but have no direct ties to it (Toronto cell).

The first tier, which forms the core of al-Qaida, is the high command and its centralized components. This tier includes most of the remaining senior leadership, likely based in Waziristan and Iran. The extent to which they are able to launch, command or call off attacks is not well known in the open source community. However, there is strong reason to believe that this high command is able to initiate attacks both in its backyard of Afghanistan and Pakistan and around the world, such as in London. The senior al-Qaida leadership currently consists largely of Egyptian loyalists of Zawahiri and Libyan commanders:

- *Atiyah Abd al-Rahman*, a 38-year-old Libyan who studied in Mauritania and became a proficient Islamic scholar and theorist. He also fought during the 1980s in Afghanistan, where he learned how to work with explosives. He reportedly served in the now defunct Libyan Islamic Fighting Group and was imprisoned in Algeria during the 1990s but returned to Afghanistan to sit in al-Qaida's inner circle by 2000. He served as al-Qaida's liaison to Abu Musab al-Zarqawi in Iraq and likely shuttles between Iran and Afghanistan, all the while forging new relationships with other Jihadist groups and leaders. He is considered one of the most senior commanders of the organization today.
- *Abu Laith al-Libi*, leader of the Libyan Islamic Fighting Group. Now in his early forties, he has been active in global Jihadism for decades. He was arrested in 1995 after the Saudis cracked down on local Jihadis in the aftermath of the Khobar Towers bombing. After escaping from al-Ruwais Prison in Jiddah, Saudi Arabia, he traveled back to Afghanistan, where he met with senior Taliban and al-Qaida officials. On July 10, 2002, he appeared in a 30-minute video in which he acted as a *de facto* spokesman for the Taliban commander, Mullah Muhammad Umar. He also promoted two websites, one of the Taliban and the other run by Saudi al-Qaida commander Yousuf al-Ayiri, called www.al-Neda.com. On June 15, 2004, Al-Jazirah in Islamabad obtained a

video showing Abu Laith and other al-Qaida members conducting a military raid. Reports indicate that in 2005 he was replaced as the senior war commander in southern Afghanistan by a Moroccan commander, Khaled Habib, and Abdul Hadi al-Iraqi. Abu Laith al-Libi appeared again on April 27, 2007 on an as-Sahab video discussing the condition of the Jihadist campaigns in Afghanistan. He also gave a eulogy for the dead Iraqi al-Qaida commander, Abu Musab al-Zarqawi (killed in early 2008).

- *Musatafa Abu al-Yazid (Shaikh Sayid)* was previously the general official of al-Qaida in Afghanistan but was promoted to commander-general of the organization in that country in May 2007. He was born on December 17, 1955 in Egypt's al-Sharqiyah Governate in the Nile Delta. He spent three years in an Egyptian prison, from 1981 to 1984, the same time-frame as other senior Egyptians in al-Qaida, including Ayman al-Zawahiri. Like Zawahiri, Shaikh Sayid too fled for Peshawar, Pakistan, where he established a close relationship with Usama Bin Laden. He became the latter's accountant in his Sudanese front-businesses and reportedly arranged funding for a variety of attacks. Throughout the mid-1990s, he worked closely with senior al-Qaida officials in a financial capacity, reportedly transferring funds to Muhammad Atta and the Islamic Movement of Uzbekistan. One of Shaikh Sayid's daughters married the son of the Blind Shaikh, both of whom were captured in early 2003. His first publicly broadcast interview appeared in May 2007 on al-Qaida's official media outlet, as-Sahab. He continues to play a senior command role in the movement.

- *Abu Yahya al-Libi*, another Libyan member of the Libyan Islamic Fighting Group, has become a popular icon and emerging leader in the Jihadist movement. He achieved cult-like status with global Jihadists after he and others escaped from US custody in Baghram, Afghanistan, in July 2005. His face now adorns al-Qaida media releases, including videotaped interviews, poetry readings and statements, all of which track precisely with the issue stances of the high-command figures. All indications point to the fact that he is the high command's designated successor to Bin Laden as chief Jihadist.

- *Muhammad Khalil al-Hakaymah (Abu Jihad al-Masri)* became a household name in the Jihadist community on August 6, 2006, when he was introduced by Ayman al-Zawahiri in an as-Sahab video. Hakaymah had been an Egyptian Islamic Group operative and propagandist and reportedly helped to facilitate the escape of a senior IG leader, Rifai Taha, from Egypt in 1981. He also worked closely with followers of the Blind Shaikh, Umar Abd al-Rahman. In the early 1990s, aided by the brother of Ayman al-Zawahiri, he traveled to Peshawar, Pakistan, where he helped to set up the Islamic Group's propaganda magazine. He befriended another Egyptian Jihadist, Abu Hamza al-Masri, and later traveled between London, Bosnia, Turkey, Syria and Germany. At his next stop, Iran, he worked with the Voice of Palestine radio station in Tehran and become chief editor of the Arab news. By mid-2001, he was back in Afghanistan, but with the start of Coalition bombing, a group of Taliban members smuggled him and 24 other leaders (including

Muhammad al-Islambuli, Abu Musab al-Zarqawi, Shaikh Abu Hafs the Mauritanian, and other training officials and military administrators) out of Kandahar.

- *Abu Ubaydah al-Masri* is an Egyptian Jihadist commander in his mid-forties who served as deputy chief of al-Qaida forces in Afghanistan's Kunar Province, a mountainous area where much fighting with US and Coalition troops has occurred. Al-Qaida's media group has dedicated increasing amounts of time and attention to promoting him in its products.
- *Khaled Habib al-Masri* is, according to some reports, dead as the result of a January 2006 missile strike in Damadola, Pakistan. Recently, however, there have been suggestions that he may not have been killed. Khaled Habib served as a senior operational commander in southeastern Afghanistan alongside another senior commander, Abdul Hadi al-Iraqi.
- *Abdul Rehman al Magribi*, a Moroccan, is thought to have been al-Qaida's commander in Pakistan, and is said to have replaced Abu Hamza Rabia, who was killed on December 1, 2005. He was Ayman al-Zawahiri's son-in-law, played a prominent role in al-Qaida media operations, and, like al-Iraqi and Khaled Habib, was reported killed in the Damadola missile strike.

The second tier of the Jihadist movement consists of those individuals and groups with some direct relationship to al-Qaida's high command. This interaction can include varying levels of support, including funding, operational guidance, manpower or other facilitation. Those groups and individuals conducting this hazy notion of violent Jihadist activity vary widely. Many are focused on local political events and agendas. Hamas, for instance, shows virtually no interest in waging 'global' Jihad. It is therefore chastised by certain individuals in al-Qaida and construed as having sold out. Bedouin groups in Egypt may conduct al-Qaida-styled terrorist attacks, but they do so not in support of some ephemeral global Jihadism, but rather as a way of expressing their very local grievances. These local Jihadist groups generally pose the greatest threat to the regime which they target, while the global Jihadist groups pose the biggest terrorist threat to Western countries as a whole. They know no territorial bounds in their desired reach and have few restrictions on the types of activity they are willing to conduct. They are consummate pragmatists in their actions but tend to have enormous egos, which become apparent when they distinguish themselves from the other terrorist chaff.

A good example of the second tier is the 2003 Istanbul cell, led by a veteran of Jihadist campaigns in Chechnya and Bosnia, Habib Aktas. A native of an Arabic-speaking town in Turkey, he gradually proceeded down the Jihadist trajectory, hosting Quranic study groups at his home during which he also showed his friends al-Qaida and other Jihadist propaganda videos.[8] He was said to have once hosted a three-dollar-per-head picnic in the hills above the Black Sea to raise funds for Jihad in Chechnya. At some point, Aktas decided to support al-Qaida directly, concocting a far-fetched plan to deploy 15 suicide operatives in a raid on the TUSIAD (Turkish Industrialists' and Businessmen's Association), which he said included a lot of "Jewish bosses." Around September 18, 2001, Aktas and several of his associates had arranged a meeting in Kandahar, Afghanistan, with Usama Bin Laden. According to some reports, Bin Laden spoke for almost the entire hour about general topics of Jihad or the state of Muslims. After breakfast, Bin Laden's military commander, Muhammad Atef, took the Turkish group aside, gave them ten thousand dollars in cash and recalibrated their attack plan. They were to conduct vehicle-based suicide attacks against Western and Jewish targets in Turkey, he instructed.

Aktas and his colleagues returned to Turkey with the money, set up a cell, and began building explosives using a hydrogen-peroxide-based recipe that he had learned in the Afghan training camps. He and his cell members then packed the mixture into large fertilizer bags. Another cell member, Gurcan Bac, reportedly spent hours on the internet honing his wiring design in chat forums and downloaded instruction manuals. The cell purchased four pickup trucks with cash and registered them to their relatives. Being security conscious, they made sure to turn off their cellphones and remove the batteries during cell meetings at their safe-house and even unplugged every other electrical device in the house.

In early 2003, Aktas began identifying suicide-bomber candidates. He chose Mesut Cabuk and Gokhan Elatuntas, who hailed from the same small home town. To prepare for the attack, Aktas sent these religiously conservative (although not fundamentalist) men to train in Pakistan. They returned home several months later radicalized and prepared to conduct a suicide operation, telling their parents that they were moving to Istanbul in order to open a computer store. Aktas also picked out Feridun Ugurlu, a young Muslim who had been a devout religious student until he visited Pakistan in 1996. On his return, his family and friends noticed, he was despondent and much more puritanical. Aktas's fourth and final suicide candidate was Ilyas Kuncak, a local spice merchant and now a pious Muslim, although previously he had served in the Turkish military and had even subscribed to communism.

On November 15, 2003, two truck bombs slammed into the Beth Israel and Neve Shalom synagogues in Istanbul, killing 27, most of them Turkish Muslims, and injuring more than three hundred others. Five days later, on November 20, two more truck bombs exploded: suicide bombers detonated their trucks at the HSBC bank and the British Consulate, killing 30 people and wounding another four hundred. Aktas and his men had fulfilled their terrorist missions, although the cell looked and acted differently than the hand-selected teams of trained operatives seen in previous al-Qaida attacks. The Istanbul group was tasked, partially funded and only loosely guided by al-Qaida's high command. Beyond that, there was little hands-on control or coordination, particularly after al-Qaida's chief of external operations, Khalid Shaikh Muhammad, was captured in Pakistan in spring 2003.

The third tier of the Jihadist movement comprises those individuals, cells or groups who emerge without direct assistance, training or support from any official al-Qaida element. Some call them "self-starters," others refer to them as practitioners of "home-grown terrorism." Crucially, they come to the movement of their own volition. They may be guided by teachers, friends, mentors or religious figures, but they largely drive their own radicalization. This book coins a new term for such enthusiasts of the global Jihadist ideology: *Jihobbyists*.

Arguably, al-Qaida has always been more focused on inspiring Jihobbyists than achieving anything else. It was they whom Bin Laden and his core commanders had hoped to motivate through spectacular actions like 9/11. Few senior al-Qaida leaders expected to bring the United States to its knees militarily or economically with the attacks of 2001. But Bin Laden hoped that they would serve as a wake-up call to Muslims. Al-Qaida's senior leadership understand that organizations are fleeting, but they also know that ideas—manifested in self-sustaining, organically adaptable, global social movements—can be enduring. A Jihobbyist may be an enthusiast of the global Jihadist movement, someone who enjoys thinking about and watching the activities of the groups from the first and second tiers, but generally they have no connection to al-Qaida or any other formal Jihadist groups. And it is unlikely that they will ever actually *do* anything that directly supports the movement.

So Jihobbyists may do it from the comfort of their home computer or their local coffee shop, but they are still actively seeking to move forward the Jihadist agenda. By hosting Jihadist websites, designing propaganda posters, editing al-Qaida videos, recording soundtracks (*nashids*) for those videos, compiling speeches from famous Jihadist shaikhs and packaging them into easily downloadable files or writing training manuals, these individuals help to form the base that keeps the movement afloat. Some become obsessed with the brutal beheading, sniper or explosives videos. Others would rather spend their time reading thousand-page books about the history of the movement.

Those individuals who feel compelled to support the movement in a more direct way may seek out others who are like-minded and engage in what this book refers to as *preparatory Jihad*. These activities also may not have any direct connection to terrorism or terrorist organizations. They do, however, serve to acculturate practitioners into the Jihadist mindset because these individuals will now have direct relationships with others, which serve to increase peer pressure, usually pushing forward commitment to the Jihadist movement. Preparatory Jihad might comprise playing paintball with a group in order to learn and practice military maneuvers or watching videos with friends in order to cheer on Jihadist groups in Iraq, Chechnya, Somalia, Afghanistan, or elsewhere. It might include conducting surveillance on potential targets, formulating attack plans, performing a daily Jihadist exercise regime, or learning how to prepare explosives via recipes downloaded from the internet. Sometimes those engaged in preparatory Jihad will have been inspired by individuals who are plugged into more formal organizational networks, through either al-Qaida or one of its affiliate groups. Other times, these groups organically emerge within a community. Typically, cells that move forward toward planning an attack do have contact with someone who has trained in an al-Qaida or other Jihadist camp, participated in military campaigns in Bosnia, Chechnya, Afghanistan or Iraq, or is involved with an active terrorist organization. This connection helps move those who are comfortable supporting the preparatory Jihad further down the radicalization path, toward waging violent Jihad themselves.

Take, for instance, the group of 18 Muslim men in Toronto who were arrested by the Royal Canadian Mounted Police during the summer of 2006. According to media reports, this group of mostly naive, religiously puritanical teenagers seems to have come under the sway of an older, radical hardliner who prompted them to take action. The two suspected cell leaders, Fahim Ahmad and Zakaria Amara, reportedly met this more senior figure at an Islamic center in a small suburban town outside Toronto. While their mentor had no formal religious role at the mosque, he reached out to young people through informal activities, such as camping and sports. Under his tutelage, the boys reportedly began watching Jihadist videos and communicating with other like-minded individuals in Bosnia and the United Kingdom. They even started wearing combat fatigues to their mosque.

Over the course of the next year, this group of Canadian boys allegedly began reading, talking and thinking more about the Jihadist movement, and eventually became convinced that they had to act on their grievances with the Canadian government. According to the *Washington Post*, the group discussed plots, including detonating truck bombs against targets in Toronto. They also considered storming the Canadian parliament building, taking the members hostage and beheading the Prime Minister unless Canada immediately withdrew its troops from Afghanistan.[9] So, with virtually no known ties with al-Qaida's official structure or its regional networks, this cell emerged, evolved and very nearly executed its actions on its own.

The major shortcoming with any tiered model of al-Qaida, however, is that it overly preferences al-Qaida's high command as being the core of the Jihadist movement and implicitly downgrades the importance of groups and individuals the further they are from that core. But as more knowledge becomes disseminated globally, the position of any group or organization in this model will have almost no correlation with the damage that they have the potential to inflict against a given target. It is critical, therefore, to think of al-Qaida and similarly minded groups as parts of a very complicated puzzle rather than as a specific organizational entity.

The Jihadist clash of civilizations

Although relatively few supporters of the global Jihadist ideology ever make it to the battlefield, many adherents still seek to live their lives in accordance with that doctrine. Jihadists living in the West see themselves as having to face daunting challenges in nearly every aspect of their daily lives. The reason why Muslims cannot remain in the West, Jihadists believe, is that Western civilization is inherently bankrupt and in a state of perpetual war with Islam. Proof, they argue, is everywhere within Western civilization. The visceral revulsion held by Jihadists for Western culture drips from the pages of their writings. Take an essay popular within Jihadist internet forums entitled *Some Examples of Kufr [Disbelief] and Haram [Un-Islamic actions] in the Schools of the Kuffar [non-Muslim] States*.[10] Representative of broader Jihadist thinking on the evils of Western culture, this argues that Western civilization is predicated on mind control and social engineering. Muslim children, therefore, must be prohibited from attending Western schools because they will be subject to temptation, corruption and indoctrination.

In the Western educational system, the author explains, intermingling between boys and girls is allowed, even encouraged. Students learn about un-Islamic topics such as evolution, cloning and the indestructibility of energy in their science classes. They are forced to sing and play songs on instruments that are designed to propagate Western culture, nationalism and non-Islamic religions. Children are mandated to make Valentine cards, Halloween crafts, Christmas presents, Thanksgiving costumes, Easter eggs and civic holiday decorations, all of which are weapons of cultural warfare. Physical education classes force children of the same sex to change clothes with no privacy. Then they play games, intermixing with the opposite sex. Western schools teach sexual education courses in their required curriculum. In these classes, the author writes, teachers show students pictures and videos of naked people. They promote sexual intercourse as a casual activity. They openly accept homosexuality and promote the notion of equality between the sexes. Students also learn about contraception and abortion.

The essay continues that Western youth study the fundamentals of capitalist economics, with lending money, or usury as Jihadists see it, cast as a legitimate and necessary financial tool around which the entire global economic system revolves. Western students are transformed into "neo-colonialists" who view international trade as a way to exploit Muslim wealth and labor. They study geography, embracing false ideologies like nationalism and distorted concepts like "our land," "our flag," and "our nation." They read literature that corrupts any sense they may have of social justice or morality. In their history classes, Western children learn to idolize civilizations that have contributed material progress to humanity while furthering the oppression of mankind. Western history is the history of democracy and political change towards factionalization and division. Children are taught that the majority decides on humans to legislate over the community by means of democratic elections. Reason is preferenced over revelation.

For global Jihadists, Western education creates an army of moral relativists and multiculturalists, the author argues, viewing multiculturalism as a way for Western governments to counteract the growth of Islam as a way of life in Europe and North America. In short, compromise with the West is an impossibility as its entire civilization is based on beliefs, views and actions that look to subvert Islam. The only solution is disavowal, purification and preparation for war.

2 Doctrine and schools

Everywhere you look into its lands, there are Mujahidin saying:
 NO SURRENDER.
And in every side of its hills there are men saying Allahu Akbar,
 NO PERSECUTION.
We have planted its lands with our heads held high so it grows into glory
 and blooms.

The Base, Jihadist Forum Administrator

In his book, *Millat Ibrahim* (*The Religion of Abraham*), the global Jihadist scholar Abu Muhammad al-Maqdisi, calls on Muslims around the world to live by the doctrine of *al-Wala wal-Bara*.[1] Although there is no precise English translation for this phrase, it roughly means two things. First, that Muslims must have unquestioning loyalty towards God: a Muslim ought to be loyal and loving to all that is in accordance with God's law, or *Sharia*. Second, Muslims ought to reject and disavow all that contradicts *Sharia*, especially polytheism, democracy and those who advance such "deviant" ideologies.

This "loyalty and disavowal" concept is a central doctrine for most adherents of the Jihadist ideology. Al-Qaida's number two, Dr. Ayman al-Zawahiri, wrote a book entitled *Al-Wala wal-Bara*.[2] The popular Jamaican-born firebrand Abdullah Faisal recorded a 94-minute audio lecture exclusively on the topic.[3] The emir of al-Qaida in Iraq, Abu Umar al-Baghdadi, heralded the concept in a 2007 audio address.[4] The popular al-Qaida commander in Afghanistan, Abu Yahya al-Libi, has repeatedly discussed the concept in his public lectures. And internet Jihobbyists obsess about the ways in which they can better apply *al-Wala wal-Bara* in their daily lives. In fact, the "loyalty and disavowal" concept is one of the five doctrinal legs upon which today's Jihadist movement stands. The other four doctrines are: *Tawhid* (unity of God), *Aqidah* (creed), *Takfir* (excommunication) and Jihad (struggling). It is this particularly explosive cocktail of ultra-conservative doctrinal elements, mixed with a flair for waging spectacularly catastrophic acts of violence, that separates Jihadists from the other schools of Salafism, even the most hardline of them.

Salafism

Jihadism cannot be extricated from the religious and ideological context from which it emerged: Salafism. This first appeared in Egypt at the turn of the twentieth century as an intellectual reformist movement. The ideology was meant to push Muslims forward: to blaze a progressive path of their own, steering away from the pressure being placed on Islamic society by Westernism. The solution could be found, as is usually the case in Islamic fundamentalist movements, only through a puritanical return to Islam. But it was not the Islam of one's parents or teachers, which was a doctrine of stagnation. The Egyptian youth needed to discover Islam for themselves, which the promoters of Salafism believed could be done only through a return to the foundations of the religion: the Quran, the *Hadith* (oral reporting of the Prophet's life and teachings and the record of how they were transmitted) and the *Sunnah* (a "manner of life" including that which the Prophet Muhammad did, that which he enjoined, and that which was not forbidden by him when done in his presence). The volumes of interpretation and discussion about the various dimensions of Islam recorded over centuries could be generally disregarded: the true Islam could be found by anyone; they needed only to consult the doctrine and teachings themselves. As successive generations of young, well-educated Egyptian elites wrestled with crystallizing this infant ideology, its progressive, liberal elements would be quickly stripped away. What remained was an ideology propagated by Egypt's most educated and disenchanted youth who demanded a purer, more comprehensively Islamic society.

The Egyptian Islamic activist Hasan al-Banna and his followers provided a means for Egyptian youth to channel this collective anger in the 1920s by establishing the Egyptian Muslim Brotherhood, or Ikhwan, movement.[5] Until his death in 1949, Banna helped the Muslim Brotherhood work toward restoring the Islamic Caliphate, defending against the further encroachment of Western culture and preparing for war against the apostate Arab regimes. By the 1950s, the Ikhwan had established an international infrastructure for communicating, mobilizing, recruiting and fundraising. It would also gain its most well-known spokesman, Sayyid Qutb. An educated Egyptian government official well versed in English literature and culture, Qutb had the opportunity to visit and study in the United States from 1949 to 1950. He came away from the experience believing that America was nothing short of a hotbed of perversion, racism and exploitation. It was a culture, he argued, that was inherently subversive to Islam. He also concluded that Arab leaders who claimed to practice Islam faithfully while allowing tidal waves of godless secularism, exploitative capitalism and the perverse, barbaric Western culture to drown their countrymen and women must be ousted. The challenge must be met forcefully, he argued, by a vanguard of Muslims who believe in the Quran and the *Hadith* and follow the *Sunnah*. Qutb further expounded in his writings during the 1950s and early 1960s that most Muslims at the time were totally unaware that their religion was being assaulted before their eyes. Islam, due to a combination of ignorance and denial, had allegedly reached a state of darkness that it had not seen since pagan times, before God had revealed the Quran to the Prophet.

Qutb's philosophy can be summarized in four general points:

1   The social and political system prevailing in both the Islamic and the non-Islamic world is pagan.
2   It is the duty of a true Muslim to revive Islam and change paganism through preaching religion and Jihad.
3   Transforming the society of paganism into a real Islamic state is the task of the committed "vanguards" of Muslims.
4   The ultimate goal of committed Muslims is to establish *Hakimiyah*—that is, rule by God's canons on earth—to eliminate vice, suffering and oppression.[6]

In June 1952 Egypt's pro-Western government was dislodged by a domestic nationalist movement headed by Gamal Abdel Nasser. Although the Ikhwan had initially supported the coup, thinking that Nasser would move Egypt's domestic policies more in line with Islamic law, they were soon disappointed. Nasser's nationalism was not that of Islam, but of secular pan-Arabism: an ideology that merely provided another obstacle to unifying the *Ummah*, or global community of believers in Islam, in their struggle to purify their religion.

In October 1954 Nasser was speaking to a large crowd in the Egyptian city of Alexandria when a series of gunshots sounded. Although the shooter, Mahmoud Abd al-Latif, a member of the Muslim Brotherhood, missed his mark, the incident gave Nasser both the incentive and the political cover to crack down on a variety of opposition groups, particularly communists and Ikhwanis. He jailed hundreds of Egyptians, including Sayyid Qutb, under the pretense of a variety of offenses. During his imprisonment, Qutb brought his own thinking to fruition in his books *In the Shade of the Quran* and the short political manifesto *Milestones*.[7] Although he would write a number of other works, these two pieces became the must-have writings on the challenges to, and possible solutions for, re-establishing a dominant Islam.

With Qutb's death in August of 1966, followers of this the reinvigorated Ikhwan would flee the challenges of operating in the hostile domestic Egyptian environment for lands more tolerant of their conservative interpretation of Islam. No country would welcome them with more open arms than Saudi Arabia. Led by Sayyid Qutb's brother, Muhammad, and Manna al-Qattan, a generation of Ikhwan would resettle in the kingdom, where the ultra-conservative Wahabist Islam dominated. Over the next several decades, these Egyptian youth would fill the ranks of Saudi Arabia's schools, hospitals and law firms, and serve to hybridize in many unpredictable ways with Saudi Wahabism, leaving a confusing hodgepodge of schools, branches and doctrines under the single label of "Salafism." This became the new term for those once considered "Wahabi," in large part because the latter term is derisive, implying that followers of this interpretation of Islam follow the teachings of a man, Muhammad Ibn Abd al-Wahab, not those of God. So Salafism provided a much more appealing label for Saudi Wahabis.

The influence of the Egyptian Muslim Brotherhood experience cannot be overstated. As Salafism evolved from the 1960s to the 1990s, some of its key leadership would actively draw on the principles and organizational lessons they had learned from the first half of the century in Egypt. Other Salafists, particularly hardliners, would begin to reject the Muslim Brotherhood model as being too tolerant of deviant beliefs. The Brotherhood, which had advocated fielding candidates in elections and generally encouraged political engagement rather than violent measures, did not fully appreciate, the hardliners argued, just how dire the situation had become for Muslims.

From its new base in Saudi Arabia, the various flavors of Salafism began to spread across the Middle East, North Africa and South Asia. It also had a significant impact in Europe and North America. A Salafist is a Muslim who rejects traditional religious authority in favor of a narrow body of teaching, including the Quran, and the literal model established by the life of the Prophet Muhammad and his followers in the *Hadith*. Most Salafists reject many dimensions of modernity and generally disavow those rulers who do not strictly implement Islamic law, or *Sharia*.

It is from the Salafist intellectual tradition, hybridized with the ultra-conservative Saudi Wahabist interpretation of Islam, that the Jihadists find their religious authority, intellectual guidance and, ironically, largest competition. Salafists of all stripes generally believe that propagators of ideologies challenging their ability to implement *Sharia*—including, but not limited to, capitalism, socialism, nationalism, Hinduism, Buddhism, liberalism, pan-Arabism, Zionism and secularism—are inherent threats to God's law and therefore must be at least resisted and at best eliminated. While most Jihadists embrace these tenets of the Salafist doctrine, they differ from more mainstream Salafists in terms of how to operationalize it, specifically with regards to religious warfare. Whereas most Salafists renounce the use of violence in the attempt to apply *Sharia* within an Islamic land, Jihadists have placed violence at their core, shifting an important but not central tenet of Islam to the heart of their ideology. The Jihadist ideology is, however, firmly situated in the complex historical framework of Salafism. The latter word itself derives from the Arabic root *salaf*, which literally translates as "pious forefathers." More specifically, the term refers to the companions of the Prophet Muhammad and the generation of Muslims who followed.

Since the hybridization of Salafism and Saudi Wahabism, the Salafist movement has gained significant traction worldwide through the financial backing of Saudi Arabia. Saudi oil revenue empowered the kingdom to push its version of Wahabist-influenced Salafism aggressively over other forms of Sunni Islam through the establishment of mosques, schools, charities and youth centers. Contemporary discussions of Salafism are generally misleading, however, because the term has acquired such eclectic meanings. In its most basic form, it refers to a *manhaj*, or method, of consulting the foundational texts of Islam. In its more popular understanding, it is a movement, or a collection of like-minded believers who are held together by a common puritanical understanding of Islam, all of whom apply the Salafist methodology to their religion. The problem is that today, given the term's loose definition, any number of groups embrace it to describe themselves, which further blurs the meaning. This lack of specificity has significantly increased the difficulty that Western policy-makers have had in recent years drawing lines in the sand between friend and foe.

Arabic-speaking Jihadists have sought to clarify this variegated and often opaque world of Salafism to show how they are distinct from one another. As a result, they tend to be among the most astute observers of doctrinal similarities and differences among Salafists. Jihadist thinkers may divide the Salafist movement into anything from three to eight sub-schools of thought. Although these schools may be analytically distinct, they are still dynamic, overlapping and messy in reality. The fluid nature of this schema has been generally too problematic to gain popular appeal in the West. It is in the interplay between these various sub-schools, however, that the key for long-term success against the Jihadist movement might lie.

A popular article among hardline Salafists, written by a Canadian thinker, Dr. Tariq Abdelhaleem,[8] outlines eight branches of the Salafist movement:

- Establishment Salafists;
- Madkhali (or Jami) Salafists;
- Albani Salafists;
- Scientific Salafists;
- Salafist Ikhwan (Muslim Brotherhood);
- Sururis;
- Qutubis;
- Global Jihadists.

This is by no means scientific. Nor is it a comprehensive breakdown. In fact, many of the labels used in this list are considered derisive by those who fall into those categories and, therefore, are dismissed out of hand. The categories are, at best, fluid, dynamic and only rough approximations of the personalities and issues that divide the movement. However, they are significantly more nuanced than the categories currently used by Western policy-makers, analysts, and law enforcement agencies to discuss Establishment Salafists, Global Jihadists and those in between.

Each of these branches of Salafist thought look to different religious figures and texts for legitimacy and intellectual guidance. Their different religious interpretations have dramatic implications for the political, social, and economic behavior of their adherents. Can a "good" Muslim listen to music? Should a "good" Muslim boycott companies who do business with Israel? Is it acceptable for a "good" Muslim to fight to overthrow a Muslim government when that government fails to implement *Sharia* comprehensively? Each Salafist subset gives its followers slightly different answers and religious justifications to these and a variety of other questions. But the categorization provides nothing more than a rough topography of the Salafist terrain in order to help observers speak in more nuanced terms about the ideology.

Establishment Salafists

The first branch of Salafism is often referred to as Establishment Salafism. Adherents to this sub-school are obedient to the Saudi government.[9] They serve as the official *ulama*, or religious guides, whom the Saudi state backs with money, resources and a platform. The most prominent clerics in this category are Shaikh

Abdul-Aziz Ibn Abdullah Ibn 'Abd al-Rahman Ibn Baz (or Shaikh Bin Baz, as he is more commonly known) and Shaikh Ibn Al-Uthaymin. To those who fit this category, the term "Establishment" seems derisive, given its connotations of being stagnant and out of date. For those who employ the phrase, however, that is precisely the image they see. Some also refer to followers of this group as "Bazis," as a slight against those who are viewed as blindly following Shaikh Bin Baz.

Shaikh Bin Baz was born in 1910 in the Saudi city of Riyadh. He is said to have memorized the Quran by the age of 11.[10] At 16, he contracted an eye infection which left him completely blind by the age of 20. Nevertheless, he continued studying Islam under some of the most prominent conservative thinkers of his time, most of whom were teaching in Saudi universities. One of his most well-known teachers was the Mauritanian Muhammad as-Shanqiti (a name that frequently appears in the writings of a variety of Salafist shaikhs), who died in 1973 after a career of scholarship.

In the 1940s, Bin Baz openly issued a *fatwa*, making it a crime against Islam for any Muslim living in the Persian Gulf region to hire a non-Muslim. The Saudi government wasted little time imprisoning him for contradicting an established government policy of allowing the employment of non-Muslims. Thereafter, Bin Baz would dedicate his life to scholarship and teaching in line with the state's official Salafist interpretation. For his obedience, he would be rewarded with positions on senior Islamic councils and committees, serve as the chairman for international Salafist gatherings and publish books and *fatwa* for the next 50 years that millions would follow.

In the wake of the 1991 Gulf War, when the Saudi government invited American military forces into the kingdom, Bin Baz lost significant support from the more hardline branches of Salafism, particularly the Jihadists, for not condemning the decision. As the government cracked down on other Salafist activists who were criticizing the regime for allowing non-Muslim forces into an Islamic land, Bin Baz published a *fatwa* declaring the decision allowable and religiously legitimate. This was not the first time he had published such a supportive *fatwa*: in November of 1979, during the siege of the Grand Mosque in Mecca, he had issued a *fatwa* authorizing the use of French special forces to aid the Saudis in rescuing the hostages and capturing the rebels.[11] Similarly, this earlier religious edict had left him with few friends in the Jihadist community.

Bin Baz became the Grand Mufti of Saudi Arabia in 1993. While holding that position, he tried to walk the tightrope of providing religious legitimacy to the Saudi royal family, a regime cast by Muslims of all stripes as often conducting itself in a less than religious fashion, while lobbying for Salafist reforms within Saudi society. The contradictions continued as his support for the Oslo Peace Accord between the Palestinian Liberation Organization and the Israeli government served as another breaking point between him and many of his more conservative followers. As Israel was, for many Salafists, the single most pressing issue of the day, Bin Baz's tacit acceptance of its continued existence was viewed as outright apostasy by some. But given the love and respect that most Salafists held for him, even his staunchest critics trod lightly in their critiques.

When Bin Baz died in 1999, he was still the Grand Mufti of the Kingdom of Saudi Arabia, chairman of the Committee of Senior *Ulama* (religious scholars) and chairman of the Department of Scientific Research and *Ifta* (guidance). The Saudi government held a state funeral in his honor and millions of Muslims around the world mourned the loss.[12]

Another guiding light among the Establishment Salafists is Shaikh Ibn al-Uthaymin.[13] Born in 1925 in Unayzah, in the Qasim region of Saudi Arabia, Uthaymin studied under Bin Baz and several of the latter's former teachers, including the legendary Shaikh Shinqiti. He went on to mentor students from Saudi Arabia and across the Islamic world who came to study with him, issued numerous *fatwa* and preached in the Masjid al-Haram mosque in Mecca for over 35 years. By his death in 2004, he was hailed as one of the world's pre-eminent experts in *fiqh*, or Islamic jurisprudence, having written over 50 books on the topic.

The Establishment Salafists, guided by the writings and *fatwa* issued by Bin Baz and Uthaymin, generally believe in the *Tawhid Al-Ibadah* (unity of worship) as it was argued for by early conservative thinkers, including Ibn Abd al-Wahab and the medieval Islamic scholar Ibn Taymiyyah. Establishment Salafists say that they consider those who rule with anything other than *Sharia* to be sinners. They believe that not applying *Sharia* is the major act of disbelief, which necessitates that other Muslims must declare *Takfir* (excommunication) on those leaders.

Critics of this school, including Jihadists as well as a number of other more conservative Salafist subsets, argue that Bin Baz and Uthaymin were misled by the Saudi government, which claims that the Saudi constitution adheres to the Quran and *Sunnah*. To the contrary, the Jihadists argue, the laws that govern day-to-day behavior within the kingdom generally follow a secular law model.[14] As a result of their allegiance to their host governments, Establishment Salafists almost never name any of the Arab regimes or individual rulers as *kafir* (unbelievers), and they tend to approve of the state apparatus, although they will acknowledge that these regimes do not govern in accordance with *Sharia*. Establishment Salafist shaikhs are willing to overlook such sins in order to maintain their religious credentials. And while they may disagree with democracy as a system of governance on the grounds that it is not Islamic in principle, they usually do not openly oppose the participation of Muslims in the democratic process.

Establishment Salafists emphasize the more theoretical and internal application of Jihad over the practical use of violence. Al-Qaida's Usama Bin Laden and Ayman al-Zawahiri have both written scathing criticisms of Bin Baz's *fatwa* and his toleration of religious laxity. But, as is the tradition, both Bin Laden and Zawahiri pay their due deference to the Shaikh before and after slamming him in their formal writings.

Saudi Arabia's current chief cleric, the Grand Mufti, is Shaikh Abdulaziz al-Shaikh. A graduate of the Imam ad-Dawah Institute from the Faculty of *Sharia*, he is known for his conservative positions on Islamic issues as well as for his unswerving support for the Saudi ruling regime. Since 2001, he has issued numerous *fatwa* condemning terrorism and Jihadist ideology. Recently, he warned Muslim youth to beware of elements that were teaching lessons of "fake Jihad" in order to misguide the average Muslim. Like his predecessors, he is viewed by most hardline Salafists as a complete sell-out and a pawn of the Saudi regime.

Madkhali Salafists

Madkhali, or Jami, Salafists follow the religious teachings of the Yemeni Shaikh Rabi al-Madkhali and the Ethiopian Shaikh Muhammad Aman Ibn Ali Jami. Each term, although derisive because it associates the followers of this school with humans as opposed to God, is a convenient way to characterize the ideological differences of the group *vis-à-vis* other Salafist subsets. Both Madkhali and Jami were educated in Saudi Arabia. Other important, but lesser-known, ideologues of the group include Mohammad Al-Banna of Egypt and Ali Al-Halabi of Jordan.

Arab states have generally viewed the Madkhali Salafists as palatable, much like the Establishment Salafists, given their endorsement of secular and democratic forms of government and their unflinching support for local Arab regimes. With Saudi backing, the Madkhalis have firmly entrenched themselves globally, operating out of most Western countries. They have also gone online, so Muslims anywhere around the world can download Madkhali's teachings. In Saudi Arabia, members of the group are more commonly referred to as "Jamis," and are known for their hostility to any political tendency that opposes the authorities. This stance stems from the Salafist principle of listening and obeying religious authority. Madkhali's writings address a broad swath of other Islamic issues, but he is best known for his resistance to the use of *Takfir* (excommunication) of other Muslims, a practice that is frequently employed by more hardline Salafists, particularly Jihadists. Madkhali wrote on the issue:

> Of the matters that makes apparent their error and uncovers their misguidance is that it is said to them: "When can it be judged against a Muslim who testifies that there is none which has the right to be worshipped except Allaah and that Muhammad is His Messenger and who prays that he has apostatised from his religion? Is one instance [of ruling by other than what Allah has revealed] enough? Or is it necessary for him to announce that he has become an apostate?"[15]

Much of his thinking has been influenced by the teaching of a closely related branch of Salafism, known as Albani Salafism (see below). However, Madkhali adopted more extreme positions than Albani in his teachings. When Albani declared his support for two hardline clerics, Safar al-Hawali and Salman Al-Awdah, Madkhali's followers felt dismayed and confused. (Again, though, it is important to note that this taxonomy is nothing more than an analytical attempt to instil some order into what appears to be a chaotic mess of ideas and personalities.)

Madkhali came from the al-Madakalah tribe, from the Jizan Province of southern Saudi Arabia.[16] He was born in al-Jaradiyah, a small village to the west of Samitah, in 1931. At the age of eight, he began studying the Quran under the tutelage of Shayban al-Arishi, al-Qadhi Muhammad Ibn Muhammad Jabir al-Madkhali and Muhammad Ibn Hussain Makki from the town of Sibya. He would go on to study at the *madrasa* in Samitah under Shaikh Nasir Khalufah Taiash Mubaki, the regarded student of well-known Salafist Shaikh al-Qarawi. He learned the *Hadith* under other notable Salafist shaikhs, including Ahmad Ibn Yahya an-Najmi, and he studied Islamic doctrine under Shaikh Muhammad Aman al-Jami. In 1960, he graduated from the educational institute in Samitah and joined the Faculty of *Sharia* in Riyadh, Saudi Arabia, before moving the next year to the Islamic University of Medina. Once there, he studied under some of the leading Salafist figures in the world, learning Islamic doctrine under Shaikh Bin Baz, the *Hadith* under Shaikh al-Albani and *tafsir* (Quranic exegesis) and *usul al-fiqh* (research methodology) under Shaikh as-Shanqiti.

Madkhali has been a highly problematic figure for Jihadists operating in Saudi Arabia because of his mass popularity, particularly among the young. His messages have proved accessible and digestible for audiences of all ages. And with the backing of the Saudi government, he has been able to exploit technology fully, allowing him much broader reach than most clerics. He also enlisted the support of a national network of disciples who promoted his works while quietly keeping watch over the maneuvers of his competitor shaikhs, particularly the Jihadists.

Many hardliners condemn Madkhali Salafists for their criticism of Sayyid Qutb. To Madkhali and his followers, Qutb's teachings make him an apostate. Madkhalis feel Qutb's legendary interpretations of the Quran—compiled in his multi-volume set *In the Shade of the Quran*—profoundly misguided. Because of these vocal criticisms of Qutb and their rejection of violence, Jihadists have cast Madkhalis as sell-outs and even as *murji'ah* (snitches).

Followers of Madkhali Salafism generally allow for the rule of secular law in Islamic countries, justifying it as an "action" as opposed to an *Aqidah*, or Islamic creed concerned with matters of dogma and doctrine. Publicly referring to the ruling regimes of Arab states as legitimate and therefore calling for Muslims in those states to obey their respective governments, particularly the Saudi royal family, Madkhali Salafists tend to allow the implementation of democratic rule in Islamic states, although they advocate that Salafists remain apolitical in their daily affairs. They argue that the simple fact that the regime has political power proves God's desire for them to possess such ruling authority. And they are willing to designate those who oppose these governments as *Khawarij* ("those who go out"— referring to an early Islamic sect who are seen by many Muslims to have left mainstream Islam). It is obligatory, Madkhali Salafists argue, for Muslims to report individuals who deviate from these principles to the authorities.

Followers of Madkhali, who tend to be foreign residents of Saudi Arabia, Saudis from Jizan, and Kuwaitis, Jordanians and Yemenis, successfully humiliated the more hardline Jihadist clerics during the 1990s, particularly in Saudi Arabia. The words they used to greatest effect against radical Islamists, argues al-Qaida, included:

- "*Jihadi*": Anyone who believes that Jihad is a purely individual duty to fight.
- "*Takfiri*": Anyone who excommunicates Arab rulers or Muslims.
- "*Khariji*": Anyone who says it is permissible to overthrow Arab rulers.
- "*Khariji Bandit*": Anyone who actively seeks to overthrow Arab rulers.
- "*Qutubi*": Anyone who reveres, quotes or even positively mentions Sayyid Qutb.
- "*One Who Reviles the Scholars*": Anyone who criticizes the Arab religious scholars who support the ruling Arab governments.
- "*Hizbi*": Anyone who participates in an anti-establishment activist group.
- "*Dirty Groundhog*": [A traitor to one's religion, used specifically against Saudi hardline cleric Shaikh Hamoud bin Uqla as-Shuaybi in the 1990s.]
- "*Rabid Dogs*": [A generic label for extremists.]
- "*The Dog*": [Referring specifically to Usama Bin Laden.]
- "*Perennial Defender of Innovators*": [An attack against extremists for rejecting centuries of accepted historical teachings and interpretations of Islam.]
- "*Betrayer of the Salafi Way*": [Used to attack hardline clerics who step outside the bounds of mainstream Islamic conservatism.][17]

Albani Salafists

A third subset of Salafism, generally referred to as "Albani Salafism," earned its name for its followers' intellectual mentor, Shaikh Nasir Al-Deen al-Albani. He was born in the city of Ashkodera, then capital of Albania, in 1914. His father, al-Haaj Nooh Najjaatee al-Albani' had completed Islamic legal studies in Istanbul, Turkey, and returned to Albania before moving his family to Damascus, Syria. There, Albani engaged in classical Islamic studies, learning the Quran, Arabic linguistics and Islamic law, particularly the school of Islamic jurisprudence known as Hanafism.

By the age of 20, he was specializing in the *Hadith*, having been influenced by articles in *Al-Manar* magazine, which had been edited by the early Salafist Rashid Rida. Albani made an early name for himself by transcribing a massive tome by the renowned *Hadith* scholar Hafiz al-Iraqi. For books on Hanafism that he was not able to find in his home, he would visit the famous Damascus library, al-Maktabah at-Thahiriyyah. Albani's extensive studies in the library reportedly convinced the librarians to grant him a private room. They even gave him his own key for after-hours access. It is widely understood within the Salafist community that Albani's deep study of the *Hadith* led him to turn away from standard interpretations and look instead to the model of the *Salaf*, the pious predecessors of the Prophet Muhammad.

Being a Salafist, Albani soon found himself at odds with some of the local shaikhs, as well as with the local Sufi imams, all of whom publicly began to oppose his preaching. In Syria's mainstream religious establishment circles, Albani became just another "Wahabi deviant." Not everyone shunned him, however. Some leading conservative shaikhs, including Bahjatul Baijar, Abdul-Fattah and

Tawfiq al-Barzah, encouraged him to press onward, no matter how uncomfortable he became. Albani began teaching two classes each week, which were attended by both students and other lecturers. In class, he taught *aqidah* (creed), *fiqh* (jurisprudence), *usul* (fundamental beliefs), and the *Hadith*. He also began organizing monthly journeys to various cities throughout Syria and Jordan.

After a number of his works appeared in print, he was invited to teach *Hadith* studies in the new University in Medina, Saudi Arabia, from 1961 to 1963, where he also served as a member of the university board. He then visited various countries for *da'wah* (proselytizing) and to give lectures, including Qatar, Egypt, Kuwait, the Emirates, Spain, and England. He would become known as the pre-eminent scholar of the *Hadith* in recent Islamic history, publishing over one hundred books on the topic, and mentoring some of today's leading Salafist shaikhs.[18]

Unsurprisingly, Albani came under intense scrutiny from Jihadist-minded Salafists as a result of some of his views. However, as an authoritative voice in the modern Salafist movement, much like Shaikh Bin Baz or Shaikh Uthaymin, Jihadists have to show deference to him even while chastising him and his legacy. Nevertheless, a number of high-profile Jihadist thinkers are clearly critical of Albani's positions with regard to the issuance of *Takfir*. The Jihadist cleric Abu Muhammad al-Maqdisi, for example, wrote:

> And with relation to the mentioned *Shuyookh* [distinguished shaikhs] not performing *Takfir* [excommunication] on the *Tawaghit* [disbelievers]—what is apparent is that it was an incorrect *ijtihad* [Islamic interpretation] from them. We do not make permissible making *Takfir* on them for merely this mistake of theirs. And whosoever says other than this regarding our position—then they have fabricated a lie against us.[19]

Another prominent Jihadist cleric, Shaikh Abu Qatada, agreed with Maqdisi, saying that, "Shaikh Nasir [al-Albani] opposes us, but we do not do *Takfir* upon him; may Allah save us from being *Khawarij*."[20] The core tenets of Albani Salafism are close to, but subtly different from, the Establishment Salafist school, particularly with regards to their respective perspectives on Arab rulers. Establishment Salafists generally believe that current Arab governments in the Middle East ought to be viewed as legitimate but as wrong-headed in their failure to apply *Sharia* comprehensively. While Albani Salafists may publicly declare that rulers of those governments are sinning Muslims, even though they should not be considered apostates or unbelievers. Albani Salafists also advocate maintaining the *status quo* rather than calling for an Islamic uprising against Arab rulers. To them, living well under a Muslim regime, even if it is not under *Sharia*, is better than risking social chaos in an attempt to overthrow that regime. They tend to be optimistic about their ability to improve the laws and constitution of those states by gradually increasing the influence of Islamic rulings. They are willing to endure the establishment of democratic forms of civic participation, not on theological grounds but because representation allows Muslims the ability to improve their conditions by gradually introducing ever more elements of *Sharia* into society. Importantly, they reject the ideas of Sayyid Qutb, particularly in respect to Qutb's thoughts on *jahiliyyah* (ignorance). They do not call him a *kafr*, or unbeliever, however. Finally, they consider Jihad primarily an abstract, spiritual activity rather than a physical one, feeling that violence waged in the name of Jihad causes more harm than good and that those who do so, even against invaders, are *Khawarij*.

One of Albani's most vigorous advocates is the website Salafi Publications. This publishes most of Albani's writings, praises his contribution to Islam and the Salafist community and aggressively defends his reputation against all of his critics. Salafipublications.com has been involved in a widely publicized dispute over the legitimacy of scholars like Albani with another website, Salafi Publications Refutations. Consider one article written by the staff at Salafi Publications Refutations (SPR) that sheds light on the debate between the various schools. The authors from SPR acknowledge that Albani has done much for advancing Islam in the areas of the *Hadith* and *Fiqh*. They applaud him for dedicating his life to the guidance of others, teaching Islam and refuting the innovators from the groups of misguidance and error. And they rightly acknowledge that a number of Muslims, mostly non-Salafists, have criticized him posthumously. His large body of followers, SPR argues, have been unable to discriminate between hostile criticism from non-Salafis and friendly criticism from Salafists, with the result that

> These people have taken it upon themselves to blindly defend the noble Shaikh from every and all censure . . . But when these people create a movement centered around the Shaikh's errors in Kufr and Takfeer, and denounce those who oppose these mistakes and when certain individuals attempt to refute these concepts, they openly show their hatred and spite towards those who differ with the Shaikh. And this would be acceptable too except that they have even gone to the length of removing the label of Salafist and Sunnah from those who have dared to utter words of counsel and reform in this regard . . . But when these individuals go to even further lengths of evil slander and lies upon us, then we see that it is incumbent upon us to point out their deception, evil and mischief.[21]

Although much of Shaikh Albani's work is cited as authoritative by global Jihadists, his followers are curiously despised by the Jihadist community as they represent a major threat to Jihadists: in short, followers of Albani adopt very similar doctrinal positions to those of Jihadists but have very different recommendations about how to apply those doctrines. Making matters worse for Jihadists, Albani's followers tend to be one of the most active Salafist subsets in terms of spreading their teachings, particularly on the internet.

The now "reformed" Jihadist cleric Shaikh Abd al-Qadr Ibn Abd Al-Aziz (Dr. Fadl) also wrote a response to this opinion in a letter entitled *The Mainstay on Preparing Provisions for Jihad*. In it, he claims that Albani's definition of Jihad as being forgiveness, education and prayer is grievously wrong. Albani, he argues, is wrapped in evil and is not suitable to be a shaikh. He also expresses the extreme view that today's leaders throughout the Muslim world are not Muslims at all. By adopting this position, Abd al-Qadir puts himself at odds with Albani and most mainstream Salafists. For Abd al-Qadir, however, fighting apostates and those who support them is a duty more urgent than fighting Jews, who would not have rooted themselves in Palestine if it were not for these Muslim leaders.

Scientific Salafists

Scientific, or Academic, Salafists earn their name from the highly rational methods they employ to discuss and implement their version of Salafism. Adherents to this approach are regularly featured in Arab newspapers and on television because they tend to be among the most vocal on social and political issues. In Kuwait, for example, they consistently enter candidates for elections. And in Algerian public schools they openly teach their scientific version of Salafism. Important figures in the group, which has its own party called Hizb al-Ummah (Nation's Party), include Shaikh Abdul Rahman Abdul Khaliq, Abdul Razak al-Shaygi, Dr. Sajid al-Mutairi and Dr. Hamid Ali.

Scientific Salafist doctrine generally emphasizes viewing most Islamic ruling regimes today as sinners, but not as apostates. Proponents openly concede that these regimes violate the strenuous demands of Islam, but they see most of their actions as minor transgressions. The fact that these rulers have not implemented *Sharia* law is, for Scientific Salafists, an undeniable sin, but it is not grounds to excommunicate them or to declare them to be disbelievers.

One stronghold of Scientific Salafism is Kuwait. Islamic political movements there have recently been targeting the information and education ministers in an attempt to move the country's policies toward conservative Salafist doctrine. Dr. Walid al-Tabtaba'i, a member of the Kuwaiti parliament who generally rejects female suffrage, has been at the forefront of these efforts.[22] But even in Kuwait, Scientific Salafists continue to face challenges familiar to most hardline Salafist movements across the Middle East. On January 29, 2005, for instance, Scientific Salafist leaders there held a press conference announcing the establishment of their party in order to confirm the right of political pluralism and the transfer of power through peaceful means, as well as their adherence to *Sharia* and their rejection of all forms of foreign occupation. Three days later, in response to this pronouncement, the Kuwaiti public prosecutor's office charged nine of the Salafist leaders with plotting to overthrow the government and violating association and press laws, crimes which carried a maximum sentence of 15 years in prison. They were released on $1,026 bail after a ten-hour interrogation. The case never came to trial.[23]

Given that no Middle Eastern government has established a functioning *Sharia* system, Scientific Salafists accept the process of democratic participation in secular government. They do so not because they see it as being compatible with *Sharia*, but because, given the current state of affairs, it is the most rational way to achieve what is in the public interest. Democracy provides the proponents of this approach with a chance to proselytize openly through campaigns, and, more importantly, to exert control over the governance of their states. It therefore allows them to set their regimes on a trajectory toward the implementation of *Sharia*.

This version of Salafism, as opposed to some of the other subsets, generally respects the teachings of Sayyid Qutb, although Scientific Salafists tend to differ from him on theological grounds as well as disagreeing with his characterization of modern society as being in an age of *jahilliyah*, or ignorance. Although Scientific Salafists embrace the concept of Jihad as an integral part of Islam, they are careful to interpret it as being more spiritual in nature than physical: they clearly advocate avoiding physical confrontation with powers numerically and qualitatively stronger than they are, as to fight them would simply be irrational. However, these Salafists are no supporters of recent American actions in the Middle East. Dr. Sajid Abdali, former chairman of the Political Bureau of the Scientific Salafist Movement, who has been active in the Kuwaiti national political machinery, for instance, has remarked: "The Scientific Salafi Movement has said it opposes the US presence in the region and in Iraq . . . Therefore, we object to the Kuwaiti government facilities for the American troops in Iraq. Yes, we are opposed to this presence, but we do not call for violence."[24]

When pushed by the London-based Arabic newspaper *al-Sharq al-Awsat* on whether he thought that such a call for resistance paved the way for young people to engage in fighting and military action in Iraq, he answered: "No, and we affirm the legitimacy of Jihad in Iraq. However, we do not call [on people] directly to go to Iraq, [although] there are scholars and religious scholars [who take] this view."[25]

Another bastion of Scientific Salafism is Algeria. Young Algerians who had studied in Saudi Arabia carried the Salafist movement back with them during the 1980s. Even though their leader Abdelmalek Ramdani has since fled to Saudi Arabia after receiving death threats, Scientific Salafists in Algeria have continued to cause the government significant consternation by challenging the way that Islam is practiced by pressuring mosques and local imams to move toward more conservative doctrine. In 2006, during the Islamic holy month of Ramadan, for instance, a controversy erupted regarding mosques which did not adhere to the time for the end of daily fasting set by the Ministry of Religious Affairs. "Some muezzins are signaling the end of the day's fast ten minutes before the time set by law," said Bouabdellah Ghlamallah, the Minister of Religious Affairs, whose ministry runs mosques and is in charge of all their expenditures, including imams' salaries. The ministry has also warned the Algerian public of the infiltration of mosques by the Scientific Salafist movement, with Ghlamallah declaring that the country is going through a severe cultural and religious crisis.[26] Other new trends observed in some mosques include the use of loudspeakers at full volume and the reciting of Wahabi-style prayers during the month of Ramadan. The Ministry of Religious Affairs is clearly concerned by this gradual infiltration and has given instructions to help mosques guard against the movement's efforts to take them over. According to the Algerian daily newspaper *El Khabar*, police have also opened a nationwide investigation into the Salafists' spread across the country.[27]

Salafist Ikhwan (Muslim Brotherhood)

The Muslim Brotherhood has become well known to most observers of Middle Eastern politics. Since its inception in the 1920s under the direction of its founder, the Egyptian Hassan al-Banna, it has morphed into a multifaceted and disjointed political movement that looks different in each local instantiation. Well-known leaders of the Muslim Brotherhood include Dr. Isam Al-Bashir of Sudan, Omar Al-Ashqar of Jordan, and Al-Shaik Abdel Majid Al-Zindani of Yemen.

This school holds views similar to those of the Establishment Salafists, although they are much more open to the democratic process as an essential element of the Ikhwan movement. They also agree with Establishment scholars about prioritizing of spiritual struggle over physical struggle with regard to Jihad. Although they condemn Arab governments for their complicity in aiding the Zionist–Crusader conspiracy, and for failing to implement *Sharia*, they stop short of declaring the rulers *kuffar*, at least publicly. Given the situation in which Muslims find themselves, followers of this subset argue, there is a tacit consensus that participation in the democratic political process is acceptable because it allows rightly guided believers to exert some influence in restoring Islamic rule to their lands.

One of the key theoreticians of the group was Egyptian Muslim Brotherhood member Muhammad Qutb, who also influences several other Salafist subsets, including the Qutubis. In his book *Understandings that Must be Corrected* he argued:

> We must bear in mind the requirements of "there is no god but God," as the first generation understood them, as being taught by God to His Messenger . . . The first requirement is the unity of the deity and the divinity, and the unity of the names and the characteristics (that is, the unity of belief). The second requirement is the unity of worship of God alone, with no partners (that is, the unity of worship). The third requirement is the arbitration of God's law alone, with all other systems of law excluded.[28]

By not applying Islamic law comprehensively, and by implementing elements of Western-style capitalism, by inviting Western companies into Islamic lands and by allowing Western soldiers to build bases in their countries, Arab rulers are violating nearly every principle of Islam. Secular rule, no matter how one spins it, is a major problem for this group. They know from experience, however, that issuance of *Takfir* against these regimes, or anything that smacks of it, invariably leads to their imprisonment.

Sururis

The Sururi Salafists are named for their clerical inspiration, Muhammad Surur Bin Nayif Zayn al-Abidin. The Sururi approach to Salafism was developed by those Salafists who saw Surur's massive global sway, resonant propaganda network and highly organized mobilizing structures as a threat to their recruiting and fundraising efforts. Surur had been an early member of the Syrian Muslim Brotherhood, which had become increasingly radical in its thinking and violent in its actions. He was also a staunch proponent of Sayyid Qutb's writing on the state of *jahiliyah*, or ignorance, in which Islam was allegedly currently stuck. Following a series of Syrian government crackdowns against the Brotherhood in the 1950s and 1960s, Surur relocated to the burgeoning hub of conservative Salafist thought in Saudi Arabia, the town of Buraidah. He taught and preached at Buraidah College, which is affiliated with Imam Muhammad Bin-Sa'ud Islamic University. Among his students were individuals who would rise to prominence in Saudi conservative Islamist activism, most notably Salman al-Awdah. There is little doubt that Surur's Ikhwani tendencies hybridized with hardline Saudi Salafism during this time.

In his early years living and teaching in Saudi Arabia, Surur sought pre-emptively to mitigate any backlash he would receive from the domestic Islamists as a result of his teachings by using the same slogan as most Saudi hardliners: "Doctrine First." This indicated the priority of theology and doctrine over matters of jurisprudence. Surur and his followers, however, quietly continued to expand their organization and influence across Saudi Arabia, particularly during the rise of the "Islamic Awakening" movement. He saw this grassroots push among the kingdom's conservatives as an opportunity to cast his doctrinal net wider. It was also during this time, however, that the split between the senior members of the Sururis and the Jamis occurred. By the 1990s, Surur himself, Safar al-Hawali, Salman al-Awdah and a number of Awakening clerics were adopting an openly confrontational stance against the Saudi regime. As the state mustered its own religious soldiers, such as Madkhali and Jami, Surur and his followers leaned further toward the oppositionists.[29]

Followers of Surur's work generally feel the concept of *Tawhid* (God's unity as reflected in both worship and daily life) is a priority. Strong belief in pure *Tawhid* often leads one to reject democracy and representative or participatory forms of government. Because of this preoccupation with *Tawhid* in theory and practice, the group tends to be remarkably well attuned to social and political issues. School curricula, laws regulating commerce and a variety of other seemingly mundane matters are also priorities. Importantly, however, adherents are not near-sighted: their concern is almost always global in scope. They feel that from New York to London, to Mostar to Algiers, to Lahore to Manilla, Muslims are under attack. This global conspiracy, they generally argue, is being perpetrated by a coalition of Jews and Christians (spearheaded by the United States, Britain, and Israel), but it is also being tacitly supported by Arab regimes.

One Sururi follower who spoke with the London-based Arab newspaper *Al-Sharq al-Awsat* noted, "What is more important than the Sururi organization is the 'Sururi ideology.' It is the ideology that dominates the majority of the Awakening addresses in the country through audiotapes, sermons, lectures, and books and 'practically' moulds the majority into the Sururi methods and thinking." For this follower, the most important issue for Sururis is "the method."

Surur and his followers quietly continued to develop their uniquely styled Salafist–Brotherhood hybrid ideology after moving from Buraidah to Kuwait and then to the United Kingdom, where Surur established the Sunnah Study Centre in his Birmingham home neighborhood.[30] Through the center, Surur began to publish the *Al-Sunnah* magazine, which he used to codify his teachings and his ultra-conservative, yet pragmatically mitigated, political stances on a variety of issues. He also used the magazine to mobilize Muslims around the world, much like the Ikhwani movement had done. The magazine gained even wider appeal in the aftermath of the 1991 Gulf War when conservative Salafist activism began to erupt into violence, particularly in Buraidah.

It was also roughly during this time that the name "Sururis" (or "Sururiyun" for "the procrastinators") to describe the adherents of this particular method, which was best articulated by Sururi, emerged from competing subsets of Salafism as a way to marginalize the group politically, socially and religiously. As one observer of Sururi Salafism has argued,

> The Sururis have taken from Ibn Taymiyah his strict Salafi stance toward those who contradict the Sunnah from the other groups and sects, such as the Shiites. Therefore, they have drawn the "ideological content" from Ibn Taymiyah. As for Sayyid Qutb, they have taken from him his "revolutionary attitude" and completely believe his opinion.[31]

By 2004, Surur had resided in Great Britain for nearly 20 years but in that year he relocated to Jordan. His supporters claimed on their Centre for Islamic Studies website (*www.alsunnah.org*) that he was not leaving Birmingham to reconcile with the Syrian government but rather to ensure that his supporters in their schools in Oman were being well supported. With respect to Surur's position on those who had joined al-Qaida and similarly violent Islamic groups, the statement said, "These young men are not enemies of the Shaikh and he does not see them as such. He will treat them as a father deals with children who have gone astray. He will always implore God to guide them and that they return to the path of righteousness."[32]

Qutubis

Closely related to the Sururis are the 'Qutubi Salafists'—a derogatory term for an eclectic group who follow the teachings of Sayyid Qutb and those who generally advocate his principles. Adherents of this school may follow a Salafist *manhaj*, or method of looking to the foundations of Islam for guidance, but many other Salafists see little common ground between the Qutubis and themselves, more often linking them to the thinking of the hardline elements of Egypt's Muslim Brotherhood. For softer Salafists, particularly the Establishment subset, the Qutubis are unacceptably radical in both their thinking and their organization. For the Jihadists, however, Qutubis are viewed as accommodationist and weak because they do not demand violent solutions. This makes them, in Jihadist eyes, even worse than some of the more liberal subsets, because they offer an alternative for youth who might otherwise have been tempted to throw in their lot with the Jihadists.

Traditionally lumped into this category are Sayyid Qutb himself, Abu Al-'ala Al-Maududi of Pakistan, Muhadith Ahmad Shakir of Egypt, Mahmoud Shaker of Egypt, Mufti of Saudi Arabia Imam Muhamad Ibrahim, and Scholar of *Tafsir* Abd al-Rahman Al-Dawsari of Saudi Arabia. More contemporary scholars generally associated with the group include Mohammad Qutb, Abdel Majid Al-Shazlie of Egypt and Shaikh Gazi Al-Tuwbah of Kuwait. Whether these thinkers accept this designation is another question. Nevertheless, their works are most often cited by this school to justify their doctrine and activities.

The group's primary agenda is to unify the global *ummah*, to promote the doctrine of *Tawhid*, and to work toward the re-Islamicization of society through the replacement of phony Muslim Arab regimes and by stopping the influx of secularism, capitalism and Western culture into the Islamic world. Scholars supporting this subset have generally been very vocal in condemning those governments who adopt legal systems other than *Sharia*, particularly the Saudi regime. These thinkers openly declare that Arab and Muslim governments are secular and therefore stand beyond the Islamic pale. Historically, they have not hesitated to label any Muslim political officials who participate in legislating secular laws *kuffar*. Qutubis generally ground their arguments in the Quran, *Sunnah* (or model of the Prophet) and specific *tafsir* (or interpretations of the Quran), particularly those written by Sayyid and Mohammad Qutb. Furthermore, Qutubis are comfortable publicly admonishing Muslims who commit major Islamic violations with the label of disbeliever.

Hardline Qutubis strongly oppose participation in the democratic process on both theoretical and practical grounds: democracy is allegedly un-Islamic in its nature and participation in secular parliaments has not provided any benefit to Muslims. Qutubis recognize the potential danger of average Muslims, not educated in the foundational texts of Islamic theology, judging one another as *kuffar*, but they argue that they only advocate such a judgment when the accused has committed a major crime against Islam. For Qutubis, Jihad in its violent form is a viable solution for righting the wrongs of today's Islam. They do, however, identify a number of important religious stipulations for the use of violence. Adherents generally believe that Jihad should be defined as to prepare fully for struggle in whatever form is necessary, meaning economically and spiritually as well as militantly.

Global Jihadists

In many ways, today's Jihadist movement is the most successful self-fulfilling prophecy the world has ever seen. For, while Usama Bin Laden from 1996 to 1998 hailed a "world Islamic front for Jihad against the Jews and Crusaders," at that time there really was little more than a small band of well-funded and highly organized peripatetic bullies stirring up trouble and justifying it in Islam. But the more that Bin Laden and his followers kept proclaiming their existence, the more people began to believe it, and the more it became true.

As staggering as it may seem, the global Jihadist movement in its current incarnation stepped out of its adolescence and into adulthood remarkably recently (*circa* 2003), particularly in terms of its doctrinal maturity and social embeddedness. Before then, the global Jihadist movement had crawled along as a loose amalgamation of schools, personalities, doctrines and individuals. It borrowed heavily, co-opted where it could, and claimed credit when it needed to. Despite Bin Laden's attempts to spin al-Qaida as the vanguard of a globally united social movement as early as 1996, this was simply not the case. Planning and executing an operation, even one as catastrophic as 9/11, is one thing; creating a self-sustaining global movement is entirely another.

To a large degree, the Jihadist movement began as nothing more than a distillation of the most conservative and violent tendencies from the other seven categories of Salafism. It took these elements—their personalities, political stances and experiences—assembled them into an accessible and persuasive composite and began to market them as a new product. It would therefore be appropriate to view global Jihadism as a tremendously successful entrepreneurial initiative. From a corporate branding perspective, or the business of helping a corporation to create an enduring, emotional tie between itself and its consumers, al-Qaida provided a perfect vehicle to "sell" global Jihadism. Its brand was easy to remember, thanks in large part to its corporate spokesman, Usama Bin Laden. Like any public face of a brand, Bin Laden provides a single, memorable image that allows consumers to connect instantly with his product line. Many successful corporate spokesmen present a "folksy" image to their audience: it feels good to think about these people because it is easy to relate to their background, like a neighbor, grandfather, uncle or brother. If a company can persuade an audience to like its spokesman, that audience becomes more likely to purchase (and keep purchasing) the company's product. It was not global Jihadism *per se* that attracted people to the brand. It was the feelings of hope and admiration that a key demographic of Muslims felt while watching al-Qaida's chief spokesman hiking in the desert in videos or listening to his audio-taped lectures: Bin Laden became the face and personality of global Jihadism.

Besides having a likeable spokesman at its helm, however, al-Qaida had to demonstrate to its target audience—young Muslim men who were frustrated with a stagnant and politically correct Islam and disenchanted with the effect they believed capitalism and Western culture was having on their local culture—that al-Qaida was the solution, the organization that could turn the tides. In short, al-Qaida had to become the brand to beat. The attacks of 9/11 and the immediate global aftermath provided that legitimation. The organization proved that it was both willing and able to attack the most powerful country in the world on its home turf. It also gained affirmation of its position as public enemy number one when George W. Bush demanded that people choose sides: "You're either with us or against us, we mean it. There's no middle ground when it comes to freedom and terror."[33]

Since branding itself, the movement has been able to accomplish incredible feats and turn itself into a stand-alone social phenomenon that can organically adapt to environmental changes and mobilize support in a variety of social and political climates. Seven interlocking elements comprise today's global Jihadist movement:

1   A founding myth, which encompasses the history of the Prophet Muhammad and his "rightly guided followers," the deep body of medieval Islamic intellectualism that followed in that path and those contemporary Islamic thinkers who made it accessible to a modern Islam.
2   The core doctrines of *Tawhid*, *Al-Wala wal-Bara*, Jihad, *Aqidah* and *Takfir* that were clarified by the teachings, writings and lives of men like Muhammad Ibn abd al-Wahab, Hasan al-Banna, Sayyid Qutb, Maududi, Juhayman al-Utaybi and others.
3   The lessons learned from leaders trying to apply these teachings on the ground, including Marwan Hadid, Abdullah Azzam, Mullah Muhammad Umar, Usama Bin Laden, Ayman al-Zawahiri, Khattab, Yusuf al-Ayiri and Abu Musab al-Zarqawi.
4   The ongoing ideological guidance generated by scholars like Hammoud bin Uqla as-Shuaybi, Abu Muhamamd al-Maqdisi, Nasr al-Fahd, Ali al-Khudayr, Abu Qatada, Abu Basir al-Tartusi, Umar Abd al-Rahman and others.
5   The ever-expanding accessibility of information and education made possible by Jihadist propaganda groups, such as as-Sahab, al-Furqan, Sawt al-Jihad, al-Fajr, Global Islamic Media Front and others.
6   The hard-nosed strategic thinking provided by men like Abu Ubayd al-Qurashi, Abu Musab al-Suri, Abu Bakr Naji, Lewis Atiyattallah and a variety of others.
7   The increased grassroots investment of Muslims through engagement in study groups, internet forums and self-guided Jihadist curricula on every imaginable dimension of Jihad.

Global Jihadist doctrine

The modern global Jihadist movement has invented and propagated a compelling founding myth modeled on the experience of the Prophet Muhammad. That myth centers on the fact that Muhammad and his followers were obstructed from practicing their religion freely in Mecca and, facing impeding doom from those who were ignorant about the monotheism of Islam, fled to Medina in order to escape certain oppression, imprisonment and even death, consolidate their strength, expand their base and return to Mecca to spread the word of God through the blades of their swords, and set up a system of governance completely in accordance with the teachings of Allah as revealed to Muhammad in the Quran.

Aqidah

Above all else, Jihadists are concerned with perfecting their *Aqidah*, or Islamic creed, so that they can be as closely aligned with God's teachings as possible What makes matters complicated for Jihadists is that there is no single, agreed-upon *Aqidah*. The debate over what comprises the perfect *Aqidah* has inevitably caused a great deal of historical debate for Muslims of all stripes.

To declare that Allah is the Creator or the Provider is not enough to become Muslim, global Jihadists argue. A Muslim must aspire toward the *Aqidah* of *Ahl al-Sunnah*, the ways in which the first generations of Muslims sought to reject ignorance (*jahilliyyah*) and deviance (*shirk*) and instead embraced the word of Allah and lived according to the tenets of *Tawhid*, or the belief in the unity of Allah. The *Aqidah* followed by most Jihadists was articulated by the medieval Islamic thinker Ibn Taymiyyah in his book *Al-Aqidah al-Wastiyyah*. Ibn Taymiyyah described his reason for writing this *Aqidah*:

> A Shafi'ite judge from Wasit [in Iraq] whose name is Radiy ad-Din al-Wasiti visited me on his way to Hajj [pilgrimage]. This Shaikh was a man of goodness and faith. He complained to me of the people's situation in that country [i.e., Iraq] under the Tatars' [Mongols] rule of ignorance, injustice, and loss of faith and knowledge . . . He asked me to write him an *Aqidah* as a reference to him and his family. But I declined, saying: Many creeds have been written. Refer to the scholars of the *Sunnah*. However, he persisted in his request, saying: I do not want any creed but one you write. So I wrote this one for him while I was sitting one afternoon.[34]

Jihadist scholar Abu Muhammad al-Maqdisi updated Ibn Taymiyyah's work on *Aqidah* for the contemporary Jihadist movement. In some cases, Maqdisi quotes directly from Taymiyyah and other medieval scholars who had written on *Aqidah*. In his famous work on the topic, "This is Our *Aqidah*!," Maqdisi reminds readers that previous scholars, such as Taymiyyah, would go to great lengths in expounding upon the issues of their times in order to refute the philosophies of any sects that had deviated from the true path.

For global Jihadists, *Aqidah* is a key element in learning the difference between right action and wrong action in the eyes of God. Ibn al-Qayyim, a student of Ibn Taymiyyah, argued in one of his well-known books, *Zad al-Ma'ad* (*Provisions of the Hereafter*), that disbelief in Islam will eventually span the globe, leaving only a few Ghuraba (literally "strangers," but when used by Jihadists it refers to the minority of Muslims who will gain eternal life in Paradise).

An important part of perfecting one's *Aqidah* is identifying and publicly highlighting the behavior and beliefs from which one is trying to distance oneself. Jihadists divide the Islamic world into at least ten communities based on the *Aqidah* that they practice. Of these ten groups, most are considered deviant by Jihadists because of their corruption, disbelief and hypocrisy.

- "*The Apathetic*" (*Al-Zalamiyun*): For Jihadists, those Muslims that fall into this category are living in spiritual darkness because they show little concern for the affairs of Muslims. They are politically and socially unaware of what is around them religiously and do not feel connected to the Jihadist operations in places like Iraq, Palestine and Chechnya. Jihadists argue that this group of Muslims do not concern themselves with preparing to fight against apostate rulers or foreign occupiers of Muslim lands. They lump the religious group Jama'at al-Tablighi and the mainstream supporters of the Saudi government into this category.

- *"The Propagators of Disbelief"* (*Al-Zanadiqah*): Whereas Jihadists chastise the first group for failing in their *Aqidah* due to apathy, passivity and ignorance, this group is considered far worse. For Jihadists, Muslims who fall into this category are promoting disbelief, innovation and deviance couched in religious terminology and doctrine. They are the most evil of the Muslims, Jihadists argue. Current examples of this group include Salman Rushdie, whom Jihadists argue has attacked Islam using its most sacred texts and teachings. The Qadiyanis, also known as Mirzai, Ahmadi or Lahori, also fall into this category. They are a sect who do not believe that the Prophet Muhammad was the last prophet of Islam. Their founder, Mirza Ghulam Ahmad (1835–1908), claimed to be the Messiah. Jihadists, like many other Muslims, argue that this group does little but promote wrongful innovation and deviance cloaked in the religion of Islam.
- *"The Deviant Nation of Islam"*: Most Muslims, Jihadists argue, knowingly or unknowingly promote behaviors that are prohibited by Islam. In order to justify their failure to live a virtuous life and perfect their *Aqidah*, Jihadists say that these Muslims cloak themselves in the Quran and the *Hadith*. In this group, Jihadists tend to include the Nation of Islam and all government-sponsored Muslim organizations, such as the Muslim Council of Britain (the UK's representative Muslim umbrella body with over four hundred affiliated national, regional and local organizations, mosques, charities, and schools). They also include Young Muslim associations and certain scholars, such as Yusuf al-Qardawi and Hamzah Yusuf.
- *"The Desirous, the Superstitious and the Innovators"*: For Jihadists, those who fall into this category include, above all else, Sufi Muslims and those whom they believe worship things other than God and allow their human desires to guide their faith. These are Muslims, they argue, who resist submitting exclusively to Allah, and instead seek to tempt the Islamic world with their own misguided practices and beliefs. As well as Sufis, Jihadists include any mystical or revivalist trends of Islam in this category.
- *"The Evildoers"* (*Ahl ul-Fisq wal-Mujoon*): This group refers almost exclusively to the non-practicing youth of Islamic backgrounds who live in and have embraced Western culture. Jihadists are particularly concerned by their support of night clubs, cinemas, clubs, theaters, universities and colleges, and by their open fraternization with non-Muslims of the opposite sex. They chastise them for listening to music, promiscuity, drinking alcohol, smoking, taking drugs and so on.
- *"The Fake and Rotten Salafists"* (*As-Salafiyyat ut-Talafiyyah*): This category refers to those Muslims who call themselves Salafists, study the Quran and the *Hadith*, and follow the general foundations of the Salafist tradition but resist the call to wage physical Jihad. Although their *Aqidah* is more closely aligned ideologically with that of the global Jihadist movement, their reticence to follow through with any meaningful action makes them, for Jihadists, as bad as any other deviant group. Nearly all Salafist tendencies outside of the Jihadist movement itself fall into this category.

- *"The Faithful yet Silent"* (*Ahl al-Ibadah wal-Iltizam*): This category includes those Muslims who adhere to the conservative religious doctrine of Salafism and practice in their daily lives. They are the sympathizers and financial supporters of groups like al-Qaida and the global Jihadist movement in general. The main Jihadist criticism of them is therefore not on ideological or doctrinal grounds as their *Aqidah* is sound, but rather that they are silent when they should be speaking out in support of the global Jihadist movement and against its enemies. Jihadists argue that fear of being arrested or labeled a terrorist is an insufficient excuse for their lack of action.
- *"Those who Procrastinate"* (*Ahl al-Irja*): Jihadists lump those Muslims who have heard the call but delay in heeding it through physical action into this category, arguing that they separate their beliefs and their *Aqidah* from their actions. Muslims in this group frustrate Jihadists because they actively spread the idea that violence, action and physical Jihad can wait, preferring accommodation and compromise with the governments that Jihadists consider disbelievers and sinners. Jihadists characterize those in this group, particularly the Muslim Brotherhood, as relativists who believe (incorrectly) that everyone is entitled to their own opinion in order to avoid direct conflict. Jihadists also include in this category Islamic groups like the Muslim Association of Britain, the Islamic Society of Britain, the Islamic Forum Europe and the Muslim Public Affairs Council.
- *"Nationalist Muslims"*: Jihadists characterize many Muslims, particularly in Palestine and parts of South Asia, as being too deeply in love with their nation, not realizing that the entire state system is a tool of Christian oppression. Nationalism, Jihadists contend, is a disease and the main cause of disunity among Islam and the failure of Muslims to strive toward the proper *Aqidah*.
- *"The Secularists"*: This final group includes those individuals whom Jihadists believe have bought wholesale into the Western concept of separation of church and state. Members of this group, they argue, do not support the establishment of *Sharia* law and instead argue that Islam must reconcile itself with and adapt to the twenty-first century.

Tawhid

The Arabic term *Tawhid* refers to the oneness and totality of God. In its contemporary usage, it refers to the need for unity across a number of different spheres. When understood as "unity of believers," it means Muslims should seek to transcend legal and factional differences in order to overcome common enemies. When understood as "unity of belief," it means Muslims should steer away from those who innovate (*bida*) Islamic doctrine and instead return to the fundamentals as taught in the Quran, the *Hadith* and the *Sunnah*. When understood as "unity of worship," it means Muslims must learn that they cannot live a true Islamic life as instructed by God if they are living under rules that are not in complete accordance with *Sharia*. This requirement means that Muslims cannot support non-*Sharia* systems of governance, particularly secular democracy, because it puts the laws of humans ahead of the laws of Allah. So God is the only legislator and the only one who should be consulted when resolving disputes. Democracy would amount to denying the oneness of Allah (*shirk*); and it is sinful under all circumstances, Jihadists argue, because Islam does not accept that the end justifies the means.

For Jihadists, *Tawhid* is the first and most important obligation in Islam. Believing in Allah does not make one Muslim, they argue, for a person can be authentic only if they worship and obey Allah exclusively. Therefore, for Jihadists, it is not enough for one to fulfill one or two conditions of *Tawhid*; every one of the conditions listed below must be fulfilled in order for one's *Tawhid* to be valid.[35]

- *Pronouncement and assertion*: Jihadists believe that one cannot be a Muslim unless they verbally testify, "I have been ordered to fight people until they say [declare] *Laa ilaaha illallah* [there is none worthy of worship but Allah]".[36]
- *Certainty in their knowledge*: For Jihadists, a Muslim must gain knowledge about God's unity in order to avoid committing *shirk* [sins] and consequently become a *mushrik* [a sinner]. Knowledge alone is not sufficient, however. Muslims must be certain in their heart that what they believe is the only truth.
- *Acceptance and submission*: After one becomes certain in one's knowledge of God, one must fully accept what one testifies, setting all of one's personal desires (*hawaa*) aside. Acceptance, Jihadists reason, leads to absolute submission in God's law in all aspects of one's life. One's belief must seize one completely and one must live as God's slave with no *haraj* (discontent).
- *Disavowing disbelief*: Those Muslims who fail to embrace the doctrine of Tawhid are liars in the eyes of Jihadists as they claim to be Muslims but they do not believe in their hearts. It is a condition of *Tawhid*, they argue, to disbelieve in false deities and religions, and to reject the people who do. One's status as a Muslim is incomplete until one makes *Takfir* and disavows sinners and disbelievers.
- *Dying for belief*: It is pointless for one to fulfill all of the conditions of *Tawhid* and then die due to infidelity. In such a case, all of one's deeds will be lost and the individual will be damned in the afterlife.

Takfir

Most simply, *Takfir* is the practice of declaring an individual a religious apostate, saying that they are no longer welcome in the community of believers in Islam. It is a highly problematic concept for Jihadists because, although it forms part of their critical doctrinal core, it is generally unpopular: mainstream Islam has no history or tradition of judging fellow Muslims' "Muslim-ness."

Therefore, *Takfir* is where the Jihadist movement is perhaps most doctrinally weak. Most Salafists stop short of declaring that fellow Muslims are unbelievers, accepting simply public disavowal due to an individual's sins against God and Islam. But Jihadists, drawing on the writings of key figures like Taymiyyah and Wahab, view *Takfir* as a religious mandate. Consider the book by Jihadist Shaikh

Nasir bin Hamad al-Fahd entitled *Whoever Does Not Do* Takfir *of the Disbeliever is a Disbeliever*, a title that efficiently sums up his position on the matter. Fahd observes, "'Whoever does not do *Takfir* of the disbeliever is then a disbeliever' is a well-known principle, and is the third nullification of the nullifications of Islam, as mentioned by the Shaikh Muhammad bin 'Abd al-Wahab, [quoting Wahab]: 'The Third: Whoever does not do takfeer of the polytheists, doubted their disbeliever, or corrected their creed, disbelieves.'"[37] For Fahd, there are two categories of disbeliever: "The Original Disbeliever," including Jews, Christians, Hindus, Buddhists and Confucianists. Muslims who do not do *Takfir* against these groups immediately, doubts their disbelief even for a moment, or tries to correct their creed ought to be considered a disbeliever himself because this is effectively a rejection of *Sharia* texts that mention the falsehood of all creeds other than Islam and the disbelief of all non-Muslims. The second category of disbelief for Fahd is "The Apostate from Islam," which includes anyone who converts from Islam to another religion, particularly Judaism or Christianity, or anyone who nullifies their "Muslim-ness" in their actions but still claims to be a faithful Muslim. This category includes those who fail to do *Takfir* against those whom they know first-hand to be disbelievers; those who fail to do *Takfir* against those about whom they have heard reports but have no first-hand experience; those who reject reports of someone being a disbeliever and therefore refuse to do *Takfir* against them; or those who simply reject the principle by which a person has been called a disbeliever by other Jihadists. For example, if a Muslim stops praying five times daily for a year, Jihadists would call them a disbeliever and demand that the community do *Takfir* on them. Not doing *Takfir* on them is grounds for someone to do *Takfir* on them. Anyone who rejects the notion that not praying five times a day for a year constitutes a 'nullifiable' offense against Islam, and therefore is not grounds for doing *Takfir*, is also subject to being excommunicated.

Saudi Jihadist ideologue Yousef al-Ayiri noted that Jihadists "do not declare any Muslim a disbeliever for a sin he has committed, short of apostasy, until they ascertain that there is conviction." Rather, he suggests, "they declare as a disbeliever whoever utters words of disbelief or commits, or believes in, acts of disbelief, whether individually or collectively, so long as this is not done out of ignorance, misinterpretation, or coercion, which disqualify people from being declared disbelievers."[38] Before ascertaining whether someone qualifies as a disbeliever, Ayiri clarifies, Jihadists first declare *Takfir* on the act in question. Once they can identify that there are grounds for declaring the person is a disbeliever, they do so.

Abu Muhammad al-Maqdisi takes an even finer hand to the questions of *Takfir* in his book *This is Our Aqidah*. For Maqdisi, blatant infidels, including Jews, Christians, Hindus, Buddhists and so on are without question to be shunned by Muslims. They have nothing to offer but religious temptation and impurity. However, with respect to those Muslims whom Jihadists believe have nullified their "Muslim-ness," Jihadists should not necessarily declare *Takfir* on "the Kuffar and the Mushrikun and apostates." Even disobedient believers, he argues, remain within the fold of Islam so long as they remain Muslims. Jihadists only declare "disavowal towards their disobedience, corruption and sins and we do not interact with them in the manner of Kuffar."[39] To clarify, Maqdisi is saying that he does not advocate that his followers liberally declare *Takfir* on Muslims who violate Islamic law. Rather, he suggests that Jihadists should simply disavow them—a key difference—and refuse to associate with such people. (It should be noted that critics argue that Jihadists who claim to follow Maqdisi make no such careful distinction.) Taken in concert with the doctrine of *al-Wala wal-Bara*, this forms the doctrinal basis for much of the social isolation seen among Jihadist groups, even in Islamic communities.

Maqdisi does, however, believe that Jihadists should perform *Takfir* upon those Muslims who are willing to run for elected office in secular governments, vote, or support the rule of disbelieving Muslims or infidels in other ways. In short, providing allegiance or support to non-Muslims, or aiding them against Islam, he argues, is grounds for excommunication.

Al-Wala wal-Bara

Al-Wala wal-Bara, or loving and hating for the sake of Allah, is one of the most important doctrinal elements of Jihadism. Jihadists argue that the "loyalty and disavowal" concept is rooted in the Islamic *shahadah*, or the declaration of faith that all Muslims state aloud, which goes: "There is no god but Allah, and Muhammad is the messenger of Allah."

The first part of the expression, *al-Wala*, literally translates from Arabic as "loyalty" or "allegiance." The *al-Wala* concept impacts not simply on what actions and activities one feels are religiously acceptable but on the types of people with whom one can socialize. For Jihadists, it refers to how Muslims should act with those who believe and state this *shahadah*: they are to be loved, embraced with loyalty. The other part of the expression, *al-Bara*, literally means "disownment" or "disavowal." In its Islamic context, it means to reject, renounce or shun all that displeases Allah, or anything that contradicts *Sharia* law. As with *al-Wala*, this concept of *al-Bara* refers not simply to what types of behavior ought to be considered Islamic or un-Islamic, but to which human beings it is religiously acceptable to know or have as *mawlat*, or friends. In short, those who reject the *shahadah* must be disavowed entirely, purged from any daily interaction with God-fearing Muslims. Jihadists believe that most humans love one another because they see other people as a means to attain more worldly pleasure, fulfillment or profit. They go so far as to push non-Muslims out of their lives even if they are blood-relatives. All non-believers are viewed as enemies of the right *Aqidah*. Jihadists believe that their only true friends are those who adhere to the *shahadah* precisely as they do. Those beyond the pale of Islam therefore include Jews, Christians, Buddhists, Hindus, Confucianists, communists, fascists, secularists, atheists, anarchists and many others. There can be no doubt that Muslims must dissociate themselves (*al-Bara'a*) from adherents of any of these "deviant" ideologies. The harder question comes with regard to identifying when a Muslim needs to be disavowed.

Remembering Maqdisi's commentary on *Takfir*, Jihadists would rather simply disavow a deviant Muslim than call them a disbeliever. They have therefore developed a loose framework for knowing when a Muslim needs to be pushed away:

- Imitating non-Muslims in dress, language, morality or eating indicates, for Jihadists, loving that which is against Islam, and therefore against God. If an imitator of these customs does not already love the culture of non-Muslims, Jihadists argue, such imitation invariably invests a person deeper into that culture and leads them down a deviant path.
- Living in the lands of non-Muslims (*Dar al-Harb*) and not immediately moving back to the lands of the Muslims (*Dar al-Islam*) is enough to make a Muslim lose their way. This return to the holy land of Islam, or *Hijra*, is an obligation upon every Muslim, they argue. Residence in the land of non-Muslims invariably means that a Muslim will begin to feel friendship toward them.
- Muslims who aid or support non-Muslims in any way that injures other Muslims, be it military, economic or even speaking well of disbelievers and defending their honor borders on apostasy. It is grounds enough for mandatory dissociation with other Muslims, if not excommunication.
- Seeking aid, comfort or assistance from non-Muslims is also grounds for dissociation. In the hearts of non-Muslims, Jihadists argue, are feelings of hatred, betrayal, evil and subversion against Muslims: non-Muslims want to harm Muslims by any means possible and are eager to exploit the trust of any Muslim in order better to plot against them.
- Observing the holidays, festivities or celebrations of non-Muslims, merely congratulating them during those seasons or even being present at their celebrations is enough to necessitate immediate and mandatory disavowal by other Muslims.
- Asking forgiveness for non-Muslims, or praying for them in any way, or being compassionate or taking pity on them is totally disallowed.

Once Muslims fully understand what they cannot do, particularly Muslims living in the West, with regard to non-Muslim cultures, Jihadists provide them with a rulebook for what they ought to do. First, they are to flee immediately from the lands of non-Muslims and return to a Muslim country. Next, they ought to help their fellow Muslims through donations of money, goods, their labor or even defending their honor. By feeling sympathy for other Muslims whenever harm comes to them, Jihadists believe they can help create a deeper awareness among Muslims and a broader recognition that Muslims around the world are bound to one another: success in London is a success for Iraqis; failure in Iraq is a failure for the Chechens. This is the foundation, they argue, of a global Jihadist revolution.

Jihad

Perhaps the most publicly recognized (but often misunderstood) of these doctrines is that of Jihad. By now, most people probably believe that they understand enough about the word to know that it leads to nothing good. *Tawhid*, *Aqidah*, *Takfir* and *al-Wala wal-Bara* are esoteric concepts: they are the core building blocks of the Jihadist ideology of which most non-Muslims (and likely many Muslims) have probably never heard. The term Jihad, however, has become pervasive in the media and daily discourse. It usually appears in conversations about Usama Bin Laden, al-Qaida and 9/11.[40]

What remains unclear is what motivates an individual to believe that they can kill in the name of God. Also, one question must be asked: "What is the *real* meaning of Jihad?" Unfortunately, there is no single definition: Jihad, to a large degree, is whatever Muslims make of it. This ambiguity really begins with the question of *whose* Islam is being discussed. Most mainstream Muslims who regularly practice their faith will argue that Jihad may have once meant conquering in the name of God. And many will concede that, although offensive Jihad is no longer appropriate or applicable to today's world, Jihad (when understood as fighting) *is* still appropriate when Islam is attacked by outside forces.

Finding common ground in the debate about when Islam can be considered as "under attack" is the sticking point. For Jihadists, Islam has been *perpetually* under attack, beginning with the time of the Prophet, through the invasion of the Mongol hordes, Christian forces in the Crusades, European colonizers, the penetration of communist, socialist and Marxist thought into the Middle East, the establishment of a Jewish state in the form of Israel, to the globalization of Western market capitalism.

In order to defend their continuing violence in the eyes of broader Islam, Jihadists do a curious two-step maneuver: first, they try to prove that the doctrine of Jihad is inherently centered on fighting; and second, they attempt to demonstrate that terrorism is both a legitimate and a necessary form of fighting. With regard to the first point, throughout Islamic history, the meaning of Jihad has been discussed, contested and debated. The mainstream consensus is that it encompasses a wide range of activities, including fighting, but also physical, emotional and intellectual preparation for battle, providing support for those in battle, and even conducting one's own internal spiritual battle in order to purify oneself religiously. For most Muslims who voluntarily choose to participate in all of the trappings of today's fast-paced, globalizing society, defining Jihad as the application of force against those who stand in the way of one's ability to practice one's religion freely simply does not work. Jihad, whether by doctrine or by necessity, has to be concerned more with internal struggle than with external, physical struggle.

Global Jihadists argue that such thinking is a blatant misunderstanding of the concept: Jihad does not mean "any sort of struggle in the path of Allah."[41] They even argue that it is wrongly translated as "striving" or "struggling" by Muslims and non-Muslims alike. Thinking that one is waging Jihad by conducting morning prayers, or by giving a lecture about Islam at a local community center is misguided. For Jihadists, there are two meanings to every Islamic word: a *Sharia* meaning and a linguistic meaning. In its *Sharia* meaning, Jihad means *al-Qital* (physically fighting); when it is mentioned in its linguistic sense, it should be regarded as *muqayyid* (restricted) by other rules. Believing in the linguistic meaning of the term and doing activities other than fighting in the name of Jihad is much like arguing that one has successfully fulfilled one's religious duty to *zakat* (purification of oneself by giving 2.5 percent of one's annual savings to charity as an obligation) by taking a shower.

Out of frustration with what he saw as a generation of misguided Muslim youth, the Palestinian Jihadist Shaikh Abdullah Azzam sought to clarify how "Jihad" could be both an Arabic word and a *Sharia* term during the 1980s. Azzam observed that it was taken from the Arabic, *Juhud—Yajhadu—Juhdan*, referring to strength, power, hardship and taking something to the limit. For him, it linguistically derives from terms meaning to use one's utmost personal ability and strength in order to obtain the beloved or to avert the hated.[42] But in terms of its legal, or *Sharia*, meaning, Azzam pointed to the four major jurists of Islamic jurisprudence to prove his point. For the Hanafi school of Islamic law, "al-Jihad means to call the Kuffar [disbelievers] to the religion of truth and to fight them if they do not accept."[43] It means "to sacrifice one's strength and energy in Fighting in the way of Allah '*Azza wa-Jal* with one's life, property and the tongue and whatever besides."[44] For the Maliki school of Islamic law, Azzam argues that Jihad means that a Muslim should fight against a disbeliever who is not under oath or treaty with Muslims by attacking him.[45] For the Sha'afi school, Azzam says, Jihad means "fighting in the way of Allah,"[46] as well as "sacrificial striving in fighting the Kuffar."[47] And finally, according to the Hanbali school, Jihad means "fighting and to sacrifice all strength . . . to raise the Word of Allah."[48]

Once Jihadists prove beyond doubt, at least in their own minds, that the official meaning of Jihad can only be fighting, they have to clarify precisely what kind of fighting they mean: there is both *Jihad al-Talab wal Ibtida'*, or offensive Jihad, and *Jihad ud-Dafa'* or defensive Jihad. One of the more sophisticated discussions of these two concepts from a Jihadist perspective is by the Saudi ideologue, strategist and al-Qaida commander Yousef al-Ayiri. According to Ayiri, *Jihad al-Talab wal Ibtida'* refers to the call made by Muslims to non-Muslims to convert to Islam. If non-Muslims resist this call, or reject Islamic authority over them, Ayiri argues, Islamic doctrine declares that Muslims have a collective obligation (*Fard ul-Kifaya*) to fight them and conquer them so that they do. Jihad by way of conquering, some argue, is a duty for individuals only when too few Muslims collectively stand and fight on Islam's behalf. But for hardline Salafists, particularly Jihadists, offensive Jihad is an individual obligation for each Muslim (*Fard 'Ayn*), in the same way that defensive Jihad is an individual duty.

Jihadists contend that Islamic scholars have differed over the question of whether there is a minimum time limit upon Muslims to perform offensive Jihad. Some Islamic scholars have argued that Muslims must go forth in at least one expedition every year to discharge the duty of Jihad (anything more frequent is above and beyond the minimum requirement). The evidence that Islamic forces have to prove that they have completed their mission is the *jizya*—a tax paid by non-Muslims to Muslims to avoid fighting with them. As it is not permitted in the *Sunnah* to take *jiyza* more than once a year, and Jihad can effectively take the place of collecting *jizya*, Jihad too is required only once a year. More conservative scholars argue that, to the contrary, it is *obligatory* to wage Jihad against the enemy in their heartlands whenever possible. Fighting non-Muslims and going on expeditions against them whenever possible, according to Ayiri, perfectly suits the aims and objectives of fighting Jihad, which include removing corruption and spreading Islamic authority all over the world. The obligation of Jihad can only cease being mandatory when its true purpose is realized: "that being the complete control of the whole earth such that not a single hand-span is left which is not under Islamic rule or by struggling one's utmost to accomplish this."[49]

Offensive Jihad should really only become an individual duty, Ayiri argues, in the following cases:

- When a legitimate Muslim leader calls on a specific person to fight.
- When a legitimate Muslim leader orders all the people of a particular town or region to fight.
- If non-Muslims take a Muslim prisoner, every Muslim must fight to release them.
- If a Muslim happens on a Muslim army engaged in combat, they are obligated to remain and fight.

Discussing Jihadism is complicated by the fact that there is no single doctrine or ideology: it is always in motion, driven by the various individuals who develop and promote it as well as due to the constantly changing environmental circumstances in which it evolves. Without understanding the various schools of Salafism, Western policy-makers cannot possibly identify those constituencies that may be useful allies in erecting a bulwark against the spread of the global Jihadist ideology. What becomes clear after assessing these schools of Salafism is that they vary with regard to their doctrinal positions across different issues. Any attempt to generalize about Salafism or even about the global Jihadist movement is likely to provide inaccurate conclusions.

3 Ideologues

> The sword and the pen are instruments of action and speech. They are the support of nations; any nation bereaved of them will lack in strength. They are the pillars of authority that declare who shall be lowered and who shall be raised in status.
>
> Abdulrahman al-Muhajir, Jihadist internet forum senior member

Jihadist internet discussion forums occasionally sponsor question-and-answer sessions between their members and prominent Jihadist clerics.[1] In one such session, the Saudi shaikh, Ali bin Khudair al-Khudair, a senior student of the heralded Saudi Jihadist ideologue Hamoud bin Uqla as-Shuaybi, took questions from interested forum members.[2] At one point a member asked Khudair: "What do you see in those *Shuyukh* [distinguished Muslim clerics]: Abdul-Munim Mustafa Halimah, whose *kunya* [honorific name] is Abu Basir [al-Tartusi], Isam Muhammed al-Barqaawi, commonly known as Abu Muhammad al-Maqdisi, and Umar bin Mahmud, whose kunya is Abu Qatada al-Filistini?" To clarify, the forum questioner queried Khudair about his thoughts on three well-known Jihadist clerics: Abu Basir al-Tartusi, Abu Muhammad al-Maqdisi, and Abu Qatada. These "What should I think of Shaikh X?" type of questions appear almost daily on the Jihadist web forums. Jihobbyists, or those enthusiasts of the Jihadist ideology who are not connected to an official al-Qaida element, tend to be obsessed with practicing Islam to the letter. Reading and following the right teachings and teachers are key parts of getting Islam right in their minds. Rarely do Jihobbyists have the chance to ask such questions to a scholar of Khudair's caliber.

Khudair responded to the questioner as follows:

> Those are scholars of Ahl us-Sunnah [followers of the Quran, the *Hadith* and the Prophet's life], and *Tawheed* [oneness of God] and '*aqeedah* [creed], and they are from the people of Jihad and writing and teaching, and we know nothing about them except good. And what some people fabricate upon them of lies, and false statements in the matters of *takfir* [excommunicating other Muslims], then it is nothing but the making of the *Murji'ah* [those who delay judgement], and they are of Ahl us-Sunnah in the matters of *takfir* and Iman [faith], and our Shaikh Hamoud used to praise them, and recall them in good, and commend them, and defend them.[3]

This answer, as cumbersome as it may seem to someone outside of the Jihadist movement, shines invaluable light on the mindset of Jihadist ideologues. For Khudair, the only Muslim scholars worth trusting are those who adhere precisely to the words of the Quran and the *Hadith*, embody a commitment to the model of the Prophet Muhammad's life (*Sunnah*), believe completely in the principle of God's unity (*Tawhid*) and application to all things on Earth, and interpret Jihad as being inherently violent in nature.[4]

Jihadist scholars, intellectuals and ideologues serve as the movement's guiding lights: they are the men who pull the intellectual strings of the more well-known figures like Bin Laden, Zawahiri, and Zarqawi. These ideologues have provided the intellectual coherence, ideological ammunition and religious legitimation to the movement. There can be little doubt that towering Jihadist figures like Abu Muhammad al-Maqdisi, Hamoud bin Uqla as-Shuaybi, Abu Qatada, and Khudair himself, men considered by governments in the West to be of secondary importance in terms of the security threat that they pose, have wielded words with far more enduring consequences than has been understood up to now.

The Awakening

Followers of the al-Sahwa al-Islamiyya, or the Salafist Awakening movement, constituted the conservative mainstream of puritanical Sunni Islam during the 1990s. Known as the Sahwa, the movement represented a unique hybridization of two ideological strains: the ultra-conservative Wahabi interpretation of Islam in Saudi Arabia, particularly on social issues; and the progressive and highly politicized perspective of the Egyptian Ikhwan, or Muslim Brotherhood, movement.

Sahwa Salafism emerged during the 1960s, as an outcome of three interconnected phenomena: growing frustration with government crackdowns on conservative Islamic activists; a widespread feeling of humiliation from the Arab military defeat in the Six Day War against Israel; and an exodus of young, highly passionate and educated Muslim Brotherhood members from Egypt to Saudi Arabia. Under the Egyptian president, Gamal Abdel Nasser, the hardline Muslim Brotherhood members became increasingly targeted by the Egyptian government. Driven by the inspirational writings of Sayyid Qutb, the Ikhwan and their machine-like organizational skills threatened to undermine pan-Arabism. Nasser's widespread security sweeps resulted in the imprisonment of much of the organization's leadership, and killed its brightest star, Sayyid Qutb. But Egypt's devastating loss to Israel in the Six Day War in June 1967 sent the Nasser government reeling, leaving it unable to focus on many of its domestic problems. As protests grew in number and strength, Nasser called for more crackdowns. This hostile environment left many of the Islamic activists in Egypt seeking refuge elsewhere. Saudi Arabia offered that shelter.

Sayyid Qutb's brother, Muhammad, having been left to carry his brother's legacy, needed to find a way to sustain the Ikhwan's momentum. The Saudi state, reaping the rewards of its new-found oil reserves, was in dire need of professionals and teachers to maximize the country's economic growth. Muhammad Qutb and his band of young, educated Ikhwan members were able to fill that void for Saudi Arabia.[5] As these men became more deeply entrenched across the kingdom's educational and professional communities, their politically charged activism began to merge with the Wahabi puritanical reading of Islam. So, by the 1980s, Saudi Sahwa Salafism had become a confusing spectrum of beliefs and doctrines hybridizing the social activism of the Egyptian Muslim Brotherhood, Sayyid Qutb's most radical thinking about the need to wage a defensive war against those foreign influences penetrating the Middle East and their Arab government hand-maidens, and Saudi Arabia's long-standing conservative Wahabist teachings.

According to Jihadist cleric Abu Muhammad al-Maqdisi, these Awakening scholars promoted their ideas and enlightened the youth about the various attempts to secularize the Islamic *ummah*. The movement, led through the 1980s by such Saudi shaikhs as Safar al-Hawali, Nasir al-Omar, Salman al-Awdah, and A'id al-Qarni, "broke the rigidity, enlightened the youth, and kept them away from innovations and superstitions." For Maqdisi, "the awakening scholars participated in making them take a qualitative step and enlightening them to a certain stage."[6] Perhaps no man was more instrumental in advancing the march of the Sahwa Salafist movement than Safar al-Hawali.

Safar al-Hawali

The Saudi cleric Safar al-Hawali was born in 1954 in Hawala in the Baha Province of Saudi Arabia.[7] He specialized in Islamic studies at the Islamic University, Medina, during his undergraduate education and wrote his masters thesis at Umm al-Qura University on the origins and consequences of secular thought spreading throughout the Arab and Muslim world. He completed his doctoral work in 1986 under the guidance of Muhammad Qutb, one of the key interlocutors between Egyptian Ikhwan thinking and Saudi Wahabism. His doctoral dissertation examined the concept of *irja* (separation of thought and action; moral indifference) in Islamic thought, particularly with regard to such challenges as the spread of secularism. From 1988 to 1994, he directed the *Aqidah* Department at Umm al-Qura University. Thousands attended his weekly public lectures on the topic of Islamic belief and they were widely distributed throughout the Islamic world. What made Hawali so accessible and popular, however, was that he was able to take these often esoteric, complex and abstract religious ideas and apply them to the political and social realities of everyday life. He was perhaps most interested in the foreign policy reasoning and actions of the United States, particularly with regard to the Middle East.

Consider his book, *The True Promise, the Bogus Promise*, in which he lays out ten things that all Muslims must do in order to reform their religion.[8] This document serves as a roadmap for uniting the community of Muslims, or the *ummah*, under the banner of Salafism. Muslim unity is critical, he says, because the West's marginalization of Islamic global concerns will continue until Islam is no longer viable. Islam must therefore go it alone: "it is incumbent that [Muslims] spread knowledge of the *Aqidah* throughout our *ummah*, and the correct creed at all levels, in particular the *Aqidah* of *al-Wala wal-Bara*." The only way to wage this war, Hawali argues, is through the religious Establishment. Mosques and clerics must "fight this media and educational blitz" that they see launched by the West using all the tools at their disposal: "If we do not own satellites to fight their satellite broadcasts, we should at least maximize the effect [we gain] from the [only] means [we possess] in our hands." He also encourages Muslims to expand Islamic financial institutions and networks in order to avoid having to rely on those owned and administered by the West. In short, he argues in a way that is reminiscent of early Egyptian Salafist declarations that Muslims need to create their own parallel institutions and technologies in order to eliminate dependence on the West.

Hawali believed that proper Islamic education formed the bedrock of any workable reform movement. He therefore emphasized throughout his works the need to "increase the comprehension of [Awakening] students to those Quranic verses and statements of the Prophet—pertaining to the plots of the Jews" toward Muslims. Muslims must be aware of "plots and movements conspiring against us. Our advice to my brothers living in the West is that they watch these plots." While standing steadfast in their beliefs, he continues, Muslims in the West must begin to call non-Muslims there to Islam, as he sees them as living in a spiritually bankrupt society. He counsels converts to use their native status in order to penetrate the political and social institutions of Western society and advance Salafist objectives.

Together with Salman al-Awdah, Nasir al-Umar, Bishr al-Bishr and several other young Salafist scholars, these core Sahwa shaikhs forged a following of young, puritanical doctors, engineers, attorneys, professors and technocrats who were seeking to advance a reformist agenda focused on reducing widespread political corruption, fiscal irresponsibility and the un-Islamic-ness of the governing regime. What began as an intellectual reform movement quickly transformed into a widespread revolutionary movement. Incidentally, its anti-establishment momentum was indirectly aided by the Saudi family's fateful decision to invite US forces into the kingdom. Sahwa Salafism spread like wildfire both in Saudi Arabia and elsewhere.[9]

The *Sahwa* movement in Saudi Arabia became a Salafist assembly line: Hawali and Awdah worked on increasing the political, intellectual and Islamic awareness of the youth. Nasir al-Umar focused on providing ethical guidance to them. A'id al-Qarni and Ali al-Qarni lectured them about spiritual and psychological maturity and development. The Saudi authorities grew exhausted trying to rein in these clerics until things came to a head in 1994 when the instigators and ideologues behind the Sahwa movement were rounded up. In prison, these clerics faced enormous pressure to cease and desist in their radical preachings. On the one hand, this period significantly dampened their influence on the Muslim youth. On the other, however, a new generation of global Jihadist scholars were already consolidating their strength in Afghanistan, Pakistan, Jordan, Saudi Arabia and the United Kingdom.

The Taliban, an ultra-conservative student movement, had successfully taken over a large part of Afghanistan by 1996. The global Jihadist community saw in this organization their first real opportunity to establish and live in a state governed entirely by *Sharia* law. Muslims from around the world again flocked to Afghanistan, this time to support the Taliban's efforts and join the vibrant Jihadist community growing there led by Usama Bin Laden. He saw the Saudi government's arrests of the Sahwa shaikhs as troubling for the movement. They provided the intellectual guidance and, more importantly, the religious legitimacy for taking more aggressive action against the West. Once they were silenced, Bin Laden therefore lost an invaluable source of Islamic credibility, which he noted in his 1996 *fatwa*: "And, at the behest of the United States, a very large number of ulema, advocates of the call, and youth were arrested in the land of the two holy mosques. Prominent among them are Shaikh Salman al-Awdah, Shaikh Safar al-Hawali."[10]

The Saudi government released most of the shaikhs after several years but to the dismay of many hardliners, Hawali, Awdah, Qarni and other Sahwa clerics emerged substantially different from when they had been arrested. No longer did they support religious activism against the government. Rather, they began to object publicly to the droves of young Saudi men heading to what they saw as the "Afghan inferno" in support of the Taliban and al-Qaida's headquarters. The Sahwa movement, once an aggressive oppositionist faction that bucked the state at every chance, had been quieted. The shaikhs, led by Hawali, began conducting official dialogues with the Saudi government. In a transparent attempt to play to their conservative base, the clerics restarted their propaganda machines and released angry statements about the atrocities committed by the West. However, these messages simultaneously discouraged Muslims from disobeying or even criticizing the Saudi state, and clearly prohibited Muslims from conducting any acts of violence against the regime.

Salman al-Awdah

Salman al-Awdah's story tracks closely with that of his colleague, Safar al-Hawali. Awdah was born in 1955 in al-Basr, a village on the outskirts of Buraidah in the al-Qasim Province of Saudi Arabia, to a well-regarded family. He spent his early years in that village, then moved to Buraidah, where he completed elementary school and transferred to the Academic Institute, which housed some of the region's most noteworthy scholars, including Shaikh Salih al-Sukayti, Shaikh Ali al-Dali, and Shaikh Salih al-Bulaihi. Diving head-first into the institute's intellectual environment, he spent every moment he could learning from the scholars, and immersed himself in the voluminous library. His raw intellect propelled him through his bachelor's degree quickly. He earned his Masters degree in the *Sunnah* and its sciences from the faculty of *Usul al-Din* (Principles of Religion), writing the thesis *The Strangeness of Islam and its Legal Rulings in the Light of the Prophetic Sunnah*. He published that along with another 50 or so books, including: *The First Strangers*, *Characteristics of the Strangers*, *Withdrawing from Society and Participating in it*, *A Discussion with Shaikh Muhammad al-Ghazali*, *Who Has the Right to Engage in Independent Juristic Reasoning and Guidelines for Studying Islamic Law*.[11]

Awdah, like Hawali, developed a reputation for his eloquent speeches and his willingness to stand against the Saudi regime. His appeal widened as his work was disseminated throughout the Islamic world in print and on cassette. These works also won him the support of a new generation of young Muslims who were calling for comprehensive reform of Saudi society at the time. Awdah specifically courted those youth who were seeking knowledge about how they might get more involved in supporting and expanding such Islamist reform movements. Suggestions of conspiracies against Islam tended to resonate strongly with this demographic: "I believe that there is someone out there devising a plan to keep this nation of ours in everlasting silence," Awdah often proclaimed, "a plan that has led to the pervasive demoralization of society where corruption has taken its roots in Saudi society and beyond."[12] For Awdah, there is an eternal struggle between right and wrong, reform and corruption, guidance and deviation, justice and oppression. The only way that Muslims can demonstrate true commitment to Islam, he argues, is by proving that they are ready to take action for the sake of Islam (as he defines it). Awdah believed that while most clerics were busy preaching about the need for reform, few were actually seeking to change anything in the physical world. The masses, he argued, may enjoy listening to lectures about piety and righteousness, but the shaikhs have to set an example by practicing what they preach.

Awdah helped to reframe the nature of the Islamist debate: the issue of Islamic reform now transcended local grievances. He said it has no boundaries because it is an issue that concerns all Muslims, whether they are in China, India, Kashmir, Bangladesh, Kurdistan, Iraq, Turkey, Algeria, Tunisia, Egypt, Palestine, Europe, America, Russia or any other place on earth. For those who cannot be helped directly, Awdah suggested that his followers should at least shed some light on their situation and expose it to the public. He was arrested alongside the other Awakening ideologues in the fall of 1994. On his release, he resumed his activities from his home, giving lessons after the Sunset Prayer from Wednesday to Friday each week on topics such as Quranic commentary, ethics, education and personal reform. He also began supervising the website IslamToday and teaching classes and lectures over the internet and by phone to a wide range of listeners.

On September 14, 2007, the second day of Ramadan, he delivered a live, televised address directed at Usama Bin Laden. "How much blood has been spilled? How many innocent children, women and old people have been killed, maimed and expelled from their homes in the name of al-Qaida," he began. Chastising Bin Laden for murdering innocent people and radicalizing Islamic youth, Awdah blamed him for tarnishing the reputation of Salafism and Islam in general. He impugned him for spurring on civil war, plague and famine in Iraq and Afghanistan. He censured him for promoting the culture of excommunication that has torn apart families and led to sons calling their fathers "infidel." He damned him for fostering a culture of violence and murder that has led people to shed the blood of their relatives without remorse, rather than nurturing the spirit of love and tranquility that a Muslim family is supposed to possess. The vital question, Awdah concluded, is: "What have all these long years of suffering, tragedy, tears and sacrifice actually achieved?"

Aaid al-Qarni

Although Hawali and Awdah are the two most well-known names associated with the early Awakening period, other clerics had been calling for reform alongside them.[13] Consider Aaid al-Qarni, an Awakening preacher who was once dedicated to liberating Islam from the oppression of apostate Arab regimes and their Western backers. Now, though, he serves as a chief religious adviser to the Saudi government and is viewed as a sell-out by most Jihadists.

Qarni provides a striking example of how a generation of radical shaikhs could be persuaded to think differently. Like his contemporaries, he grew up in Saudi Arabia, studying at the Scientific Institute in Riyadh and the Secondary Scientific Institute, graduating from the Faculty of the Religious Fundamentals with a Masters. He earned a doctorate degree in early Islamic thought, the *Hadith*, and Islamic methodology and jurisprudence, then focused on the works of Sayyid Qutb, particularly his book *In the Shadow of the Prophet*, his interpretations of the Quran. And, similar to most other Salafist clerics at the time, he used technology more aggressively and cleverly than other Islamic clerics: more than a thousand of his lectures made their way on to widely distributed cassettes and later the internet.

Also like most of his fellow Sahwa clerics who once overstepped the Saudi government's limits for acceptable preaching, Qarni no longer advocates many of the positions that he once supported. In a May 2004 interview with *Ukaz*, he stated: "Call us what you want. Call us establishment shaikhs. Call us advocates of the sultan. The most important thing for us is to ensure that our God is pleased with us, to safeguard our homeland, and keep the ruler and the ruled united under the guidance of God's holy book." He has now become an integral part of Saudi Arabia's efforts to quash the Jihadist movement's efforts to radicalize the youth of the kingdom: "Repent to God," he told Jihadists. "Throw down your weapons and turn yourselves in, for your mask has fallen off." He now openly rejects *Takfir*, for instance: excommunication is the ideology of denunciation, he argues. It allows for Muslims on a deviant path to shed the blood of the police and the military. He also rejects the call to apply *Sharia* through force and the killing of Muslims who support Arab governments or the West.

His comments have infuriarated many within the global Jihadist community. Consider this posting on an internet forum:

> Aaid al Qarni is infamous for being a member of the Saudi mukhabarat or intelligence, and is known to interrogate the imprisoned Mujahideen. He is the one who appeared as the presenter on Saudi Television to hassel [*sic*] and question the three Shuyookh: Ali al Khudyr, Nasir al Fahd, Shaykh al 'Ulwan, on air. Furthermore, he appears quite often on Arabic satellite channels to call for walaa [alliance] and support to the Taghout in Arabia, and is also infamous for an article in a Saudi newspaper in which he called the American child as bright for toppling the Taliban government in Afghanistan, whose toppling according to him was a bounty from Allah. Scholars such as him are praised by the Apostate regimes.[14]

In short, the Awakening movement and its staunchest proponents, such as Awdah, Hawali and Qarni, fundamentally changed shape in the mid-1990s as a result of the aggressive policies pursued by the Saudi security services to quash it. Clearly, today's Sahwa Salafism has little in common with the early Awakening movement.

Rejectionists

The early Islamic rejectionists are an oft-forgotten group in debates about the development of Jihadist thought. While the Sahwa movement concerned itself primarily with external threats to Muslims in Saudi Arabia, being careful not to strike too hard against the Saudi hand that fed it, the group known by some as Rejectionists believed that the Saudi royal family and Arab regimes like them were the principal problem.

The most visible group inspired by the Rejectionist approach to Salafism was al-Jama al-Salafiyya al-Muhtasiba (JSM), which emerged in Medina in the mid-1960s. The group was established by a small cadre of religious student activists who had been actively preaching their call for Islamic purification, specifically of Saudi Arabia's Wahabism, in the city's ghettos and impoverished districts. During the 1970s, under the guidance of their inspirational leader, Juhayman al-Utaybi, the JSM members sought to find a niche for themselves and their approach in the increasingly crowded Islamist community.[15]

Juhayman directed most of his rage against the Saudi government, which he saw as embracing the cause of non-Muslims by its close alliance with foreign powers, particularly the United States. The Sahwa movement, however insightful its clerics were about the problems with Islamic society, was still reticent to advocate open revolution. For them, it was better to live under a sinful Muslim regime than create widespread chaos by rebelling against that rule. In a short period of time, Juhayman, who was in his forties, managed to recruit several hundred followers, most of whom had been students in Saudi Arabia's religious universities. Beyond this active core membership, Muslims from across the peninsula and beyond also began supporting his call for reform.

Juhayman's revolution began at 5:20 a.m. on November 20, 1979, as Muhammad bin Soubbayil, the head shaikh of Mecca's Grand Mosque, climbed the mosque's minaret in order to issue the morning call to prayer. As the shaikh drew his call to a close, Juhayman grabbed the microphone from his hands, announcing his seizure of the mosque and the triumphant return of the *mahdi*, or messiah, who also happened to be his brother-in-law, Muhammad al-Qahtani. At the same time, several hundred of his men scattered throughout the crowd of thousands of pilgrims and worshippers within the compound, moved into strategic positions, unearthed the weapons and explosives that they had secreted and opened fire on the security guards stationed inside the mosque. Juhayman continued, forcefully denouncing the Saudi state's corruption into the microphone.

His men hurried to secure the mosque, knowing that it would be only a matter of time before Saudi National Guard arrived *en masse*: the Saudi government would certainly view this act as a direct assault on its legimacy and there was little doubt that it would act authoritatively. When Saudi forces did arrive, however, they realized that the challenge posed by Juhayman's siege was greater than anything for which they had been trained. Any National Guards who tried to penetrate the compound were gunned down in their tracks by Juhayman's snipers, positioned in each of the mosque's towering minarets. After several days under the hot sun, the smell of their rotting bodies littering the perimeter began to permeate the air. The morale of the thousands of surviving forces standing guard plummeted.

As the siege dragged on, the government looked increasingly impotent to its subjects. Some began to wonder if perhaps Juhayman was right. The Saudi king, Khalid, reacted to this and tried to mobilize the official *ulama* against Juhayman and his followers. Some of these figures, like Shaikh Bin Baz, were said to have quietly supported Juhayman in his earlier proselytizing activities. But they again showed that their primary loyalty rested with the al-Saud family: Bin Baz and his fellow clerics issued a *fatwa* supporting the Saudi regime and authorizing military intervention in the sacred sanctuary in order to dispatch Juhayman and his men. Some accounts suggest that Khalid turned first to the Americans for assistance but was dissatisfied with their plan. Other reports claim that after the Carter administration's debacle with the Shah of Iran that same year, they avoided the Americans altogether, and called directly on the French.

Somewhere between November 23 and November 28, the French Defense Minister, Yvon Bourges, summoned his elite special forces team, the GIGN (Groupe d'Intervention de la Gendarmerie Nationale), which was under the command of Captain Paul Barrill. A highly decorated special forces officer, Barrill was ordered to select his best men and depart on a private plane to Riyadh immediately. Upon his arrival in the kingdom, he and his men were converted to Islam in order to pre-empt any criticism from the Saudi religious Establishment about non-Muslims setting foot in the holiest of mosques in the kingdom. However, Saudi officials were in a state of great confusion, and the chief of staff of the National Guard, General Osman, was not allowed to report clearly to the French group what was happening. All Barrill and his team had was a rough proposal that he received while boarding a plane for the city of Taif, on the outskirts of Mecca.

The challenge posed by the siege was that the complex was expansive (an estimated 65,000 square feet), consisting of winding hallways, corridors, hidden passageways and underground galleries. Furthermore, the French team did not have a firm count of the number of adversaries that they would be facing. And it turned out that Juhayman's men had been smuggling in weapons and explosives in coffins over a period of several weeks in preparation for the attack. Barrill donned Arab clothing and conducted reconnaissance around the mosque in order to avoid being recognized as a foreigner. As he walked through the area, he could hear stern lecturing emanating from the minarets of the mosque, calling for the people to leave behind the injustice, corruption and perversion of the state and turn again to Islam.

The French, in conversations with their Saudi counterparts, learned that the working plan to end the siege was to flood the mosque with water and then send massive electric currents through it in order to kill the rebels. Barrill liked the idea of avoiding a frontal assault, but decided gas was a more viable option. The French team was reportedly able to obtain blueprints of the compound's many entrances and exits from the Saudi construction firm that had recently renovated it, the Bin Laden Group. However, Barrill was short of both men and supplies, so he asked the leaders of the National Guard to provide their 30 best officers and 60 soldiers in small teams. He also requested canisters of gas, five hundred pounds of explosives, a quantity of detonators and fuses, gas-masks, flak jackets, and other equipment. In less than 48 hours, the equipment and *matériel* arrived in a disguised presidential plane from France.

On December 3, Barrill's team began preparing for the assault. They trained machine-guns on the sniper positions in the minarets and wired at least 15 of the 22 cellar entrance gates with explosives so that small teams of French and Saudi soldiers could enter and shoot in the dichloride gas, which would paralyze Juhayman's army before the storming teams entered. Then, acting on orders from the Saudi National Guard's commanding colonel, Barrill's men executed their plan. The machine-guns opened fire, blasting away at the sniper positions. Explosive charges detonated throughout the afternoon and evening around the perimeter of the compound. Proceeding to the next phase, the soldiers moved in nearly three tons of dichloride gas through the now open cellar gates. By the evening, the storming team felt confident that it had subdued the rebels enough to enter the mosque. Juhayman's hero, Muhammad al-Qahtani, was killed in the course of the raid, as were hundreds of innocent pilgrims who had been taken hostage.

In the aftermath of the Grand Mosque seizure, the Saudi government was ruthless in demonstrating that such acts would not be tolerated. It publicly beheaded 63 insurgents, including Juhayman, across eight different cities on the peninsula as a vivid reminder to those who were considering revolt. Most of Juhayman's writings were destroyed. What little the Saudis could not stamp out now resides primarily on the global Jihadist library website run by Abu Muhammad al-Maqdisi, a Jihadist cleric who fully embraced his teachings.

According to Thomas Hegghammer and Stephane Lacroix, Juhayman revived several important concepts from the writings of hardline Wahab scholars of the nineteenth century, such as Sulayman bin Abdallah al-Shaikh and Hamad bin Atiq. The first of these is *millat Ibrahim* (the religious community of Abraham), which is an allegorical reference to the "true" Islamic community that purges itself from associations with all forms of impiety. Maqdisi internalized this phrase so much that he penned one of his most popular books around the notion. The second concept popularized by Juhayman and Qahtani, according to Hegghammer and Lacroix, is *awthaq ur al-iman* (the strongest bonds of faith), which refers to the ties that bind Muslims with one another. Maqdisi would later draw on this concept in his thinking about the *ummah* (community of Muslims), *Tawhid* (the unity of God) and *al-Wala wal-Bara* (allegiance to fellow Muslims and dissociation from infidels).[16]

Jihadist ideologues

With the collapse of the JSM and the death of Juhayman al-Utaybi and Muhammad al-Qahtani, the Rejectionist strand of Islamist thought began to fade. By the 1990s, two hegemons were left wrestling for control: a rebranded Sahwa Salafism, one that was kinder and friendlier to the Saudi state; and the violent oppositionists of the global Jihadist strain. A new generation of fire-breathing scholars had grown up between the 1960s and 1990s, and they were ready to fill the power vacuum left by the quieting of the original Sahwa shaikhs. First among them was Hammoud bin Uqla as-Shuaybi.

Hammoud bin Uqla as-Shuaybi

Abu Abdullah Hammoud bin Abdullah bin Uqla bin Muhammad bin Ali bin Uqla as-Shuaybi al-Khalidi, or Shaikh Uqla as-Shuaybi as he is more commonly known, came from the Aale Jinah region of Saudi Arabia, a member of the Bani Khalid tribe.[17] His family migrated from the Eastern Province of the Arabian Peninsula to Shaqra, then to al-Qasim, where they settled. Uqla was born in the city of as-Shaqqah, one of the northern districts of Buraidah, in al-Qasim Province, in 1925. At six years old, at the prompting of his father, he learned to read and write from local religious men, including Shaikh Abdullah bin Mubarak al-Omari. The next year, he contracted smallpox and lost his eyesight. By the age of 13, he had memorized the Quran, and began working with his father pollinating date-palms and cultivating their farmland.

In 1946, Uqla traveled to Riyadh, again at the prompting of his father, and began to study with Shaikh Abdul-Latif bin Ibrahim al ash-Shaikh, a well-known Islamic scholar at the time. He then went on to study the writings of Ibn Taymiyyah with Shaikh Muhammad bin Ibraheem Aal as-Shaikh, and continued his studies with the leading scholars of Saudi thought, including: Shaikh Bin Baz, who taught him *Tawhid* and the *Hadith*; Shaikh Muhammad al-Amin Ash-Shinqiti; Shaikh Abdur-Rahman al-Afriqi (a *Hadith* scholar); Shaikh Abdul-Aziz bin Rashid (a scholar of *Fiqh*, Islamic jurisprudence); Shaikh Abdullah al-Khulaifi; and Shaikh Hamad al-Jasir, who taught him composition and dictation. He learned grammar and rhetoric from Egyptian scholars, Yusuf Umar Hasanain, Abdul-Latif Sarhan, and Yusuf ad-Daba.

At Imam Muhammad bin Saud University, Uqla taught courses in *Tawhid*, *Fiqh*, the *Hadith*, rhetoric and grammar, and supervised a number of students at Masters and doctoral levels. Many of these eventually became prominent Saudi officials, including Abdul-Aziz Aal-ash Shaikh, Mufti of Saudi Arabia and head of the Committee of Senior Scholars; Dr. Abdullah bin Abdul Muhsin at-Turki, Minister of Islamic Affairs; Dr. Abdullah bin Muhammad bin Ibrahim al ash-Shaikh, Minister of Justice; Dr. Saleh bin Fawzan al-Fawzan, a member of the Committee of Senior Scholars; Judge Abdur-Rahman bin Salih al-Jabr; Judge Abdur-Rahman bin Ghaith; Shaikh Abdur-Rahman bin Abdullah bin al-'Ajlan, former Head of the Courts, Qasim Province; Shaikh Sulaiman bin Muhanna, head of Riyadh Courts; Abdul-Aziz bin Abdur-Rahman as-Sa'id, head of the Committees for Enjoining Good and Forbidding Evil; Shaikh Muhammad bin Muhawass, head of Investigation and Prosecution; Hamad bin Faryan, Attorney of the Ministry of Justice; and Ibrahim bin Dawud, Attorney of the Ministry of the Interior. Among his other students were: Abdul Qadir Shaibah al-Hamad; Abu Bakr al-Jaza'iri; Muhammad Aman al-Jami as-Somali; Rabi al-Madkhali and Muhammad bin Salih al-Uthaymin. In Qasim, he taught Salman bin Fahd al-Awdah and the hardline shaikhs Ali bin Khudair al-Khudair, Sulayman al-Ulwan, and Nasr al-Fahd. He also penned a number of important Jihadist treatises, including: *The Supreme Imamate*; *Demonstrable Proofs on the Certainty of Iman in Allah and the Last Day; The Preferred Statement Regarding the Ruling of One who Seeks Assistance from the Disbelievers*; and *Supporting the Taliban*. Finally, he produced a collection of approximately a hundred *fatwa* that include criticism of certain current issues and explanations of his other religious rulings.

According to a popular biography appearing on several global Jihadist websites, Uqla was not just a brilliant scholar but an emotionally dedicated supporter of Jihadist revolutionaries:

> Most of his night was spent in supplication for the Mujahideen in Afghanistan ... Whenever there was any good news he would cry with happiness and whenever there was bad news he would cry out of sorrow. Whenever anyone defamed the Mujahideen, he would become extremely angry. His students used to know the current situation of the Mujahideen just by looking at his face as he entered his circle of knowledge.[18]

Uqla was one of the first scholars on the Arabian Peninsula to issue a public *fatwa* calling upon all Muslims to support the Taliban. And after the attacks of 9/11, he issued another, calling upon Muslims to support the Taliban and the mujahidin in Afghanistan against American and Coalition forces. Many of his students reportedly answered his call and went to Afghanistan. Undoubtedly, some of them were consequently killed.[19] When asked about the Islamic legitimacy of the Taliban, Uqla explained:

> The Taliban Regime in Afghanistan has been proven to fulfill these factors, so it is the only country in the World in which there are no man-made laws and legislations. Rather, indeed its legislation is established on the *Sharia* of Allah and His Messenger in the Courts of Law, in the ministries, in the governmental circles and in other establishments.[20]

Shortly before he died, Uqla issued a letter to the Islamic scholars in Pakistan, together with his students Shaikh Sulaiman ul-Alwan and Shaikh Ali al-Khudair. He also wrote a letter of encouragement to the commander of the Taliban, Mullah Muhammad Umar.[21]

Nasr al-Fahd and Ali al-Khudair

Nasr Ibn Hammad Ibn Humayd al-Fahd and Shaikh Ali Ibn Khudair Ibn Fahd al-Khudair form two of the three legs in the "Takfiri Troika," with the third being Ahmad al-Khalidi. These scholars provided legitimation for the use of *Takfir* (excommunication) to justify heinous attacks against political and ideological enemies of global Jihadism.

Fahd was born in Riyadh in 1968.[22] He had a distinguished academic career, graduating from the Imam University, the University of *Sharia* in Riyadh, and in 1991 he earned his doctorate and was appointed dean at the University of the Principles of the Religion (Usul al-Deen) in the Department of Creed and Modern Ideologies. He grew increasingly radical in his preaching and was arrested in September 1994 for his subversive teachings. When he was released in 1997, he no longer had his faculty position so he began focusing his time and energy on highlighting two major points: the apostasy of Arab regimes and the need for Muslims to wage warfare against Jews and Christians.

Khudair was born in 1954 in Riyadh. In high school he began diligently studying the Quran and reciting it under the tutelage of the renowned Salafist shaikh Abd al-Rauf al-Hannawi. Khudair also worked privately with Shaikh Ali Ibn Abd-Allah al-Jardan and the judge Muhammad al-Muhizi before beginning his undergraduate work. He graduated from the Usul al-Deen Faculty at the Imam University in 1982, then went on to study *Tawhid* and *Aqidah* with Uqla until the latter's death. Khudair also studied under Shaikh Muhammad Ibn Salih al-Mansur for four years, under the legendary Shaikh Muhammad Ibn Saalih al-Uthaymin for four years and with Shaikh Abd-Allah Ibn Muhammad Ibn Abd-Allah al-Husain.

This impressive pedigree qualified Khudair to teach on matters of *Tawhid*, *Aqidah* and *Fiqh* in the hotspot of global Jihadist thinking, Buraidah. At first, he had no more than five students in each class, but as he became increasingly respected in the area for his knowledge, his student base exploded. Among his students were Saudi judges, doctors, teachers, and preachers. During this time he ardently defended the actions of the Jihadists in his written work and lectures.

Both Fahd and Khudair have also written a number of highly militant treatises. Fahd issued the first *fatwa* in 2003 authorizing the use of weapons of mass destruction against enemies of Islam,[23] while both men expounded on the various types and degrees of infidelity. They sanctioned the killing of women and children in the defense of Islam. They chastised those who refused to act in the name of their religion and provided religious cover for attacking the United States. And they loudly urged those Muslims around them to declare *Takfir* against the Saudi regime.

Today, the work of these two scholars is among the most widely translated into other languages, particularly English, by global Jihadists. Of particular interest to Western Jihobbyists are Fahd's authorizations to attack the United States. Their impact on defining the nuance and fury behind global Jihadist ideology should not be underestimated. As Chapter 6 on Saudi Arabia shows, however, both Fahd and Khudair would eventually be encouraged to recant nearly all of their positions and earlier writings.

Sulaiman al-Ulwan

Sulaiman Ibn Nasir Ibn Abd-Allah al-Ulwan, or Sulaiman al-Ulwan, was born in the Saudi town of Buraidah in 1969.[24] He was the fourth of nine sons. Ulwan begin his schooling in 1983. After completing middle school, he attended high school for 15 days before dropping out and dedicating himself to total immersion in the study of Islamic law by reading the books of the great. He married in 1989 and subsequently had three sons, the oldest of whom is Abd-Allah.

During his early days, he demonstrated an impressive ability to memorize extensive texts, showing deep understanding of Islamic writings on *Sharia*. At first, he focused upon the medieval writings of thinkers like Ibn Taymiyyah, Ibn al-Qayyim, the Imams of Najd, Ibn Rajab, the *Sirah* (Prophetic Biographical Accounts) of Ibn Hisham and *Al-Bidiyah Wan-Nihiyah* of Ibn Kathir. He also visited with four different scholars daily, one after each call to prayer. He would then shift his focus to the schools of *Fiqh* and the selected opinions of Ibn Taymiyyah, Ibn al-Qayyim and Ibn Hazm, claiming that he spent over 15 hours daily reading, memorizing and reviewing these texts.[25]

As al-Ulwan's reputation grew in the conservative community of Saudi Arabia, he was banned by authorities from teaching in the mosques. Reportedly, Salafist Shaikh Bin Baz himself petitioned the government several times to allow him to do so, all of which were denied. He returned to Medina where he would continue working with other prominent Jihadist clerics such as Uqla as-Shuaybi, Nasr al-Fahd and Ali al-Khudair. In his introduction for Nasr al-Fahd's book, *The Exposition Regarding the Disbelief of the One that Assists the Americans*, Ulwan argued:

> In our current times, the legions of *Kufr* and the heads of the devils—America, Britain and their allies—have struck an alliance to wage war against Islam and its people among the Taliban and the other Islamic lands, all under the guise or name: "The War on Terrorism" . . . It is obligatory upon all of the Muslims, everyone according to his capacity, to assist our brothers, the *Mujahidin*, in the path of Allah with wealth, life and tongue.[26]

Singing the common global Jihadist refrain, one advanced in Saudi Arabia by his mentor, Uqla as-Shuaybi, Ulwan similarly believed that Islam was under attack by a Zionist–Crusader-led campaign against the world. This initiative was being directed in the Middle East locally by their running dogs, the Saudi royal family. Muslims, therefore, had only one option: to fight back.

The best way to assess Sulaiman al-Ulwan's importance to the global Jihadist movement is by his impact. He has shaped the movement in both direct and indirect ways. First, one of al-Ulwan's religious students was Abd-al-Aziz Bin-Abd-al-Rahman al-Umari al-Zahrani. The latter was born in Ghawran, a village of al-Makhwah, in the al-Bahah region of Saudi Arabia. His father was a religious scholar who taught in the local mosque. Like many Saudi youth seeking knowledge from the conservative clerics, he moved to Qasim, where he studied *Bulugh al-Maram* (classical Islamic teachings) under men like Shaikh Muhammad al-Uthaymin, Shaikh Khalid al-Mushayqar, and Shaikh Salih al-Fawzan. He also studied the Prophet's sayings under al-Ulwan, Shaikh Abd-al-Rahman al-Shamsan, and Shaikh Abdallah al-Ghulayman. He reportedly memorized the Quran in two months, the works of the early Islamic thinker al-Bukhari in one year, the *Arba'in bi al-Sanad* (classical Islamic teachings) in one year, and *Umdah al-Ahkam* (classical Islamic teachings). Rather than staying in Saudi Arabia to preach, he left to fight in Afghanistan, where he would be chosen to participate in the 9/11 attacks against the United States as a hijacker on the first plane to hit the World Trade Center. Al-Ulwan would subsequently issue a *fatwa* praising the 9/11 attacks.

In 2002, al-Ulwan, along with Uqla as-Shuaybi and Ali al-Khudair, celebrated the leadership of Taliban commander Mullah Muhammad Umar in a long letter. "Commander of the believers," they wrote,

> We—the collective scholars—are honoured to have the likes of you attributed to our nation, because you have affirmed, in reality, the supremacy and honour of the believers. You were not satisfied with declaring that you are the dominant, rather you confirmed this great meaning through your noble deeds, as the dominance in the land is not merely the material dominance, rather its most important and its greatest, is the dominance of religion and moral values.

For them, Mullah Muhammad had given Muslims around the world a lesson, through actions, that was a continuation of the lesson from the Jihadist experience in Afghanistan against the Soviets: "when Afghanistan was on the verge of crumbling into the hands of the secularists and the Communist and the Rafidhah [i.e. Shia]—and just when our hope for the fruits of Jihad was about to cease, you revived the hope in the Ummah . . . And then you took control of Afghanistan and implemented the *Sharia*, Allah be praised."[27]

A less direct indication of his impact is provided by who reads his work. In the Jihadist bestseller *39 Ways to Serve and Participate in Jihad*, the author, Issa Muhammad al-Awshan, provided an ideal Jihadist reading list, including al-Ulwan's *A Guide to Explain the Fine Points of Islam*, *Tendencies of the Savior*, *God's Triumph is Near*, *Ruling on the Obligation of Jihad against the Crusaders* and *Let Us Die that We May Attain Martyrdom*.

Although al-Ulwan's friends were *persona non grata* within Saudi Arabia, his direct family relationships with Yusuf al-Ayiri, one of the most dangerous and powerful al-Qaida figures in post-9/11 Saudi Arabia, would inevitably lead to his demise. Al-Ulwan supported his brother-in-law's efforts in organizing al-Qaida in the peninsula. On April 28, 2004, Saudi police took al-Ulwan into custody at his home for his support of al-Qaida's terrorism in the kingdom. His arrest sent the al-Qaida internet forums into a frenzy, speculating about his whereabouts and the circumstances of his arrest. Little was heard from al-Ulwan until March 2007, when Prince Nayif, Minister of the Interior, allowed him and his two brothers to visit their ailing father, Nasir al-Ulwan. As a gesture of goodwill, the prince even had Nasir al-Ulwan transferred to a top-tier hospital with a reputable intensive-care unit. Jihadists on the internet celebrated this good deed: "May God reward Shaikh Nasir al-Umar with all the good and also Prince Nayif Bin-abd-al-Aziz"; "May God heal Shaikh Nasir al-Ulwan, reward Shaikh Nasir [al-Umar], release Shaikh and speaker Sulayman al-Ulwan and his brothers, and bless Prince Nayif."[28] Sulaiman al-Ulwan nevertheless remains in prison.

Abu Muhammad al-Maqdisi

The man known today as Abu Muhammad al-Maqdisi was born Isam Muhammad Tahir al-Barqawi in 1959 in the hotbed town of Barqa, near Nablus, Palestine.[29] By the age of four, his family had emigrated to Kuwait, the country in which Maqdisi would spend the remainder of his youth.[30] After completing his secondary education, Maqdisi, who was eager to study Islamic law in the Islamic University in Medina, would instead be compelled to follow the path directed by his father, studying science in the University of Mosul in northern Iraq. At this time he became an Islamist activist. He began communicating with a variety of Islamist movements and organizations, some of which were reformist offshoots of the Muslim Brotherhood. He also established contact with Salafists of all kinds, including the rejectionist branch of Juhayman al-Utaibi and the JSM. Among the biggest supporters of Juhayman's teachings during the 1970s was a small band of puritanical Islamists known as al-Ahl al-Hadith (Followers of the Sayings of the Prophet).[31] This group, with whom Maqdisi aligned himself early on, had not yet sanctioned violent Jihad, instead placing a stronger emphasis on intellectual inquiry and religious purity. Although Maqdisi would move from this position, as would Juhayman himself, the former would be forever marked by a belief that the pen is mightier than the sword.

Al-Ahl al-Hadith drew its ideological inspiration from Juhayman's pronouncements which were published throughout Kuwait by the Dar al Taliah al Taqadumiyah (Progressive Vanguard) publishing group.[32] One of Juhayman's closest associates in Kuwait, who helped to spread his teachings, was Abdel Latif al-Dirbas, also known as Abu Hazza. Imprisoned immediately after Juhayman's attack on the Grand Mosque, the Saudi government forcibly returned Abu Hazza to Kuwait upon his release several years later. By chance or design, Maqdisi and Abu Hazza would become brothers-in-law, providing Maqdisi with a direct channel into the thinking of Juhayman and his followers.

Maqdisi's major questions at this time centered on clarifying the state of oppression of Islam, identifying how *Sharia* could be applied in today's world, finding a consensus position on what Islamists should do *vis-à-vis* Arab regimes whom they viewed as apostates, and planning a roadmap for establishing Heaven on Earth in the form of global Islamic rule. For answers, he looked backwards, devoting himself to studying the books of the medieval Islamic scholar Ibn Taymiyyah and his student Ibn al-Qayyim. He traveled to Medina, Saudi Arabia, and began reading the books of Muhammad bin Abd al-Wahab, his students, sons and grandsons and the local religious scholars there. This experience crystallized Maqdisi's thought in many ways.

The Saudi environment was polarized in the aftermath of Juhayman's seizure of the Grand Mosque. Although the official line had to be that the clerical establishment rejected him and his teachings, there were nonetheless some clerics who advocated his beliefs. Shaikh Muqbil ibn Hadee al-Wadi'ee, a prominent Albani Salafist, for instance, praised the principles of Juhayman and his revolt, without of course backing his claim of having identified the *mahdi*. Maqdisi's own name would be introduced into the Saudi Salafist dialogue due to his open support of another hardline cleric, Abdullah ad-Duwaish, who would publicly criticize Sayyid Qutb, the founder of the Egyptian Muslim Brotherhood movement, for 181 errors made in his book *In the Shadows of the Quran*. In short, Duwaish contended that Qutb was both ideologically soft and religiously undereducated.

Maqdisi then set off for Pakistan and Afghanistan, where he would meet Islamist groups who came from all regions of the Islamic world. He became increasingly involved in educational activities and wrote his foundational book, *Millat Ibrahim* (*The Religious Community of Abraham*).[33] Juhayman's life and teachings had been influencing Maqdisi's thinking for years, and this book would be the first of many allowing him to work out these principles formally, applying them to a revised ideological perspective. Consider this passage in *Millat Ibrahim*:

> Where are the writings of Juhayman and the likes of him . . . which were full of and enriched with *Tawhid*? Why doesn't the government fund these and encourage them, despite the fact that he did not even declare the disbelief of them, in those writings? Or could it be that it is a *Tawhid*, which opposes the compromise with the *Tughat* and their desires and that he spoke about politics and discussed Allegiance and Disavowal [*al-Wala wal-Bara*] and the Oath of Allegiance [*Bay'ah*] and Leadership [*Imarah*].[34]

Another book by Maqdisi, *The Manifest Proofs of the Disbelief of the Saudi State*, a scathing indictment of the Saudi government and its *ulama*, would become widely read by Jihadist fighters inside Afghanistan. It was smuggled across the Middle East, earning Maqdisi few friends inside the Saudi regime. Despite his criticisms, Maqdisi would return several times to the kingdom. In 1991, he visited the northwestern city of Hail, where he saw the powerful sway that the oppositionist Salafist teachings coming from the thinkers of Medina (including Juhayman and his JSM movement) held over the young men whom he met. Although Islamism was relatively new to the city, Maqdisi saw that in a period of two years most of the city's young men had embraced the ideology.

Back in Afghanistan Maqdisi came into contact with Abu Musab al-Zarqawi. A high-school dropout and petty criminal, Zarqawi was not the kind of man whom one might expect a high-brow Jihadist intellectual like Maqdisi to befriend. They would, however, find mutual utility in each another and their friendship blossomed. Maqdisi was the consummate academic, quiet in demeanor and reflective. Zarqawi was brash, loud and popular among the fighters. Together, they created a global Jihadist recruiting network, Bayat al-Imam, which they used to coordinate the movement of Jordanian fighters in and out of Afghanistan.

In late 1992, Zarqawi and Maqdisi left Afghanistan and returned to Jordan, only to find a country that was more culturally deviant and religiously disappointing than they had imagined. Then, in 1994, the Jordianian government signed a peace treaty with the devil, in the form of Israel. The Palestinians had already signed the Oslo Accords the previous year. Unemployment was up and the morale of most Jordanians was down. For Maqdisi and Zarqawi, the country looked ripe for a Jihadist revolution. In an interview with *al-Neda* magazine, Maqdisi said it was "swarming with *Irja* [hesitation to act] groups who wander about it in joy". He began teaching both public and private lessons emphasizing the concept of *Tawhid*, with all its implications and obligations. Meanwhile, Zarqawi began publicly condemning the government and denouncing mainstream clerics who supported it. Among those criticized were the Muslim Brotherhood, Jordan's only viable domestic opposition group, which, like most Brotherhood groups across the Middle East, agreed to support the ruling establishment in exchange for being allowed to participate openly in government. For those Jordanians with sincere grievances against the ruling regime, the Brotherhood offered little. A vast underground network of Jihadist groups, staffed primarily by Afghan veterans, emerged as a result of this growing public hostility.

Maqdisi also tapped into current events of the day, which revolved around the upcoming democratic elections for the Jordanian Legislative Council. He decided to focus aggressively on explaining to the people how much supporting democracy and elections violated Islamic doctrine, writing an essay entitled "Democracy is a Religion," which he had his students print and widely distribute. He also delivered public speeches in which he explained the concept of *Tawhid* and openly invited the people of Jordan to denounce man-made laws, to disbelieve in the Legislative Councils and to refuse to take part in it.

Maqdisi used this time to transform his recruiting network into an underground terrorist cell. According to Mary Anne Weaver's account of Zarqawi's life, the group's first operation was in Zarqa, in 1993.[35] Zarqawi had ordered one of his followers to bomb a theater showing pornographic films. The would-be bomber apparently got so distracted by the film playing that night that he inadvertently blew off his own legs. According to a court testimony that Maqdisi denied, he provided Zarqawi with grenades, which the latter added to the stockpile of weapons and explosives that he was developing in the cellar of his family's home. Given his high-profile criticism of the Jordanian regime, the security services were tracking Zarqawi closely. Before long, they would raid his family's home, finding the arsenal. Zarqawi was arrested, along with several other cell members, including Maqdisi, for possession of illegal weapons and participating in a banned group. In the lead-up to their arrest, Maqdisi's house had already been raided seven times, with his door broken, his home searched, and his books and writings confiscated.

Maqdisi was taken to the infamous Qafqafah jail in northern Jordan, while most of the rest of the group, including Zarqawi, was sent south, to Swaqah jail. Deprived of contact with his followers, Maqdisi nevertheless began the next phase of his proselytization campaign while in Qafqafah. One of his first moves while there was to write a booklet entitled "O Two Companions of the Prison! Are Many Different Lords Better or Allah, the One, the Irresistible?" in which he discussed subjects relating to *Tawhid*, the Jihadist ideology in general and the dangers of democracy in particular. He and his supporters began to pass the work around the other inmates, and as his minions were released back into Jordanian society they took copies of the booklet with them. As was typically the case with underground Jihadist literature, it became a hot commodity among Islamists inside Jordan during the 1990s.

Maqdisi's impact began to manifest itself more, both within and outside the Jordanian Islamist communities. For instance, when armed attackers struck an office of the Jordanian intelligence service, some of the arrested perpetrators confessed to having known Maqdisi in prison and even carried some of his writings with them. In the al-Ulya explosions in Riyadh, in November 1995, a Jihadist group blew up a training center of the Saudi National Guard. Abd al Aziz al-Muthim, who masterminded the attack, had been traveling frequently to Jordan, bringing back Maqdisi's books, listening to his teachings, and promoting his ideas.

In the immediate aftermath of the Riyadh bombings Maqdisi was transferred out of Qafqafah to Swaqah. He could not have been more delighted. Once reunited with his old students, including Zarqawi, they began to organize their activities inside the jail. Maqdisi established a study and prayer group, one that he hoped would become a platform for proselytizing and studying material that was not being taught in the prison's mosque, which was staffed by more conventional imams. The popularity of Maqdisi's group dramatically surpassed that of the mosque, not simply because his teachings were so compelling, but also because Zarqawi—the consummate thug and now *amir*, or religious commander, of the prison—helped to "persuade" other inmates to attend.

Maqdisi did not limit his Jihadist recruiting initiatives to inmates, however. He prepared a series of lessons in essay form for consumption by prison guards, officers and managers, as well as any intelligence officers who might be in the prison. Whenever members of parliament visited the jail in order to review conditions, he made sure to give them one of his books—*Unveiling the Falsehood in the Provisions of the Constitution*—which scrutinized the Jordanian Constitution and sought to expose the corruption that he saw in the Legislative Council.

Maqdisi and his prison followers also established a magazine called *Majallat at-Tawhid*, for which inmates wrote articles. Maqdisi's own writings refuting articles written by parliamentarians against Jihadist thought that he read in local newspapers would invariably be leaked out of the prison and into the hands of a growing band of youthful followers hungrily waiting for his next pronouncement. When he could receive visitors, Maqdisi was called on by young men from across Jordan, most of whom he had never previously met. They had read Maqdisi's work and asked him to advise them on various questions, as well as requesting *fatwa* from him on specific problems that they were having. He would give them copies of his prison writings as well as custom-written responses to their queries, which they would subsequently publish for a broader audience to read. As a result, the authorities began to restrict the visitation hours and carefully inspected those who were allowed to visit Maqdisi and his followers, both on the way in and going out. In order to deter the almost continuous parade of young men waiting to visit, the security agencies began tracking those who did, later detaining them to inquire about what they were seeking from Maqdisi, why they were reading his works, where they had obtained them and who else they knew who read such material.

Inside prison, the guards began to separate the rest of the inmates from Maqdisi's group so they could no longer recruit new followers into their movement. They prohibited anyone else from communicating with the group, reportedly punishing anyone who took Friday prayers with them or was caught reading Maqdisi's writings. For the most part, Maqdisi encouraged his followers to wait patiently and endure whatever punishment was meted out. However, he advocated active resistance if someone insulted their religious position or forced a follower to shave his beard, and members of the group would congregate at the doors of the prison, disobeying orders, refusing to follow the daily timetable and refusing to enter their cells at night. They would damn the prison guards and managers for their religious indiscretions, quoting passages of the Quran and the *Hadith* in support. After numerous violent clashes, the guards, who sometimes used tear gas in order to end the resistance, agreed to stop insulting the religious approach of Maqdisi's group. Maqdisi, though, was transferred to the primary jail of the Jordanian secret service, where he was questioned extensively about fomenting revolutionary thought while in prison, about how his writings were smuggled out of the prison and about the identity of his group members and associates. After 50 days of chastising his interrogators with Islamic damnations, he was moved back to the main prison and then to a small penitentiary in the suburb of al-Balqa.

Although the Jordanian government eventually released him, they rearrested him following a thwarted 2002 terrorist plot against government targets in Amman. Although a Jordanian court acquitted Maqdisi of all the charges leveled against him, he remained in solitary confinement for six months before being released on June 26, 2005. He reportedly remained silent and met only with his family until July 3, when he met with officials from the Jordanian Intelligence Department, who told him that he was free to give press statements. Thereupon he began accepting invitations to be interviewed by the press and television. Most of these interviews centered on his disagreements with Zarqawi. He scolded Zarqawi for his use of excessive violence and for causing bloodshed in Iraq, particularly against civilians and the Shia. He also complained about the fact that Zarqawi was using the name Tawid wal-Jihad for his terrorist group in Iraq because that was the name of Maqdisi's website: "This has caused much harm to the ideology I espouse," he said in one interview.[36] Maqdisi also railed against Zarqawi for his use of photography and the filming of terrorist attacks, and particular beheadings, which he saw as not only gratuitous but counterproductive:

> I previously warned of such operations that kill tens of innocent Iraqis and that do not differentiate between woman and child, civilian, military, or American occupier. This was contained in my messages from detention in the Qafqafa prison. They were entitled "Contemplation of the fruits of Jihad between ignorance of *Sharia* and ignorance of reality." They incorporated 18 stances in which I brought out the essence of my advice for every advocate and Mujahid among those who belong to the Salafi Jihadi Current,

including a position on what is taking place today on the level of Jihad action, especially the issue of explosions that occur on the streets of Muslim countries including Iraq.[37]

Advocates of Zarqawi saw Maqdisi's comments as traitorous, referring to them as *muraja'at* (revisionist). Maqdisi argued that he drew his conclusions from the core of global Jihadist ideology and from his own previous work. He noted in press interviews that he had previously counseled Zarqawi on the dangers of suicide attacks in the training camps of Harat, Afghanistan, and said that while he himself had sanctioned suicide attacks in specific cases, he could not do so when dozens of civilians were killed alongside a few soldiers or policemen.

Not more than a week later, Jordanian authorities again rearrested Maqdisi, which came as a surprise to many, given the anti-Zarqawi statements he had been making. According to the London-based *al-Quds al-Arabi*, this arrest was likely a result of the fact that the Jordanians had learned Maqdisi was planning to contact some Muslim clerics taking part in the First International Conference of Muslim Scholars (which was sponsored by the royal palace in Jordan) and challenge them to a debate. The Jordanians decided to arrest Maqdisi in order to avert any embarrassment he might cause the government.[38] During Ramadan in 2007, the still-incarcerated Maqdisi began an open-ended hunger strike, demanding to be either tried or released.

Abu Qatada

Just behind Maqdisi in terms of influence stands another major global Jihadist ideologue, Shaikh Omar Abu Omar. Better known as Abu Qatada al-Fillistini, he was born in Bethlehem, Palestine, in 1960 and later moved to Ra's al-Ayn, a neighborhood in Amman, where he became politically active as an oppositionist preacher. While in Jordan, he recruited and fomented Jihadist awareness among the youth of the country.

In 1990, he traveled to Peshawar, Pakistan, where he served as a professor of *Sharia* sciences. Peshawar, at the time, was a Jihadist hotspot: the Afghan Jihad had just concluded and thousands of *mujahidin* were milling about, looking for their next campaign. Fighters from various backgrounds and ideologies flooded into Pakistani cities, particularly Peshawar. According to some reports, Abu Qatada made a number of enemies there because of his ultra-radical stance and public candor. When Kabul, Afghanistan, reopened and the fighting ceased, he traveled there in order to visit some old friends, including Maqdisi. Some reports suggest that Abu Qatada had previously met Maqdisi in Kuwait and then in Zarqa, Jordan. Their friendship is one of mutual respect and ideological agreement.

In 1993, Abu Qatada left Pakistan and settled in London, being granted political asylum one year later. By this time he had already started his own Jihadist group in Jordan, al-Islah wal-Tahadi (Reform and Challenge). However, this group remained under the radar until 1998, when it detonated bombs outside an Amman hotel, a school, and under the cars of two government officials. Although the blasts caused no casualties a Jordanian military court found Abu Qatada and eight other alleged members of the organization guilty of conspiracy, and sentenced Abu Qatada *in absentia* to 15 years' imprisonment.

In the safe environment of Britain, though, Abu Qatada was feverishly writing articles and books and issuing *fatwa*. Some of his more famous books, which were printed and distributed widely across the Western Jihadist community, are *Jihad and Interpretation* and *Between Two Methods*, in which he tediously explains the primary features of the Jihad ideology, as well as the philosophy of change, its core tenets, and its historical evolution. Jihadism, for Abu Qatada, is a comprehensive, cultural movement based on the concept of *Tawhid*:

> During the phase of Jihad for the establishment of the Islamic State, the earth will be purified of the crows of evil and owls of immorality. Those midgets who are falsely called thinkers will be chased and liquidated group after group of secularists, communists. So we pave the road with their skulls. Let the world say we are barbarians, for that is what we are. Let them say we are terrorists. Yes, that is what we are; the word appears in Islamic terminology. We shall cut off the heads of journalists, for they are corrupters. We are not in need of the Pharaoh's magicians. Let people call us the enemies of thought and opinion. Yes, we shall set up the Islamic State with fire and iron, as this is what God prescribes to purify gold of impurities and rubbish.[39]

Jihad was mandatory. Hesitation was sinful. Anyone who stood in the way of waging Jihad was the enemy.

Abu Qatada's writings and recorded sermons seethe with fury against Arab governments. All Muslims have an immediate obligation, he said, to wage all-out warfare against these rulers until they are eliminated.[40] Arab states have become nothing more than instruments for subduing and controlling the Islamic world. Ministries of Information spread "heresy and apostasy, immorality, vices, beautifications of sins and fornication. They call to the trash and mindlessness of destructive Shirk beliefs." Ministries of Justice legalize all that is immoral, sexual and barbaric. Arab financial institutions, which are run by the government, promote usury. Ministries of Education have corrupted a generation of youth who have graduated from its schools and institutions. Arab governments have propagated theories of coexistence, which, for Abu Qatada, are merely ways to marginalize the doctrine of *al-Wala wal-Bara*.

There is little doubt that Abu Qatada stands among the most important Jihadist ideologues of his era. Since October 2002, however, he has been held by the British government under its terror laws, sidelining him in terms of his ability to preach, write and radicalize. In 2004, he appealed against his detention but without success. The appeals commission decided that there was sufficient evidence to conclude he had been "concerned in the instigation of acts of international terrorism," while its chairman, Mr. Justice Collins, said, "The appellant was heavily involved, indeed was at the center in the United Kingdom of terrorist activities associated with al-Qaida . . . He is a truly dangerous individual and these appeals are dismissed."[41]

Abu Qatada was eventually freed on bail in March 2005, but he was made subject of a control order to limit his movement and contact with others. In August, the British government took him back into custody pending extradition to Jordan, where, as mentioned above, he has been found guilty of terrorism offences in his absence. In December 2005, he made a video appeal to the kidnappers of British peace activist Norman Kember in Iraq. The recording, made inside Full Sutton jail, near York, was broadcast in the Middle East. Even such good behavior, however, did not help his efforts in early 2007 to appeal against the deportation decision.[42]

Indicating the importance of Abu Qatada in the global Jihadist movement, al-Qaida's High Command released a video statement in May 2007 in which his impending deportation was addressed. Senior al-Qaida leader Abu Laith al-Libi announced that the organization was prepared to conduct a prisoner exchange with the UK to secure the release of Abu Qatada. The British government did not respond.

Sayyid Imam

Among the global Jihadist ideologues covered in this chapter, few are more complex than Sayyid Imam Abdul Aziz Imam As-Sharif. Born in August 1950 in the city of Bani Suwayf, southern Egypt, Sayyid Imam, who is also known as Abd al-Qadir ibn Abd al-Aziz, memorized the Quran as a young boy and began writing deep, reflective essays on Islamic issues as a teenager. He attended the Faculty of Medicine in Cairo, graduating in 1974 with top honors, and then served as a vice-chairman in the surgical branch of the College of Ophthalmology. At the same time, he started to support the growing underground movement of violent Jihadism bubbling in Egypt and met another young Egyptian physician who was similarly inclined, Ayman al-Zawahiri.

Sayyid Imam, or Dr. Fadl as he came to be known within Jihadist circles, was accused of involvement in the assassination of Anwar Sadat in 1981, but he was able to escape to Pakistan before he was arrested. He became the director of the Kuwaiti al-Hilal Hospital in Peshawar and used this position to bring Zawahiri to Pakistan in 1986. At this time, Sayyid Imam married a Palestinian woman, with whom he had four sons and one daughter. He then married a Yemeni woman from the city of Ebb, with whom he had another daughter. From Peshawar, he played a senior management role in one of the top two Egyptian terrorist organizations— Egyptian Islamic Jihad. Although this group had not at this point waged any large-scale attacks, the winding down of the Jihad against the Soviets in Afghanistan provided a new cadre of highly skilled Egyptian fighters who were eager to return home and start conducting operations.

As influential as he was in catalyzing Jihadist thinking in and around Peshawar, Sayyid Imam's writings between 1988 and 1992 would have an even greater long-term impact. Two of his books, *Risalat al-Umdah Fi I'dad al-Uddah* (*Foundations in Preparing for Jihad*) and *Al-Jami fi Talab al-I'lim al-Sharif* (*The Comprehensive Book about the Pursuit of Glorious Knowledge*), are core Jihadist texts: over the past decade, they have been found in the hands of terrorist cells worldwide. Other writings, such as *The Five Ground Rules for the Achievement of the Tradition of*

Victory or Its Absence, The Manhaj of Ahl As-Sunnah Wal-Jamā'ah and *The Refutation of the Doubts Concerning Bay'ah and Imārah*, are actively shared in their original Arabic and in English translation online.[43]

Sayyid Imam also served as a senior adviser for other Jihadist intellectuals, such as the Syrian Abu Musab al-Suri. The latter had established an early friendship with Ayman al-Zawahiri and would come to know Sayyid Imam as the senior religious figure in the Egyptian Islamic Jihad group. He would later say: "I wish to thank al-Shaikh Dr. Abd al-Qadir Ibn Abd al-Aziz . . . His acquaintanceship, his books, and his conversations have left a great impact on me intellectually."[44] Suri also provided important details about Sayyid Imam's thinking on some of the most controversial Jihadist methods, including suicide bombings: "He said to me: that they were not permitted because he could not find any strong text to support suicide operations. He thought about it a long time, until he found permission for it in Almighty Allah's saying: *Take not life, which Allah made sacred, except by way of justice and law* (Al-An'am: 151)."[45]

By 1991, Sayyid Imam had passed the leadership of Egyptian Islamic Jihad to Ayman al-Zawahiri. However, he would remain the group's senior ideologue, providing religious cover for the series of unpopular attacks that Zawahiri carried out in Egypt from 1992 to 1995. In late 1993, though, as the Pakistani government began cracking down on the militants in Peshawar, he and his family fled to Sudan. Details are sketchy about this time in his life, but his support for global Jihadist activities started to ebb. One important factor in this seems to be a book entitled *The Bitter Harvest*, which is traditionally attributed to Zawahiri. According to some Jihadist accounts, Sayyid Imam actually wrote a great deal of the text, and he assumed that he and Zawahiri would publish the book under the auspices of Egyptian Islamic Jihad. So when Zawahiri accepted sole credit Sayyid Imam was infuriated.

In November 1993, the Vanguards of Conquest, a violent offshoot of Egyptian Islamic Jihad, launched a strike against the Egyptian Prime Minister, Atif Sidqi. The cell had been ordered to conduct a careful reconnaissance in order to minimize civilian casualties, but what had seemed like a perfect spot for the attack proved devastating for the group. They had mistakenly believed that a girls' school directly across the street from where they planted a car-bomb was under construction when in fact it was in session. When the bomb exploded, the Prime Minister escaped unharmed. However, a 12-year-old girl attending the school was killed by shrapnel. The Egyptian government seized the opportunity to portray the incident as an attack by terrorists on innocent Egyptian people, rather than an attack on Atif Sidqi, a man for whom few Egyptians had any sympathy. Government-supporting news-papers published photos of the girl's parents sobbing and pictures of the girl herself in her early childhood.

Nearly a thousand members and supporters of the group were arrested in the aftermath of this and several subsequent attacks. The Egyptian government executed several of the group's key domestic leadership, dealing a fierce blow to Zawahiri and Sayyid Imam, who were attempting to maintain control from abroad. Sayyid Imam's frustration with Zawahiri and their Jihadist enterprise led him to renounce his position within the organization and return to practicing medicine. He left Sudan for Yemen, where he began work in the Hospital of the General Revolution in the city of Ebb, south of the capital, Sana. From there he went on to the Dar As-Shifa Hospital. Little more is known about his time in Yemen; he simply sought to remain under the security radar, and seemed intent on putting his Jihadist past behind him.

That past inevitably caught up with him, however, as the Yemeni government arrested him on October 28, 2001 as a result of the massive pressure placed on it by the United States in the aftermath of 9/11. Sayyid Imam remained in a political high-security prison in Sana for two years and five months before being turned over to the Egyptian authorities on February 28, 2004. He had previously been found guilty *in absentia* in Egypt for his role in Egyptian Islamic Jihad. He was not heard from again until 2006, when the Egyptian government announced that he was playing a leading role in helping to renounce terrorism, violence and the Jihadist movement within its prisons. This announcement shocked, disappointed and confused Jihadists around the world but went almost completely unnoticed in the West.

In November 2007, Sayyid Imam released his much-anticipated book, *Tarshid al-Jihad fi Misr wa al-Aalam* (*Rationalizations on Jihad in Egypt and the World*). Serialized in the Egyptian daily *al-Masry al-Youm*, the book is already being hailed within official Egyptian circles as the definitive renunciation of violence by one of the most influential Jihadist thinkers alive today.[46] It is an attempt to counter his own and others' earlier works by way of a *Fiqh*-based series of clarifications and reconsiderations. The Jihadist use of violence in trying to overthrow Islamic governments is both counterproductive and religiously unlawful, Sayyid Imam now argues. *Dawa*, or the practice of publicly calling others to Islam, is a much safer, effective and religiously justifiable way to channel one's grievances against a regime. Sayyid Imam prompts Muslims to use non-violent methods to reform (*al-Islah*) laws that are not in accordance with *Sharia*. He advises that Muslims should flee state persecution (*al-Hijra*) when necessary instead of fighting, or isolate (*al-Uzla*) themselves from corruption that cannot be escaped. Muslims ought to pardon (*al-Afw*) the harmful actions of others, forgive (*al-Safh*) their enemies, shun (*al-I'rad*) those who advocate un-Islamic behavior and maintain patience (*al-Sabr*) in the face of seemingly insurmountable challenges. According to Sayyid Imam, when judging whether to employ violence, particularly against an Islamic government or foreign tourists, one must always consider whether the potential damage of such an act outweighs the potential benefits. Since violence only leads to death, destruction and further violence, Sayyid Imam concludes that it can *never* be justified within Islamic law and must, therefore, never be applied on religious grounds. Furthermore, on practical grounds, he suggests, armed action against an entrenched power simply makes no historical sense: after decades of violence in Egypt, for instance, Jihadists have yet to overthrow the ruling regime. His approach, therefore, is to maintain an ideological commitment to applying *Sharia* on Earth, but to reject the use of violence against governments who fail to apply it. He can therefore maintain his Salafist credentials while also appeasing his Egyptian overseers.

Rationalizations is just one in a series of recantations emerging out of the Egyptian government's initiative to quash radicalism within its borders. The leadership of Egypt's other major terrorist organization, al-Gama'a al-Islamiyya, led the charge in 1997 by announcing a formal ceasefire, which they followed in 2003 with a renunciation of violence altogether by publishing two books: *Al-Riyadh Bombing: Rulings and Repercussions* and *River of Memories*.[47] As reward for their moves toward reconciliation, the Egyptians released over nine hundred imprisoned members of al-Gama'a.

One of Egyptian Islamic Jihad's first retractions came in March 2000 from the Egyptian Islamist now living as a political refugee in Germany, Osama Ayyub. His attempt to reform the Islamic Jihad ideology generated only limited support, though, most notably from Shaikh Ahmad Yusuf, the emir of the Bani-Suwayf group, and Shaikh Nabil al-Mughrabi, who was serving two life sentences in an Egyptian prison.[48] During the summer of 2004, two more senior Islamic Jihad figures, Nabil Na'im, a senior leader since Zawahiri had left him in charge in the mid-1980s, and his colleague Ismail Nasr, drew up a "draft document" entitled *Visualization*, in which they rejected violent attempts to overthrow Islamic governments and urged the al-Azhar University scholars publicly to readdress the issue. Like Ayyub, Na'im and Nasr could generate only limited support from within the imprisoned Islamic Jihad ranks: Shaikh Ahmad Yusuf Hamdallah, Dr. Ahmad Ujayzah and Shaikh Amal Abd-al-Wahab were the only major figures to support the move. The competing al-Marj group, led by Majdi Salim, and the Abu-Za'bal group, led by Ahmad Salamah Mabruk, rejected the initiative on the grounds that Na'im lacked the religious qualifications to authorize such a revision. Enter Sayyid Imam.[49] In 2006, with the support of the Egyptian government, he began lecturing with his long-time colleague Abd-al-Aziz al-Jamal to imprisoned members of various Jihadist groups in the al-Fayyum prison on the legal limitations of armed action. As the highest-ranking Islamic scholar in any Egyptian prison, Sayyid Imam commanded respect across various Jihadist subsets that neither Ayyub nor Na'im could muster. But *Rationalizations* has caused a stir among his former colleagues, who have now launched a coordinated response.

After submitting *Rationalizations* to the al-Azhar scholars for review, Sayyid Imam faxed a statement to *al-Sharq al-Awsat* announcing the impending release of his retractions. Ayman al-Zawahiri responded speedily, observing in a video message in July 2007:

> I read a ridiculous bit of humor in *al-Sharq al-Awsat* newspaper, which claimed that it received a communiqué from one of the backtrackers, who faxed it from prison . . . I laughed inside and asked myself, "Do the prison cells of Egypt now have fax machines? And I wonder, are these fax machines connected to the same line as the electric shock machines, or do they have a separate line?"[50]

Al-Qaida's ideological hitman, Abu Yahya al-Libi, followed Zawahiri's comments in a speech two months later. Rather than interpreting Sayyid Imam's abandonment of Jihadist principles as an ideological defeat for the Jihadist movement, he characterized it as just another weapon being wielded in the Crusaders' "war of ideas." Muslims, he suggested, ought simply to dismiss the news as a result of torture, brainwashing and blackmail.[51]

Muhammad Khalil al-Hakaymah, a former al-Gama'a member who has since pledged allegiance to al-Qaida's senior leadership, was next, producing a six-point response to *Rationalizations*. In it, he says that Sayyid Imam tarnished his religious credentials the moment he broke from Zawahiri in 1993. He accuses him of misrepresenting the reality of Jihadist armed action and implies that he was little more than an armchair ideologue even when he was aligned with the movement. Now in prison, Sayyid Imam has shown just how weak he is, buckling under Egyptian government pressure. Hakaymah then compares him unfavorably with another imprisoned Egyptian Jihadist ideologue, Shaikh Umar Abd al-Rahman.[52]

Global Jihadist ideologues are forced to live between two worlds: a rhetorical one that is ideologically pure and allows their grandiose statements and damning indictments; and the real world, where they are forced to mitigate, posture, quiet, compromise and occasionally back-pedal. There can be little doubt that no matter how complicated the challenges posed to them by governments, thinkers like Fahd, Khudair, Maqdisi and Abu Qatada will continue to adapt and seek to trigger a revolution. They are the backbone of the global Jihadist movement. Without them, none of the violence or rhetoric could endure or make sense. The challenge for governments is not simply how to mute these hateful voices in the short term but how to deal with their legacies over the long term. And a great many of them need to be addressed: the scholars discussed in this chapter are but a handful of the global Jihadist core cadre.

4 Strategists

What unites us first and foremost is TAWHEED, then Jihaad. If a person dies not intending to do Jihaad, then he will die on a branch of hypocrisy. But if a person dies fighting the Jews while he hasn't Rejected Taghoot, he will die Mushrik. So before jumping on the bandwagon, learn your Tawheed, because Jihaad without Tawheed will only end up in a bloodbath of confusion.

Umm Umar, Jihadist internet forum senior member

On June 25, 1996 a truck packed with over five thousand pounds of plastic explosives detonated outside the Khobar Towers complex in the densely populated urban environment of Dhahran, Saudi Arabia. At the time, the Khobar Towers housed nearly half of the 2,500 US military forces based in Saudi Arabia, mostly US air force personnel. Nineteen US servicemen were killed in the blast and more than 500 other people were injured, 240 of whom were American.

Feeling the international pressure to identify the perpetrators, Saudi state security began rounding up known religious radicals whom they suspected may have been involved in plotting or executing the attack. One Saudi caught up in the sweep was Yousef al-Ayiri. Known in the global Jihadist community by the name Shaikh Yousef bin Saleh, or by his *nom-de-guerre* "Al-Battar" (the "Severer" or "Swift Sword"), Ayiri had trained at al-Qaida's famed al-Faruq camp in Afghanistan, served as a bodyguard for Usama Bin Laden in Sudan, and fought alongside other Arab Jihadists in Somalia. His Jihadist credentials were therefore impeccable. When Ayiri returned to the Arabian Peninsula in the mid-1990s, he is said to have met with a Saudi shaikh, Salman al-Awdah, to whom he described the ongoing initiatives of Usama Bin Laden. At the time, Awdah reportedly responded favorably, indicating that, "It's an honor for me to be one of the soldiers of Abu Abdallah [Bin Laden]."[1] Working from Dammam, the largest town in the eastern region of Saudi Arabia, and then from Kosovo, Ayiri dedicated himself to supporting Jihadist activities in Bosnia in the mid-1990s. He reportedly collected donations and even crafted a two-week physical fitness training program for Jihadists preparing to fight there. But not long after the Khobar Towers bombings, he found himself facing the interrogators in prison in Dammam, charged as a leading plotter in the attack.

This experience left him loathing the Saudi governing regime. Other extremists who had been similarly picked up during the security sweep later described how they saw him being carried out on a stretcher, shaved beardless, after each interrogation session because of the toll that the beatings and whippings had taken on his body. After enduring days of this treatment, Ayiri requested a meeting with the prison director in order to make a confession. The director agreed to hear him and ordered the guards to bring him to his palatial office. Once there, security officers crowded around Ayiri, each holding a pen and paper, hungry to notate the details of his confession. The director walked in and asked bluntly: "What have you got? Go ahead and make your confession." Bound and shackled, Ayiri looked up from his chair and replied, "I am aware of the embarrassment that you are experiencing for not knowing who carried out the bombing. I will volunteer to confess that I am the one who carried out the bombing and I am prepared to pay with my life as a price for this." Infuriated, the director hurled a glass ashtray at Ayiri's face, then shouted to the guards, "Take him out and discipline him!" When asked later why he made the confession, Ayiri replied, "By God, I could not take the torture any more. I was close to losing faith. Death is more merciful than this torture." After more days of intense interrogation, a Saudi intelligence officer came to see him in his cell. "Good news," the officer told Ayiri. "We know the real culprit. He is not one of you. He is from the al-Rafidah [Shia Muslims], but don't tell anybody!"

Although charges were soon dropped against Ayiri and the other Jihadists for involvement in the bombing, they were found guilty on lesser charges, such as "declaring the society infidel," and sentenced to varying prison terms.

Upon his eventual release, Ayiri recommitted himself to waging violent Jihad against the Saudi regime. He reestablished contact with Usama Bin Laden and began writing studies on *Sharia* for the Voice of the Caucasus website. The Chechen Jihad had struck a deep chord within Ayiri. He knew the much-heralded Saudi commander in Chechnya, Khattab, with whom he often corresponded about guerrilla warfare strategy. Ayiri worked to raise funds for the Chechen *mujahidin* but quickly became distracted with studying and supporting the Taliban in Afghanistan. He went so far as to try to connect the Taliban's director, Mullah Muhammad Umar, with one of the most highly regarded Jihadist-leaning shaikhs in Saudi Arabia, Hammoud bin al-Uqla as-Shuaibi. In 2000, several Taliban ministers visited Ayiri in Mecca, Saudi Arabia, and through them he scheduled a phone conference between Shaikh Uqla and Mullah Muhammad. In order to make it to Uqla's house in al-Qasim Province in time for the phone call, Ayiri and his Taliban guests decided to drive through the night. Several hours into the trip, though, the driver, tired and blurry-eyed, hit a stray camel in the road, flipping over the car. Although none of the group was injured, the car was a write-off and they missed the phone call.

Saudi intelligence detained Ayiri after this incident and held him for nearly a year in jail. He was released in August 2001 and wasted little time in returning to the Jihadist world, both physical and virtual. He had always been comfortable using technology and believed that the internet was the logical means to push the Jihadist creed globally. He assumed the screen-name Azzam in tribute to his hero, Abdullah

Azzam, and began frequenting Jihadist chat-groups and discussion forums, where he engaged in debate and hunted for new recruits. He also started writing and publishing books.

Ayiri's first book, released just weeks after 9/11, was entitled *The Truth about the Crusader War*. In it, Ayiri sought to establish the religious validity of the attacks and to call the Islamic nation to action. It spread rapidly throughout the Jihadist community, reportedly even to Bin Laden, who was surprised that Ayiri could have written such a detailed treatise so quickly. Ayiri also showed the book to his brother-in-law, the renowned Jihadist shaikh Sulayman al-Ulwan, who quietly passed it throughout the Saudi Salafist establishment. His later books include *The Balance for the Taliban Movement* and *The Role of Women in the Jihad against the Enemies*, and he wrote a series of articles entitled *Landmarks on the Path of Jihad*. He found that one of the most effective vehicles for communicating his call for global Jihad was his own newly formed Center for Islamic Study and Research. For example, he posted a series of articles on the implications of America's military intervention in Iraq on the Center's website.

Key strategists

One often hears discussion in the counter-terrorism community about the need to know al-Qaida's strategy. But this question is slightly misguided. There is no single Jihadist strategy. There are, however, Jihadist strategists. These thinkers, including Abu Ubayd al-Qurashi, Abu Bakr Naji, Yousef al-Ayiri, Abu Musab al-Suri, Ayman al-Zawahiri, Abu Ayman al-Hilali, Abu Saàd al-Amali, Muhammad Khalil al-Hakaymah, Abd-al-Aziz Bin Raishid al-Anzi, Louis Atiyatallah, Abu Umar al-Baghdadi, and others, provide important suggestions, insights and strategic guidance to the Jihadist movement's senior leadership on the ground. This genre of Jihadist strategic writing, first referred to in Western counter-terrorism circles as "Jihadi Strategic Studies" by Thomas Hegghammer and Brynjar Lia, stands in sharp contrast to typical Jihadist ideological or religious texts.[2] These strategic examinations, Hegghammer and Lia argue, take a more hard-nosed approach to the real world, drawing heavily on Western military concepts and strategic thinking. Their analyses are clear-headed and focused on teasing out lessons learned from previous experience, both from the Jihadist perspective and from the experiences of their enemies.

There are several common denominators among most of these strategists. First, many of them write under pen names, keeping their true identities secret from even their Jihadist associates. Very little biographical information is known, at least in open sources, about many of the above figures. There is even debate over whether Abu Umar al-Baghdadi, the purported emir of al-Qaida's new initiative the "Islamic State of Iraq," is a real person or a media creation comprising a composite of Jihadists in Iraq and elsewhere. And virtually nothing is known about the real identity of Abu Ubayd al-Qurashi, Abu Bakr Naji, or Louis Atiyatallah.

The second common thread among these thinkers is their pragmatism. Although each of them is without question a true believer in the global Jihadist ideology, none allows his religious or ideological beliefs to hamstring his military thinking. Winning comes first, so the ideology can flex to the needs of the situation on the ground. This also means that their own popularity is of secondary concern to them. They are willing and able to advocate controversial policies, candidly to discuss mistakes made by even senior Jihadist commanders and to go for long stretches of time without uttering a word. Each, however, targets a different issue area. For Anzi, oil is the chief concern; for Naji, seizing territory and winning hearts and minds are priorities; Suri and Qurashi seek tangible metrics for assessing force strength, capability, economic viability and weaknesses in their opponents' strategic approaches.

Strategists make their writings available in a variety of formats. Some, like Hilali, Amali, Qurashi and Naji, publish short essays in popular Jihadist magazines. These magazines circulate among all tiers of the Jihadist movement, particularly among Jihobbyists, both in print and on the internet. Suri has relied mostly on publishing books. Zawahiri and Ayiri use books, articles, recorded statements and lectures as well as multimedia productions. Atiyatallah and Hakaymah have harnessed the power of internet blogs. The latter has been particularly effective by going "viral," spreading his ideas rapidly within a given population.

It is, then, extraordinarily difficult to generalize about or quantify Jihadist strategy. Doing so simply distorts the complexity and sophistication of Jihadist thinking. A better approach is to examine the writings of these strategists on a number of key issue areas. By doing so, it becomes easier to quantify a "Jihadist consensus position."

Recognize the global conspiracy to destroy Islam

Jihadists spend significant amounts of time thinking about where the movement stands. This includes defining their enemies, recognizing their friends, identifying weapons being used against them and assessing progress. Every Jihadist strategy begins with the same basic premise: that there is a global conspiracy to destroy Islam. For Abu Musab al-Suri, Islam is under attack by the establishment of a "New World Order." At the helm of this initiative, he argues, are the Jews—headed by Israel and Zionism. Behind Israel, he explains, stand "Crusaders," headed first and foremost by America, France and Britain. Then follow the rest of NATO and the apostate Arab regimes, the rulers who govern the largest "Muslim" governments in Egypt, Saudi Arabia, Morocco, Pakistan and Syria. This triangular conspiracy of Jews, apostates and Crusaders, Suri contends, wages war on Islam with a variety of weapons, including military, economic, informational and political. Muslims today fail to recognize this conspiracy, however, because of a quiet force lurking within their ranks: the *ulama*. For Suri, echoing Mao Zedong, the Islamic clerical establishment comprise the running dogs of imperialism. These government scholars have blinded Muslims' eyes and bound Muslims' hands. For Suri, they have delegitimized themselves with their willingness to support the enemy and so can no longer serve as a religious reference point for Muslims today. Due to them, Muslims have failed to understand that they have an individual religious duty to wage violent Jihad. In his "Call to Islamic Global Resistance" of December 2004, Suri stated that every person waging active Jihad must have what he calls a "battle doctrine." The mental orientation of any soldier, he explained, persuades him that he is the morally superior one in war. All the revolutionary movements of the past have employed a program for such education and empowerment of its soldiers, ensuring that the mindset of each and every warrior held the right set of beliefs. If Muslims simply fight their enemies using words then Islam is sure to fall, Suri argued, given the extent to which enemies of Islam employ "machine guns, flogging, rape and defamation." He recognized, however, the complexities that surface when Muslims employ force against other Muslims, and suggested that if Muslims "battle these people with weapons then [they] will lose Muslims and might fall into an area which is not legally permitted in Islam."

One part of Suri's battle doctrine is to degrade the legitimacy of the Islamic scholars who support ruling Arab regimes. They seek to divert the attention of the youth from their primary goal, which for Suri is fighting. The only way for one to wage an effective fight, Suri argues, is to first decipher the struggle's basic power equation. In the global Jihadist fight, Suri explains that the power equation is: Jews + Crusaders + Apostates + Hypocrites against the Movement (spearheaded by al-Qaida). At the forefront of Suri's "hypocrite" category are the official religious *ulama*. Then come the leaders of the Islamic Awakening movement, whom he says have become corrupted in their faith. These scholars, Suri argues, seek to convince Muslims that the concept of Jihad can be waged through words and non-violent means. Once Jihadists have internalized the core component of this battle doctrine —that Islam is facing a global conspiracy to destroy it—strategists are able to push forward.

View the United States as the vanguard of this conspiracy

Jihadist thinker Abu Ubayd al-Qurashi focuses on two strategic themes in his writings: demonstrating that the United States is less powerful than it portrays itself; and arguing that the Jihadist movement is on the rise around the world. For Qurashi, exposing the former catalyzes the latter.

To achieve this, Qurashi feels that the enemy's own data and logic need to be used against it. And no Jihadist strategist is better than Qurashi himself at doing just that. In his 2002 article "A Lesson in War," he conducts a nuanced distillation of Carl von Clausewitz's legendary treatise *On War*: "There are two fundamental principles behind all strategic planning that ought to guide all other considerations . . . First, getting to know the enemy's center of gravity when one is planning for war . . . Second, being sure to direct all available force against this center during the great offensive.[3] Military strategists in the United States, Qurashi explains, have embraced Clausewitz's "center of gravity" concept since the First World War, so much so that they have locked themselves into this mode of thought and now cannot break free from it. American strategic planners have failed to formulate an effective strategy for defeating al-Qaida because Clausewitz's theories are premised on fighting a centralized hostile adversary with a unified command structure, not a decentralized network. Defeating an adversary whose cells are connected only by electronic means of communication, whose targets are often selected years in advance and whose command structure is extremely resilient against military and law enforcement strikes requires a fundamentally different mode of thought, one the United States has yet to identify.

Qurashi examines the best American strategic thinking in order to understand power. He holds the thinking of Ray Cline, whom he calls "one of the best CIA experts at the peak of the Cold War," in high esteem and makes it the core of one of his major strategic arguments.[4] After serving as Deputy Director of Intelligence (DDI), Cline published *Secrets, Spies and Scholars: Blueprint of the Essential CIA* (1976), in which he articulated the following equation about power: $Pp = (C + E + M) \times (S + W)$, where Pp = potential power; C = critical mass; E = economic capability; M = military capability; S = strategic purpose; and W = will. This equation, although originally drafted to assess the power of countries, could also be used to assess the power of organizations and groups that wish to establish a state or an entity, according to Qurashi. First, he breaks down the variables. By "critical mass," Qurashi understands Cline to mean land, location, population, and so on. By "economic capability," he believes Cline means gross national product. One's "military capability" refers to the number of troops, the budget, and so on. "Strategic purpose" refers to the overall strategic vision, goals, and so on, while "will" is the degree of conviction of the elite and the masses. Fighting enemies, at least according to this equation, must therefore be grounded in reality, not in illusions.

For Qurashi, when Islamist movements claim to possess power but do not seek to acquire some of these variables, they are doomed to fail. When Islamist movements join a fight for an Islamic state with very little in terms of material preparation, they will not succeed. And when Islamic movements concentrate their efforts on aggrandizing economic power and thereby ignore the remaining variables, they are destined to fail from the outset. By applying Cline's power equation to the al-Qaida organization, Qurashi argues that it possesses a considerable degree of potential power. For instance, Afghanistan, a land strategically well located in geopolitical terms, fulfills the land requirement.

In its current war against the United States, Qurashi argues, the Jihadist movement needs to develop an intimate understanding of combat power. To do so, he suggests that it should employ an equation written by war researcher and retired colonel T.N. Dupuy, whose book *Understanding War: History and Theory of Combat* (1987) identifies combat power (P) as being a function of the number of troops (N) multiplied by variable factors (V) multiplied by the quality (Q) of those troops, or $P = NVQ$.[5] Although the overall number of troops is tilted in favor of the Americans in Afghanistan and Iraq, the Jihadists have a large potential pool from which to recruit. By this, Qurashi means the world's population of well over a billion Muslims. With regard to the quality of the forces, Qurashi argues that the balance is undoubtedly already in favor of the Jihadist movement because its soldiers not only wage war with deep religious conviction (rather than for profit, which he argues drives American soldiers) but live a Spartan life that turns them into fierce warriors, superhumans. More important than either of these, however, are the variable factors, which Qurashi predictably argues are all in favor of the Jihadists: they have the initiative; they possess the element of surprise; they choose the scenes of operation; and they choose the type of combat interaction. Americans, on the contrary, continue to struggle with trying to understand what comprises the Jihadist mindset.

Use Jihadist judo: turn the West's strength against it

For Qurashi, the Jihadist movement is vastly outmatched, undergunned and over-powered. It is the ultimate David versus Goliath story, he argues. This vast power asymmetry is not necessarily a bad thing, however. First, the movement's scarce resources have made it more flexible, more creative and more resilient. It is able to harness existing resources in ways that help to amplify its projection of strength. Second, being the underdog always makes for good propaganda. The Jihadist movement has been able to spin itself as a small but dedicated populist force seeking to defend the freedom of the oppressed and downtrodden. Although this image is far from the reality, the Jihadist propagandists have been able to sell it convincingly.

Qurashi believes that identifying power inequalities between the West and the Jihadist movement is important for developing a viable strategy. The imbalances that he sees center on the following points:

- *Inequality in force strength*: It is a war between a strong party that possesses all the necessary land, sea and air capabilities and a weak side with limited troops. However, the weak side is intelligent and possesses great will-power.
- *Inequality in information technology*: America possesses the technological and informational tools to obtain and deliver data. Despite the enormous gap in resources, though, it has lost the battle of information. The 9/11 shocked the global village with scenes of destruction that devastated the symbols of US economic and military might and subsequently afflicted the world's stock exchanges with a malady that exposed the frailty of the US economy. Furthermore, all of these scenes were transmitted by the enemy's own technological tools at no cost whatsoever to the attackers.
- *Inequality in the structural position and global legitimacy*: America is speaking for a state while al-Qaida is speaking for the people. America's point of reference is democracy while al-Qaida's are the Quran and the Prophet's tradition.
- *Inequality in space*: America wants to control areas and bring them under its dominance while al-Qaida seeks to operate throughout the world irrespective of borders, and so strike where and when it wants.
- *Inequality in objectives and time horizons*: Al-Qaida is looking to the future while America wants to maintain the status quo.

These power inequalities, Qurashi argues, lead to one conclusion: al-Qaida can and must turn its enemy's strengths against itself. The martial arts philosophy of judo, where an individual turns a formidable opponent's strength against him, best defines this form of strategic thinking. Although Qurashi himself does not use the concept explicitly, it is clearly informing the ways in which Jihadist strategists think: hijacking American planes and using them as weapons against the symbolic targets of the Pentagon and the World Trade Center is a good example of this strategy in action.

Qurashi builds much of his strategic framework around the thinking of ancient Chinese military strategist Sun Tsu. Drawing from the latter's *The Art of War*, Qurashi tries to address the massive power imbalance between Western military strength and Jihadist forces by advancing three of Sun Tsu's strategies:

- "The best war is turning the tables on enemy plans after they have been worked out."
- "If your enemy is superior in number and military hardware, make good use of the terrain by spreading out on rugged mountains and lanes."
- "Force the enemy, who is superior in number, to deploy his army in a certain way that suits you best and make your army ready to face all forms of reorganization."

With these three strategies, Qurashi argues that Jihadist fighters will be able to offset the West's military superiority and not only live to fight again but run the West ragged by forcing it to try to nab elusive Jihadist cells. Regarding the first strategy, Qurashi advocates that Jihadist groups must be flexible in their thinking. If the Coalition forces try to force Jihadists into urban areas, they ought to flee to rural areas and hide in the mountains. But they ought to wait until the West has formulated and begun implementing its plan in order to maximize the paralysis that will ensue. With regard to the second strategy, Qurashi believes that the rugged terrain of places like Afghanistan and Pakistan helps to preserve Jihadist forces and capabilities by allowing them to decide when and where to engage Coalition forces. This ensures prolonged periods between encounters, thereby eroding the morale of Coalition forces. With regard to the third strategy, he applauds the ways in which Jihadist fighters have deployed in the mountains after their withdrawal from the towns, which has forced the United States to divide rather than consolidate its forces. This strategy makes Coalition forces more vulnerable and beatable when they face the small Jihadist fighting cadres.[6]

Exploit the West's weaknesses

Qurashi tries to highlight what he believes to be America's "hidden weak points" by examining the studies that Western strategic analysts have written about the real or imagined security gaps and dangers threatening the safety of American society.[7] To Qurashi's mind, the security threats that American policy-makers fear most are:

- acquisition of weapons of mass destruction;
- perpetration of naval and maritime attacks;

- attacks on oil installations, tankers, pipelines and refineries;
- employment of cyberterrorism;
- strikes on key hubs, including electrical grids and nuclear power plants, financial institutions, and the "911" emergency telephone network;
- connections between Jihadist groups and organized crime syndicates.

The strategy that America is following in an attempt to thwart these threats, and to repress the Jihadist movement in general, is nothing more than the "same old strategy" of containment that George Kennan developed in 1947 and which the United States applied against the former Soviet Union. Such recycling of outmoded strategies, Qurashi argues, shows the absence of creativity in this administration and the obsolescence of its planners, who are still living in the age of the Cold War. The latter have not appreciated the ways in which today's conflict against the Jihadist movement differs from that against the Soviet Union. Whereas the USSR was a vast state whose vital interests could easily be understood and thus countered through a variety of conventional state instruments, the Jihadists are difficult to monitor, since they exist in the shadows and on the periphery. The application of America's containment strategy, he argues, has been wrong-headed. Instead of limiting themselves to Afghanistan and concentrating on achieving victory there, they extended their forces around the world, and especially in Iraq.

Another top-level Jihadist strategist, Abu Bakr Naji, elaborates on the impossibility of trying to govern everywhere. There is no doubt that American power vastly overwhelms that of its opponents, including the Jihadist movement. Nonetheless, the United States is not powerful enough to impose its authority from the core to the periphery unless those peripheral countries submit entirely of their own accord. Therefore, the United States relies on proxy powers, particularly the Arab regimes, to do its bidding. And further, Naji argues, it employs what he calls "a deceptive media halo" in order to portray its massive military and economic might as benign, even benevolent, but omnipotent. This halo, much like the *faux* Russian village of Potemkin, is little more than a façade designed to deter closer examination of what is happening. According to Naji, the United States started believing the lies that it had told about its power. And that national hallucination, another strategist, Muhammad Khalil al-Hakaymah, explains in his book *The Myth of Delusion*, is the reason why the attacks of 9/11 were not thwarted.[8] Using America's own government reports, news and research, Hakaymah's book tries to expose the extent of the failure of the American intelligence services. According to Naji:

> When a state submits—whatever the extent of its ability—to the illusion of the deceptive power and behaves on this basis, that is when its downfall begins. It is just as the American author Paul Kennedy says: "If America expands the use of its military power and strategically extends more than necessary, this will lead to its downfall."[9]

He also targets American social cohesion. For Naji, all of the military power in the world is worthless without the cohesion of society and its institutions. What Naji wants to prompt is cultural annihilation, which includes the "corruption of religion, moral collapse, social iniquities, opulence, selfishness, giving priority to [worldly] pleasures and the love of the world over all values."[10] Direct military confrontation by Jihadists against the United States, particularly in Middle Eastern countries like Iraq and Afghanistan, helps the Jihadists to expose the deceptive media halo, to point to America's weaknesses and, importantly, to remove the "aura of invincibility" that America projects.

Understand that perception is reality

America's war against the Jihadist movement is one of perceptions. The United States uses its deceptive media halo so effectively, Qurashi contends, because "America made headway in history only by using media and psychological warfare and various kinds of fraud and deception." He painstakingly examines how American President Theodore Roosevelt played a prominent part in inciting newspaper owners to inflate the sinking of the battleship *Maine* in the Cuban port of Havana in order to have an excuse for starting the Spanish–American War, with the goal being to supplant Spain's colonial authority in the Caribbean Sea and the Philippines. He also details how political elites dragged the American people into the First World War by recounting fictions that Belgian infants were being killed by the brutal Germans. The Second World War, he suggests, had hardly broken out before America had an effective apparatus for political propaganda and for informational and psychological warfare. The expansion of the war in Vietnam came about because of the infamous Gulf of Tonkin episode, which was fabricated by the American machinery of deceit. It was claimed that North Vietnamese torpedo boats had attacked an American warship. President Lyndon Johnson hastened to exploit the story to extract a resolution from Congress granting him sweeping authority to involve America in Vietnam.

Because Jihadists know of all these incidents, the strategy of dropping millions of leaflets on places where al-Qaida is present, urging its fighters to surrender, has been singularly unsuccessful. As Qurashi says:

> The stupid leaflet that pictured Shaikh Usama Bin Laden—God grant him victory!—without a beard and in a European suit, to suggest that he had fled the battlefield and left his followers, was too inane for consideration. The leaflet that pictured two piercing eyes above an alleged picture of Mullah Umar—God grant him victory!—meaning that "we are watching Mullah Umar and have been able to photograph him close up"—may have caused more laughter than fear, especially after it become clear that the picture was not Mullah Umar, but only a minor protocol official of the Islamic emirate.

He also scorns "the acrobatic movements of giant bombers that would draw a figure eight in the sky to terrify the Jihadist fighters and command them to surrender at eight o'clock in the morning."

If the Jihadist movement is to wage an effective counter-propaganda effort against the United States, Qurashi contends, it must be based on scientific principles, including:

- identifying American information strategy and propaganda products;
- pointing out contradictions in these products;
- strongly attacking the weak points in US propaganda;
- ignoring US propaganda when it is accurate or convincing;
- responding to US propaganda through action not simply words;
- pointing Muslim attention to the US policy-makers and individual leaders who are guiding information operations against the Jihadists;
- taking the initiative in terms of information operations from the United States.

The American propaganda apparatus, he explains, seeks to sow disunity among global Jihadists by spreading false rumors on internet sites (a policy that the United States government does not follow and cannot implement by law) and creating websites that falsely claim to be in touch with al-Qaida. America, he argues, is also trying to control sources of information, with regard to both the educational curricula of schools throughout the Middle East and audio, video and cable broadcasting. He claims the American phrase "information dominance" is proof of this policy, and says that Muslims need to oppose it forcefully and comprehensively.

In his September 10, 2007 video release, Shaikh Abu Yahya al-Libi offered the United States several unsolicited tips for the prosecution of its "war of ideas" against al-Qaida.[11] Although his comments brought al-Qaida propaganda to new heights of arrogance, it must be said that his recommendations are nothing short of brilliant. Policy-makers who are serious about degrading the resonance of the Jihadist message, therefore, would be remiss to ignore his strategic recommendations simply because of their source.

Abu Yahya, a senior member of al-Qaida, is one of the world's foremost experts on the strengths and vulnerabilities of the contemporary Jihadist movement. He became a household name within the counter-terrorism community when al-Qaida made him a prominent figure in its propaganda following his July 2005 escape from detention at Bagram air base in Afghanistan. Over the next two years he became the High Command's attack dog, chastising a variety of Muslim groups for failing to follow the proper path: the Shia, Hamas and the Saudi royal family bore the brunt of his rage.[12] Al-Qaida also promoted Abu Yahya's softer side, though, showing him reciting poetry and informally dining with his students. He has therefore become the Jihadist for all seasons.

Obviously, Abu Yahya's decision to volunteer strategic advice to the United States was neither a gesture of goodwill nor an indication of self-destructive tendencies. Rather, his comments embodied the explosive cocktail of youth, rage, arrogance and intellect that has made him a force among supporters of the Jihadist movement. By casually offering his enemy a more sophisticated counter-ideological strategy than the US itself has been able to implement or articulate to date, Abu Yahya's point was clear: the US lags so far behind the global

Jihadist movement in the war of ideas that al-Qaida has little to fear in the foreseeable future.

His strategic plan for improving America's counter-ideology efforts centers on turning the Jihadist movement's weaknesses against itself. He first suggests that governments interested in weakening the ideological appeal of al-Qaida ought to focus on amplifying those ex-Jihadists (or "backtrackers," as he calls them) who have willingly renounced the use of armed action and recanted their previously held ideological commitments. Using retractions by senior thinkers and religious figures who have established followings within the Jihadist movement helps to sow seeds of doubt across the movement as a whole and deters those on the ideological fence from joining. Although Arab governments, most notably the Saudis and the Egyptians, have successfully utilized this approach for decades, there may be particular value in broadcasting such retractions in the West. In November 2007, for instance, as we saw in the previous chapter, the legendary Egyptian Jihadist thinker Sayyid Imam released a book renouncing his earlier commitment to violent Jihadism.[13] As could be expected, given his eminence in the movement, the story made front-page news across the Arab world. In the English-language media, however, it registered little more than a minor blip. The media's lack of interest in such a major ideological victory against global Jihadism is due to the fact that few in the West appreciate Sayyid Imam's significance to groups like al-Qaida. Raising Western awareness of Sayyid Imam's renunciation might persuade scores of English-speaking Jihobbyists—who are currently downloading thousands of pages of his earlier writings—to debate the issue. Can and should they still read his works even though he has renounced al-Qaida? Why did he renounce the Jihadist movement? These are the questions that they need to be prompted to ask themselves and one another. Abu Yahya suggests that the public media can play an effective role in publicizing ideological retractions, particularly by conducting interviews with these reformed scholars, publishing their articles and printing their books. Enthusiastic promotion of the retractions will also help to redirect public attention away from the role of the host government in soliciting the retractions in the first place. And the more distance the reformed scholars have from their host governments, the more they are likely to be perceived as legitimate.

Second, Abu Yahya recommends that the United States should both fabricate stories about Jihadist mistakes and exaggerate real Jihadist mistakes whenever they are made. These may include blaming Jihadist terrorism for killing innocents, particularly women, children and the elderly. But he does not stop there. Jihadist mistakes should not simply be highlighted as anomalous or extraordinary: rather, governments ought to characterize them as being at the core of the Jihadist methodology. In short, governments need to convince their populations that the murder of innocent people is a central part of global Jihadism. The most effective way to pursue this strategy, he contends, is to exploit mistakes made by any Jihadist group, whether al-Qaida or not, by casting that action as being emblematic of the entire movement. Abu Yahya calls this strategy of blurring the differences between al-Qaida and other Jihadist groups when it serves propaganda purposes "widening the circle." Pursuing it offers the United States significantly more exploitable opportunities for discrediting the actions of the Jihadist movement writ large.

Abu Yahya provides two clarifying examples of existing counter-propaganda initiatives that he found to be effective in damaging the Jihadist movement's credibility. The first was the rumor about an al-Qaida constitution that makes death the penalty for quitting the organization. Although Abu Yahya claims that no such policy ever existed, he says that the story effectively portrayed al-Qaida to the Islamic world as a small group of fanatical thugs who are bound by no moral code. He also points to how the Saudi and Algerian governments successfully characterized Jihadist terrorist attacks against government targets in their countries as really being attacks against the *people* of those countries. By downplaying the official nature of the buildings and focusing instead on the human victims, casting them as powerless and ordinary, both the Saudis and the Algerians were able to "move emotions" and "whip up storms" among the public against the Jihadist movement.

Abu Yahya's third strategic point deals with the Egyptian government's prompting of mainstream Muslim clerics to issue *fatwa* that denounce the Jihadist movement and their actions. He shudders at other Muslims' use of "repulsive legal terms, such as bandits, *Khawarij* [the sect that left] and even *Karamathians* [*al-Qaramitah*], extreme fanatics" when referring to the Jihadists. He also points to the effectiveness of special committees of scholars who try to deprogram Jihadists in prison. These rehabilitation programs, which are now operating in Egypt, Yemen, Saudi Arabia and Singapore, have become a central part of these countries' efforts to defeat the Jihadist movement, at least in the war of ideas.[14]

For his fourth recommended strategy, Abu Yahya suggests strengthening and backing Islamic movements far removed from Jihad, particularly those which favour a democratic approach. He also counsels governments to push these mainstream groups into ideological conflict with Jihadist groups in order to keep the Jihadist scholars and propagandists busy responding to their criticisms. This approach is designed to strip the Jihadist movement of its monopoly on setting the debate and instead unleash a "torrential flood of ideas and methodologies which find backing, empowerment, and publicity from numerous parties" who are against it. There is no doubt that the Jihadist thinkers are most threatened by groups like the Muslim Brotherhood and Hamas as well as mainstream Salafists. This is because these groups draw on many of the same religious texts and appeal to the same constituencies for recruitment and financial support.[15] Groups like the Muslim Brotherhood, however, are significantly more palatable to their host governments than Jihadists. This bitter rivalry between Jihadists and more moderate groups could be usefully exploited by governments interested in testing al-Qaida's stamina.

Next, Abu Yahya recommends aggressively neutralizing or discrediting the guiding lights of the Jihadist movement. His point is that not all Jihadists are replaceable: there are some individuals who provide a disproportionate amount of insight, scholarship or charisma. These individuals include key ideologues like Abu Muhammad al-Maqdisi, Abu Qatada and (formerly) Sayyid Imam; and senior commanders like Khattab, Yousef al-Ayiri and Abu Musab al-Zarqawi. In order effectively to degrade the Jihadist movement's long-term capacity, Abu Yahya suggests, these figures need to be silenced, leaving the movement "without an authority in which they can put their full confidence and which directs and guides them, allays their misconceptions, and regulates their march with knowledge, understanding, and wisdom." The consequence of this power vacuum, he argues, will be that "those who have not fully matured on this path or who are hostile to them in the first place [will] spread whatever ideas and opinions they want and cause disarray and darkness in the right vision which every mujahid must have."

Finally, Abu Yahya advises the United States to spin the minor disagreements among leaders or Jihadist organizations as being major doctrinal and methodological disputes. He suggests that those fissures can be deepened by using them as the basis for designating new subsets or schools of thought. These fractures can also serve as useful inroads on which targeted information operations can be focused: such an environment becomes a "safe-haven for rumor-mongers, deserters, and demoralizers, and the door is left wide open for defamation, casting doubts, and making accusations and slanders," he explains. This "war of defamation," as he terms it, leaves the Jihadist propagandists almost impotent in that no matter how they try to defend themselves, dispel misconceptions and reply to accusations, their voices will be as "hoarse as someone shouting in the middle of thousands of people."

Adapt to the situation on the ground

The Jihadist movement has employed a variety of proven techniques from historical revolutionary wars, guerrilla actions and insurgencies. Its record of success in using those techniques has, however, been mixed. Qurashi believes that the failures have resulted from the movement making the mistake of applying pure military theory without adapting it to specific time and place. He also feels that it has consistently failed fully to integrate the other dimensions of warfare, including political, social, psychological, ideological and economic instruments, in its campaigns.

With the goal of making Jihadist military commanders more sensitive to local contexts, Qurashi examines the work of US military strategists who wrote "The Changing Face of War into the Fourth Generation," an article published by the *Marine Gazette* in October 1989. In their article, William S. Lind, Keith Nightingale, John F. Schmitt, Joseph W. Sutton, and Gary I. Wilson predicted a radical change in the nature of wars and how they are managed, which they called "fourth-generation warfare." Agreeing with their conclusions, Qurashi expresses the belief that the Jihadist movement's natural operating style is ideally suited to this new generation of warfare.[16] To his mind, most of the wars fought by Jihadists in the past two decades have been "guerrilla wars of attrition." This reality is a manifestation of the circumstances in which the movement tends to find itself: undermanned, under-resourced and outgunned. Although the enemies of the movement have "carefully examined guerrilla warfare by going back to several in-depth studies on this subject," Jihadist commanders have, for the most part, been able to adapt their tactics and operations successfully to the conditions on the ground, exploiting any gaps left by their enemies. Two important tactical adaptations have occurred in the midst of this fourth-generation warfare, Qurashi notes, which have led to significant strategic advances for Jihadists. First, the mainstreaming of suicide operations in Jihadist attacks represented not simply a new method of attack but a strategic "landmark" for the movement, proving its worth time and again for achieving militarily aims and generating powerful psychological victories on the battlefield and beyond. Second, a more recent addition to the Jihadist movement's strategic arsenal has been the sniper attack. Shooting has long been an important source of power, Qurashi argues. The Prophet Muhammad recognized it. The medieval Islamic scholars noted it. It is time that the Jihadist movement recognized that "the advance in weapon technology has produced extremely accurate firearms and vision-aiding accessories and gadgets that muffle the sound and hide the firing glare."[17] Qurashi relates the story of Assili Aitsev, who became a Soviet hero during the Second World War when he helped to turn the course of the battle of Stalingrad by killing 40 German officers in ten days, causing panic in the occupiers' ranks. Above all else, his unerring aim "revived the will of resistance among the Russians, particularly at the entrance to Stalingrad."[18] Similarly, the Americans, during the same war, suffered great loss of morale because of snipers, particularly during the battle of Kwajalein in 1944, when Japanese sharpshooters stopped the advance of the US 7th Infantry. The same thing happened repeatedly during the Vietnam War, Qurashi tells his readers. In short, throughout recent history, single individuals have managed to terrorize entire divisions.

In the Jihadist movement's own experiences in Afghanistan, sniping became a key component of their strategy at the beginning of the Soviet invasion. Although their weapons were outdated, particularly the Lee-Enfield rifle, the Jihadist fighters had success shooting from great distances. The Soviets, by contrast, soon realized that their Kalashnikovs were not very effective at a distance of more than 300 meters, and therefore they were forced to reconsider their strategic rules of engagement with the Jihadists. In response, they trained special teams of snipers and sent them to the field in Afghanistan, equipped with SVD 7.62 sniper rifles. In this conflict Chechen Jihadist snipers became legendary for their ability to target enemy commanders with astonishing accuracy. Their skill led to some operational successes but had far greater impact in terms of terrorizing Soviet forces. Qurashi emphasizes that by hitting extremely distant targets, a sniper inflicts more casualties on the enemy, restricts its movements, instills fear in the hearts of its soldiers and weakens their resolve, particularly if they fail to eliminate the shooter quickly. It is a tactic that can be employed across all theaters of operation and during day or night. And most importantly, like suicide bombing, it has critical strategic implications because it forces the adversary's hand.

Seize and govern territory

Territory equals power for Jihadist strategists. Consider Ayiri's writings on Afghanistan. To him, that country empowered Jihadists to pursue their most important goals. Chief among them, he argued, was the establishment of a religiously legitimate government in an Islamic land. A true Muslim state would facilitate the restoration of the Jihadist spirit and stand as a model to refocus the people's commitment to Jihadism. Historically, Jihadists could point to Afghanistan, Ayiri wrote, as the blueprint for how to remove all aspects and symbols of polytheism and superstition from a society and create a culture of war against all enemies, including the Crusaders and their agents. It became a staging ground for defending the causes of Muslims worldwide. Jihadists who were based there supported oppressed Muslims all over the world. They provided aid to fighters in Chechnya, Kashmir, Burma, and elsewhere, and offered shelter to immigrants and fighters who had been forced by their governments to leave their homelands. In a very real sense, Afghanistan became the crucible for the creation and establishment of a truly global Jihadist movement. Muslims from all over the world could unite there under a single banner and attend training camps dedicated to advancing the global Jihadist ideology.[19]

Abu Bakr Naji also believed that the need for the Jihadist movement to seize, retain and govern territory more broadly could not be overstated in its importance. Territory gives Jihadists a location for consolidating their strength: it provides a way to give their forces the rest and relaxation that they need to be effective in combat. It allows the movement to begin implementing *Sharia* law on Earth, which is a religious mandate that most of the world's Muslims disregard. Finally, it provides the Jihadists with a way to start winning the hearts and minds of Muslim constituencies. Naji's theory of how to seize ground is remarkably similar to that devised by previous insurgent strategists, particularly Mao Zedong. For Naji, Jihadist military forces are best used to conduct what he describes as "vexation and exhaustion" operations against critical infrastructure and key economic targets within a region where the United States is militarily involved. These operations include repeated and unpredictable strikes against changing targets, such as oil pipelines, key installations, tourists, bridges and more. The goal for Naji is to force American elite forces to grow vexed and exhausted as they try to combat and preempt an elusive force. He argues that this should cause the American forces, as well as those of the host nation, to pull out of peripheral areas in order to concentrate their protection on these key targets. Oil pipelines, for instance, are easy targets for terrorist operations. It is almost impossible for security forces to protect every foot of pipeline since they cover thousands of miles; and it is equally impossible to tighten the security measures at every pipeline. Governments that control the oil fields therefore have to choose between amassing their forces in order to protect certain stretches of key pipelines and protecting other vital targets, including population centers. The withdrawal of the elite American forces and best local forces creates what could be called "security vacuums" in the periphery, zones that will invariably be filled with chaos and competition by a variety of factions (including local warlords, tribal leaders, crime syndicates, traffickers and so on) trying to seize control in the area.

If the Jihadist forces are well prepared, Naji anticipates that they ought to be able to take control of these areas and manage the "savagery" that will have ensued after American and local security withdrawal. Winning the hearts and minds of local Muslim populations is key in this. It should not be a difficult task, Naji explains, because the chaos and conflict resulting from power competition will inevitably leave residents of a region feeling scared and desperate for order, an order that the Jihadists should be ready and able to provide.

For Naji, effective territorial governance by the Jihadist movement includes a number of elements:

- establishing and maintaining enduring domestic security institutions (e.g., police);
- providing food and medical treatment for the people;
- setting up defensive fortifications and developing fighting capacities;
- implementing *Sharia* law among the people;
- inculcating the Muslim youth in these areas in order to form a "fighting society at all levels and among all individuals;"
- working for the spread of scientific knowledge and expertise;
- building global Jihadist spy networks and a domestic intelligence agency;
- winning the loyalty of Muslims by buying them off;
- forcing doubters of the Jihadist approach to bite their tongues until they are true believers or until they are "put in check;"
- preparing for attacks against all enemies of Islam, which includes plundering their money and terrorizing them until they express a desire for reconciliation;
- establishing coalitions with other like-minded oppositionist forces.

In January 2007, Jihadist thinker Uthman Bin Abd al-Rahman al-Tamimi published "Informing the People of the Birth of the Islamic State" on the (now-defunct) Jihadist website Tajdeed. In it, he justifies the establishment of the Islamic State of Iraq (ISI). He makes the point that building such a state takes both time and patience. Governance, as Naji conceives of it, does not instantly appear. For Tamimi, global Jihadists in Iraq today are in control of areas of land that are far greater than the area in which the Prophet Muhammad established his first state. Therefore, he sees a specific *Sharia* requirement for establishing the state. Those who criticize the ISI's lack of sovereignty or its ability to provide security for its people must realize, he explains, that Islamic sovereignty was not complete in the first Islamic state, Medina:

> Medina at that time was home to many groups of Jews who had great military capabilities and economic resources in the region. In addition, the enemies of the Islamic call and its followers were present inside and outside Medina. But that sovereignty started to grow and to expand after the legitimization of Jihad gave the young state an increasing momentum of power and influence built on a solid base.

Although the control of territory is essential in the establishment of a state, Tamimi argues that the very notion of "control" must be rediscovered within Islam. It is not simply about administrative tasks or performing functions, as is the case in modern states. Tamimi argues that *Sharia* does not require the adoption of a specific type of organization or administration in a growing Islamic state. Therefore, there is no need to place emphasis on the official facilities of the state.

Win in Iraq

Most Jihadist strategists view the American military presence in Iraq as a blessing from God. It serves as a rallying flag upon which to call Islamic movements from all over the world to unite for the purpose of organizing and fighting the world's sole remaining superpower. For these strategists, the Jihadist movement is waging nothing short of a war of liberation in Iraq against the United States and its local proxies.

Jihadist strategies who have written on the topic of Iraq agree that America invaded in order to capitalize on Iraq's important strategic position within the Muslim world, using it as a staging ground for American military forces in order to help buffer Israel from her Arab neighbors. But Iraq, they argue, is just one piece of America's war, which they view as global, comprehensive, immoral, unending and religious in nature.

Jihadist strategists therefore argue that Muslims have only one solution: to resist. Islam must rebuff America's physical advances into the Arab world by developing a multi-pronged strategy for victory in Iraq. This includes: rejecting Arab media and cultural institutions in Islamic countries which do not adhere to or promote the establishment of *Sharia* law; reviving the spirit of Jihad as a mobilizing force in order to expand the base of Jihadist fighters; and uniting with Muslims from around the world in order to drive the United States from Iraq. Muslims must stop thinking in terms of Iraqi fighters and "foreign fighters," a label that Jihadists tend to argue has been invented by the United States.

Qurashi argues that US policy-makers made several important misjudgements in Iraq:

- Iraqis returned to religious, not national, identification;
- failure of the transplant Iraqi politicians brought in to rule Iraq;
- the 100,000 Iraqi soldiers expected to help security and stability operations around the country instead melted back into the civilian population.

Jihadists must capitalize on these misjudgements, it is argued, by extending the duration of the war, drawing the United States deeper into a protracted conflict whereby Jihadist fighters can encourage Western forces and Western publics to grow weary with the effort, cause the troops and their families to lose morale and cause Western nations to expend massive amounts of money in a losing cause. They must increasingly use highly trained units of Jihadist fighters who can inflict precise and devastating blows against American forces, and Amali believes that they must do so more broadly and more aggressively throughout Iraq.[20]

Jihadist strategists believe that America's military occupation of Iraq has led to several benefits for their cause. It has heightened regional instability and hostility among Arab Muslims toward the United States. It has inadvertently created a new platform for the expansion of Iranian influence. It has led to the withering of America's historic partnerships with European nations. And it has inspired countries like North Korea, who fear that they might be next on the list of America's targets, to develop weapons of mass destruction more aggressively.[21]

Shaikh Atiyatallah says that the signs of victory in Iraq and Afghanistan against "the armies of the libertine nation, the leader of the cross, America" are looming on the horizon, and warns that this phase will be characterized by craftiness, scheming and deception to "divide the believers, create strife, distort facts, and divide [their ranks]."[22] Atiyatallah is referring here specifically to the "lies and fabrications" that were made by Mish'an al-Jaburi, the owner of the al-Zawra satellite station, about the Islamic State of Iraq.

Atiyatallah advises members of the ISI that success can be achieved only when those Muslims participating in the movement publicly prove that they are "the most righteous, the most meritorious, the most deserving, and most entitled in religion and politics." They are to do this, he argues, across all fields of life, including religion, morality, military and physical strength, social strength and community service, among other things. He cautions the youth against hurrying to pass judgment on people in this matter, and says they should not be hasty in applying *Takfir* (excommunication) suggesting that they should surround themselves with religious experts in order to gain more sophisticated, correct religious rulings.

Provinces where the Jihadists already have a firm hold, such as al-Anbar and neighboring Diyala, ought to be used as bases from where to spread their influence. By slowly engulfing surrounding territory from these strongholds, be it towns, villages or even individual streets, the ISI will grow.

Domestically, according to some Jihadist strategists, the Iraqi Sunni population needs to support the establishment of the ISI by taking the following steps:

- organizing and using whatever political instruments they have available to stymie American "colonization" efforts or the establishment of a functioning Shia-led democracy in Iraq;
- propagating the call to violent Jihad, particularly among the youth;
- resisting efforts by the United States to gain people's support and trust;
- setting aside internal rivalries in order to focus on the task at hand, which is removing Western forces from Iraq;
- capitalizing on the mistakes of the United States, whom Jihadists argue lack experience in "colonization" operations;
- targeting America's military weaknesses and steering clear of its strengths;
- encouraging terrorist attacks on the oil sector in Iraq in particular;
- targeting individual American soldiers in the name of the Jihadist movement wherever and whenever one has the opportunity;
- using every military means at their disposal (including missiles, mortars and mines);

- avoiding hasty, uncalculated decisions that could strategically backfire on the movement.

There is no doubt that, for global Jihadist strategists, Iraq has become a land of opportunity for them to close the wide gulf between their organizations and the Muslim base to whom they appeal for support and protection as well as from which they recruit and fundraise.

Target oil

For Jihadist strategists, the global capitalist economy is the pillar on which the Western states are founded and the source from which they are fueled. It is the god that the West worships. It is one of the primary tools that the West uses to dominate, exploit and prop up countries around the world, but perhaps nowhere more importantly than in the Middle East. In short, global Jihadists argue that Muslims have little choice but to push against the West's use of economic exploitation, by which it colonizes the Islamic world and plunders its oil. Jihadists must wage what they call "economic Jihad," which is striking against an enemy's economic viability. It is waged in order to seize key assets from the possession of non-Muslims, particularly those in Islamic lands and can be used to bring down an enemy's domestic economy. Or it can refer to those measures taken in order to defend Muslim wealth and resources from being seized by non-Muslims in the first place. One way of waging economic Jihad is by launching economic embargoes or boycotts against Western countries, companies or products. When Muslims face situations where non-Muslims have seized Muslim resources and are benefiting from them at the expense of Muslims, Jihadist strategists argue that Muslims must fight, even if it means destroying those resources in order to avoid enhancing their enemy's position. Perhaps no Muslim resource seems more important to Jihadists than oil. In some of his writings, Abu Bakr Naji suggests that while Jihadists ought to be constantly looking to strike any kind of target permitted by Islamic law, they are best advised to focus their efforts on hitting economic targets, particularly those in the oil sector. The strategy of targeting oil facilities is highly contentious, though, even within the Jihadist movement. Some argue that it adversely affects the movement's public popularity because it attacks what many Muslims view to be their countries' very life-blood.

For Jihadists, natural resources such as land, water, oil, grass and minerals cannot be owned: they are collectively shared with humans by God. The imprisoned Saudi shaikh Abd-al-Aziz Bin Raishid al-Anzi takes Naji's thinking on the topic one step further in his book *The Religious Rule on Targeting Oil Interests*, published by Yousef al-Ayiri's Center for Islamic Research and Studies in 2006. In the relatively short 63-page text, Anzi painstakingly examines the targeting of oil in the Middle East, looking at Islamic jurisprudence regarding oil in general, the key dimensions of economic Jihad with respect to subverting one's own resources, and prescriptions and proscriptions for waging attacks on oil facilities. While the concept of destroying the village in order to save it strikes many as problematic,

Anzi claims that it is strategically preferable and that numerous precedents for it can be found throughout Islamic history. In 1191, for instance, he discusses the Islamic city of Acre, which was under siege. In desperate need of provisions and arms, the city eagerly awaited supplies coming by ship. Before they arrived, however, enemy forces surrounded the ship and prepared to take all the cargo. Presented with the quandary of losing a ship full of arms, food and other supplies to the enemy, the Islamic crew opted to sink the vessel and drown. And in that same year the legendary Islamic military commander Saladin decided to destroy Asqalan (Ashkelon), one of the great Islamic cities, rather than allow it to be sacked and plundered by invading enemy forces: "The demolition of the city," Anzi quotes the general as saying, "will be tolerable if it is in favor of the Muslims."

By "oil facilities," Anzi clarifies that he means oil wells, oil refineries, oil pipelines, oil trucks and tankers, seaports from where oil is exported, and the individuals who support the exploitation of oil in the Middle East, including both the Western companies based there and the local Muslims who are willing to work with them. All of these categories are fair game for terrorist attack, Anzi argues. By striking these targets, he says that the Jihadists will catalyze a number of global processes: oil prices will increase, which hurts the major industrialized nations most; fear will spread of future attacks; and if the attacks are large enough, oil production and refinement will decrease, leading to a rush to buy whatever oil is available, which will obviously exacerbate global oil shortages. Western companies must therefore increase the resources that they expend on safeguarding their facilities and personnel. This means conducting more and deeper background checks on employees and expanding physical anti-terrorism measures. All of this uncertainty also causes an upsurge in insurance premiums. Higher insurance premiums and security costs for oil corporations translate into an overall net increase in the price of oil. With increased terrorist attacks against oil targets in the Middle East, Anzi notes, other corporations are less incentivized to take the risk of investing in those sectors or even those states. Increased costs of oil and petroleum products also pressures Western governments to dedicate increased funding into researching alternative sources of energy in order to pacify their domestic populations. However, Anzi and others who support terrorist attacks against oil facilities in the Middle East are not blind to the fact that they will likely face a domestic public backlash in those countries.

In his message "Declaration of Jihad against the American Occupiers of the Country of the Two Mosques," even Usama Bin Laden warned against targeting oil wells. Anzi responds by making an important distinction between targeting a country's oil *supplies* as opposed to its oil *facilities*. Oil is an invaluable resource for Muslims, he argues. The facilities discussed above, however, are nothing more than the tools used by the West in order to harvest and plunder that resource from Muslims. Nonetheless, most Muslims will be unable to make that distinction, he believes, and will view the intentional sabotage of this commodity as being inherently un-Islamic. He also concedes that attacks on oil facilities clearly hurt Muslim populations in several ways. Most significant is that in the aftermath of a major attack against Western oil facilities, Western states will almost certainly deploy military forces into the region in order to protect those facilities from further terrorist operations. Alternatively, making the cost of doing business so high in the Middle East, many corporations will significantly downsize their operations if not leave altogether, leading to domestic economic hardship: the thousands of Muslims who are employed by the corporations will lose their jobs, domestic investment will plummet, and environmental and ecological consequences are likely to be severe and costly to address. Future oil revenues may also decline as the West researches into alternative sources for energy. Despite all of these negatives, however, Anzi unswervingly claims that sabotaging Arab facilities in their own lands is preferable to allowing Western corporations access to their oil.

Anzi and Naji are joined by a third strategist who argues in favor of a targeted Jihadist campaign against oil facilities. In his article "Bin Laden and the Oil Weapon," Adib al-Bassam argues that such a campaign is already under way but needs more emphasis.[23] The process began, he explains, with al-Qaida's attack on the French oil tanker *MV Limburg* in October 2002, and continued with a Saudi al-Qaida group's assaults on the al-Khubar facility and the Buqaiq refinery. It has since been implemented in Iraq by Jihadist groups attacking pipelines and wells but only in a limited fashion. The Buqaiq attack should serve as the ideal model for future global Jihadist ventures, Bassam contends, because:

- Al-Qaida chose a suitably large target—the Buqaiq refinery is the world's largest oil-refining complex. Most exported oil passes through it and when operating at full capacity it can handle up to nine million barrels per day. The capacity of the pipelines carrying oil from Buqaiq to the port of Yanbu (another target of al-Qaida violence) was even enlarged in response to growing American oil needs after Iraqi oil exports stopped in 1991.
- The cell compiled highly accurate information before the attack was carried out, it was executed with precision and the operatives were able to extricate themselves successfully.
- The operation represented a daring penetration of a location defended by tight security, which makes for great propaganda.

If Muslims cannot reclaim stolen wealth, Bassam writes, they should destroy it. The party that stands to lose most from attacks on the oil industry is the United States. Indeed, oil has been the lifeline of the wars that the United States has waged against Muslim countries. Fuel, explosives, many tools, clothing, and even some foodstuffs have oil as their chief raw material. Just as weapon sales are prohibited during internal fighting, oil sales to the United States must be declared a prohibited act, Bassam argues. The sale of oil must be prevented by any means, even if that means destroying it. If one has to choose between several kinds of evil, one must choose the least harmful, so no zealous Muslim should denounce attacks on oil installations.

The current compulsive use of energy and the culture of US addiction to oil will require several decades to change. Hence the United States will still need the Middle East in the foreseeable future. Its oil will remain an easy target for all the enemies of the United States and its point of weakness for decades to come. Therefore, Bassam concludes, it is necessary to strike oil installations in all the regions from which the United States imports petroleum. The objective is to block or at least reduce its imports by all possible means by targeting oil wells, pipelines, loading docks and tankers. The attacks should include every method that will reduce the US's ability to obtain oil, force it to adopt decisions that it has been avoiding for some time, confuse and suffocate its economy, and threaten its economic and political future.

Expand global Jihadism

Al-Qaida's number two, Ayman al-Zawahiri, is the consummate terrorist. He has dedicated his life to waging violent Jihad against all those who stand in the way of applying *Sharia* law. But since 2003 this senior al-Qaida leader has been sidelined by the broader Jihadist movement. He was physically on the run, trying to elude capture by a massive military and intelligence campaign that was designed to find him. And with the rise of Abu Musab al-Zarqawi, an immensely popular and operational commander considered off-the-reservation by al-Qaida's High Command, Zawahiri lost much of his ability to influence the movement. He was reduced to watching news reports in order to find out what Zarqawi, the new posterboy of global Jihadism, was up to in Iraq. Zawahiri even drafted a deferential letter to Zarqawi, asking to be kept more closely informed about the situation on the ground.[24] There can be little doubt that Zawahiri, who once stood in the eye of the global Jihadist storm, now felt alienated and marginalized as never before.

In order to reestablish his position at the top of the movement, Zawahiri began to modify his public rhetoric: the *ummah* now became his target audience and the topics he discussed were increasingly social and cultural in nature. For instance, in February 2004, he addressed the issue of France's government banning the *hijab*, or headscarf, in its schools. Zawahiri called this an "additional indication of the extent of the Crusaders' rancor harbored by Westerners toward Muslims."[25] Freedom, for Western countries, is sacred so long as it is the "freedom to steal the wealth of others and plunder their resources. But when freedom becomes a means of resisting the West or choosing Islam as a way of life, Jihad and resistance, it becomes terrorism, narrow-mindedness and fanaticism that should be dealt with by tank shells and aircraft missiles."[26] Zawahiri tried to convince Muslims that cultural acts like the headscarf ban are no different to other forms of more obvious hostility against Islam:

> Banning the *hijab* in France is consistent with the burning of villages along with their people in Afghanistan, demolishing houses over their sleeping residents in Palestine, and killing the children of Iraq and stealing its oil under false pretexts . . . It is consistent with tormenting prisoners in the cages of Guantanamo and torturing Muslims in the prisons of our leaders, the friends of the United States.[27]

The need for social reform could not be clearer, Zawahiri argued.

His next step was to demonstrate that the reform offered by the United States and the West was insufficient. "America has nothing to do with reform," he proclaimed. "The alleged American reforms can never achieve for us our independence or pride." True reform "begins by planting the will of resistance in [Muslim] hearts and the hearts of [their] children and coming generations."[28] In early 2005, Zawahiri clearly explained the cultural warfare in which he saw himself engaged:

> The freedom we seek is not the low and despicable freedom of America. It is not the freedom of the banks of usury, giant companies and misleading media. It is not the freedom of destroying others for material interests. It is not the freedom of AIDS, prostitution and same-sex marriage. It is not the freedom of gambling, alcohol and family disintegration. It is not the freedom of using women as a commodity to lure customers, sign deals, draw travelers and promote goods. It is not the freedom of double standards or dividing people into robbers and robbed. It is not the freedom of Hiroshima and Nagasaki. It is not the freedom in the trade of torture equipment and support to US friends in the regimes of oppression. It is not the freedom of Israel to annihilate Muslims, destroy the al-Aqsa Mosque, and Judaize Palestine. It is not the freedom of Guantanamo or Abu-Ghurayb. It is not the freedom of carpet bombing, seven-ton bombs, cluster bombs, leaflet dropping, depleted uranium, and the destruction of villages in Afghanistan and Iraq. It is not the freedom of the Halliburton Government [a reference to one of the largest private US contractors operating in Iraq] and its sister bloodsuckers. It is not the freedom of manipulating weapons of mass destruction and their development, while banning others from doing so. It is not the freedom of five big powers—including four Crusaders—to manipulate decision-making in the international community.[29]

Above all else, Zawahiri wants freedom for Muslims. By 2005, his message was that only through the creation and nurturing of a global Islamic resistance movement could Jihadism thrive around the world. Coincidentally, this was also the year when Abu Musab al-Suri's *A Call to Global Islamic Resistance* became a must-read for Jihadists, particularly in the aftermath of his November 2005 capture.[30] This global resistance movement, in Zawahiri's eyes, is built on three pillars:

- Belief in the absolute rule of *Sharia*.
- Belief in the need to liberate Muslim lands from anyone not applying *Sharia*. Movement adherents must agree that it is impossible to hold any free elections, establish any independent government or safeguard their dignity while American forces are based and the state of Israel exists in the Middle East.
- Belief in the need to liberate humanity by disavowing vices within society, particularly those introduced by Western capitalism, consumerism and market forces, and embracing virtue, understood to be codified in *Sharia*.

For Zawahiri, the social movement of al-Qaida looks quite different from the rest of the organization. As a grassroots, organic, and socially rooted movement, al-Qaida must possess a number of qualities, especially patience, for success will take time and there will be many challenges along the way. This is a multi-generational campaign that Zawahiri believes will not be won or lost in his lifetime. It must, however, be fought.

It was on his threefold foundation that Zawahiri proceeded over the course of the next two years, slowly piecing together the social movement of global Jihadism. His strategy is divided into two parts. The first half consists of grassroots action in order to change corrupt and corruptive regimes. There is no single prescription for change, he argues, because every country has its own circumstances and conditions. But work for change does have some general characteristics, which he identifies. He also believes that Jihadists must recognize the need for winning popular sympathy for the movement's arguments and grievances. Widespread mobilization and action are crucial, and these can be manifested in several ways: terrorism; a violent coup; a mass popular uprising or mass public disobedience; guerrilla warfare; armed political resistance; and so on. Muslims need to challenge what they believe to be falsehood and declare the truth in its face, even if that leads to sacrifice of wealth and self. For this process to succeed, he feels that an organizational vanguard, such as al-Qaida, must continue to be active, dedicated to fueling social change, guiding progress, and taking advantage of any opportunities that present themselves.

The second half of Zawahiri's long-term plan is to transform al-Qaida from a vanguard elite to truly a popular movement that could rapidly deploy Muslim men to such fields of conflict as Afghanistan, Iraq, and Somalia, having previously prepared and trained them, much like the Afghanistan model of the 1980s. All enemies of the movement, he explains, particularly Jews and Crusaders, must be repelled wherever they threaten Muslim interests. Success in its defensive campaigns would invariably provide the Jihadist movement with the breathing space that it so desperately needs to conduct further military preparation.

Beyond the military component, however, Zawahiri prioritizes the need for an integrated media strategy to help Muslims better understand *Sharia* and become versed in reality, not in the distorted world in which most Muslims live as a result of the deceptive propaganda war being perpetrated by the Americans and their agents. For him, the need to entrench the social institutions of a global revolution could not be more important. This includes expanding the skill-sets of movement activists, widening the recruitment base of potential new participants, promoting education and awareness, and emphasizing global connectedness.

Part II
Practice

5   Propagandists

a)   What if the Mujaahideen had never carried a camera with them to the battlefield?
b)   What if the Mujaahideen had never created hundreds of links nearly everyday in order for people to watch the video?
c)   What if the Mujaahideen never had the appropriate program to make their videos look nice?
d)   What if the Mujaahideen had never created a Jihaadee forum to communicate their media to the public?
e)   What if the Mujaahideen had never created a strong system to protect the forums from being hacked by the enemies?

Unknown Jihadist internet propagandist

On September 19, 2007, internet Jihobbyists began buzzing about an upcoming video release that was advertised in several Jihadist discussion forums. As-Sahab Media, al-Qaida High Command's official media outlet, had posted an animated banner describing a new video entitled *The Power of Truth*. This featured a rotating series of still images from the video, including pictures of Usama Bin Laden, Ayman al-Zawahiri, Mustafa Abu al-Yazid, Abu Musab Abd-al-Wadoud, an Arab journalist, and the American counter-terrorism analyst Michael Scheuer. The next day as-Sahab uploaded over one thousand copies of the same file to the internet. It could be freely downloaded just by clicking on any of the links and then watched and burned to a DVD for wider distribution.

The Power of Truth begins with footage of an airplane cockpit and a voice-over of Muhammad Atta, the 9/11 cell leader, ordering passengers on board American Airlines Flight 11 not to move. It then cuts to a clip extracted from a Western documentary featuring American counter-terrorism observer Peter Bergen discussing al-Qaida's planning process for the 9/11 attacks. The video moves quickly to recorded poetry of Shaikh Mahfuz Ould al-Walid praising the attacks, with scenes of the Twin Towers aflame in the background, before cutting to the video's host, Ayman al-Zawahiri.

Sitting before a bookcase bulging with leather-bound Islamic texts, Zawahiri begins by commemorating the death of Maulana Abdul Rashid Ghazi, a cleric at the Lal Mosque in Islamabad, Pakistan, who was killed during a recent government raid. Although Ghazi had never been considered a member of al-Qaida, Zawahiri curiously inserts his name in a list of some global Jihadist legends, including Mullah Mansour Dadullah, Abdullah Azzam and Hammoud bin Uqla as-Shuaybi. The video then cuts to cannibalized Western documentary footage of former FBI profiler Clint Van Zandt discussing the structure and tactics of al-Qaida before shifting to al-Qaida leader Mustafa Abu al-Yazid meeting with Mullah Dadullah in Afghanistan. The video then briefly cuts to footage of terrorist attacks in Iraq played against the background of the May 2, 2003 speech by President Bush on the USS *Abraham Lincoln* in which he says, "Major combat operations in Iraq have ended in the battle of Iraq. The United States and our allies have prevailed." It then shows more Western documentary clips of former Defense Policy Board adviser Richard Perle boldly speaking about America's military success in Iraq before cutting to footage of retired general Jack Keane and retired major general John Batiste discussing the errors in judgement that were made in deciding to go to war.

This cat-and-mouse style is both compelling to watch and brilliantly executed. *The Power of Truth* creates an ironic symphony of accusation, evidence and damnation by using testimony from Western counter-terrorism analysts and footage of American policy officials, all under Zawahiri's baton. Viewers hear from operational commanders like Abu Omar al-Baghdadi, the purported leader of the Islamic State of Iraq, while Iraqi Shia government officials are shown working side-by-side with Americans. Viewers get to see senior American officials making the case for war and then immediately watch two American soldiers complaining about being hoodwinked into joining the army and posted for the third time to Iraq.

As-Sahab has learned that great TV can be made by using existing footage of American authors and journalists such as Robert Baer, Jim Hoagland, Arnaud de Borchgrave, and Robert Steele taking the Bush administration to task and splicing this with recordings of Bin Laden talking about the "big profits" made by US companies in Iraq and Zawahiri rhetorically asking, "Why should the American soldier make sacrifices when he knows that the concern of his . . . political leadership is making profits and amassing treasure?" Viewers of *The Power of Truth* can listen to audio recordings of Malcom X discussing Western intervention in the Third World and to reports of the various guerrilla resistance campaigns being waged against the "white man." As-Sahab also uses footage of former CIA official Michael Scheuer to reinforce the point that US foreign policy is a continuing problem. *The Power of Truth* counterpoints President Bush, Vice-President Dick Cheney and Secretary of Defense Donald Rumsfeld discussing Saddam Hussein's supposed weapons of mass destruction program with testimony from weapons inspectors Hans Blix and David Kay explaining how wrong the Bush administration was in its assessments.

Although this video is among the most sophisticated and hard hitting produced by as-Sahab to date, it is representative of a growing trend in global Jihadist propaganda: using the West's own words to condemn it.

The global Jihadist propaganda machine has become virtually unstoppable. Various cells and media outlets produce upwards of ten new films each day, so the number of videos floating around the global Jihadist web forums is staggering. Those products that feature specific individuals, are stamped with organizational logos or are posted on to high-profile websites have more Jihadist authenticity than others. These films tend to receive wider distribution and often stimulate more discussion among Jihobbyists than other propaganda products. Zawahiri and as-Sahab are perhaps most effective in what is known as "agenda-setting" behavior: they inform Jihadist discourse, shape the debate and introduce new issues into the Jihadist ether. Once these issues take hold in the Jihobbyist web world, there is no telling where they will head. Sometimes web discussions are little more than flashes in the proverbial pan. Other times, they can lead to serious actions in the "real world." However, few observers of the Jihadist movement have reflected on the kind of dynamic interplay that has pervaded the Jihadist propaganda business for decades. This business has assumed a life of its own, and unfortunately it is not well understood outside of the movement itself. In order fully to appreciate where the movement stands today, we must delve into the roots of Jihadist media initiatives.

Historic Jihadist propaganda

In the late 1920s, a 20-year-old Egyptian, Hasan al-Banna, was incensed with the religious malaise he saw taking hold among his generation. Politically active since a young age, particularly against the effects of British colonialism on Egyptian society, Banna began tracing the cause of the Egyptian youth's drift from the path of Islam to the growing secular, Western and Christian influences in his country. The only solution to the resulting social, political and economic problems facing Egyptian society was to be found in a full-scale return to a purer Islam, Salafism. Banna sought counsel from the writings and teachings of leading Salafist intellectuals, including the Egyptian shaikh Muhibb al-Din al-Khatib, the Syrian intellectual Muhammad Rashid Rida, then editor of the renowned Salafist magazine *al-Manar* and protégé of the esteemed Salafist thinker Muhammad Abduh, the well-known Salafist shaikh Ahmad Taymur Pasha, and Muhammad Farid Wajdi. Frustrated by what he viewed as the religious impotence of Egypt's senior religious establishment, or *ulama*, most of whom taught at the renowned al-Azhar University, Banna began pressing the clerics directly to combat the rising tide of counter-Islamic thought. Based in Cairo, al-Azhar University was the timeless hub of Islamic religious authority for the Muslim world. Its shaikhs were recognized as the leading Islamic lights of their era. For Banna and the growing body of Islamic reformers in Egypt, however, they were a disappointment, because they had succumbed to the pressure placed on them by Arab governments to steer clear of politically divisive issues. Banna and his like-minded reformist colleagues chided al-Azhar's senior clerics for standing by idly while Muslim youth both in Egypt and around the Islamic world continued to deviate from the path of what he saw as true Islam, a path illuminated by the puritanical lenses of his own Egyptian Salafist perspective. If the *ulama* was unwilling to push the reformist agenda, aggressive action, they argued, would need to come from the bottom up.

In an effort to impede the waves of secular thought seeping into Egyptian society, two of Banna's early mentors, Shaikh al-Khidr and Ahmad Taymur Pasha, joined with him to establish a Muslim youth organization known as Jam'iyat al-Shubban al-Muslimeen (Association of Muslim Youth). Rooted in a Salafist interpretation of Islam, this group of Islamic reformers addressed issues such as Egypt's broken education system, its public health crisis, its rampant socio-economic disparity, and the growing insignificance of the Islamic world *vis-à-vis* the West. Banna also helped to found *Majallat al-Fath* (*Conquest Magazine*), a journal that he hoped would become the organ in which to discuss these issues from a Salafist perspective.[1] Because Banna's message of Islamic reform appealed to a broad cross-section of Egyptian society (although it resonated most with the educated professional class), he found a great deal of backing for *al-Fath*. Through the assistance he received from the director of the Salaffiya Bookstore and owner of a printing press Shaikh Muhibb al-Din al-Khatib, the magazine rapidly grew in popularity among the Salafist literary community.

In 1930, feeling the pressure of the Islamic reformist trend, al-Azhar began issuing its own magazine, which was known at first as *Nur al-Islam* (*The Light of Islam*). Banna's colleague and mentor, Shaikh al-Khidr, had been appointed chairman of this monthly periodical.[2] He had previously published the Salafist magazine *al-Saada al-Uzma* (*Greater Happiness*), targeted at the North African Islamic community. From its launch in 1903 it featured contributions from Tunisia's top Salafist minds. But in 1911, with the declaration of war by Italy on Libya, Khidr's publication became rabidly anti-colonial, focusing predominantly on inciting Tunisian Muslims to join the Libyans in resisting Italian occupation. Once the French seized control of Tunisia, however, Khidr could no longer freely publish his magazine and he eventually made his way to Egypt. By 1932, another of Banna's mentors, Muhammad Farid Wajdi, had succeeded Khidr as chief editor of *Nur al-Islam*, which was soon rebranded as *Majallat al-Azhar* (*al-Azhar Magazine*).[3]

Egyptian Islamists published a variety of periodicals over the next two decades. Banna and his colleagues appreciated the massive impact that journals like *Majallat al-Fath* or *Majallat al-Azhar* could have in recruitment and mobilization, and as the Society of Muslim Brothers evolved into a more formal organization Banna continued to stress the importance of ideological writings. The Ikhwan's publication section, Qism Nashr al-Dawa (Propagation of the Message), urged members to read useful books in order to increase their erudition, and Banna even proposed sending Ikhwan students to the American University in Cairo in order to take courses in modern journalism.[4] The Ikhwan leadership used this and other media outlets as effective tools to provide ideological education for both their followers and new recruits. Banna's own articles laid out the core tenets of the puritanical Islamist ideology that he and his followers were espousing. The periodicals also reproduced many letters and communiqués sent by the Ikhwan core leadership to the Egyptian government in protest over the prevailing social norms, political institutions and economic system that consistently failed to meet the demands of *Sharia*. *Al-Fath* endured until 1940, the same year that another stalwart publication in the Egyptian Salafist community, *al-Manar*, breathed its last gasp, when also under Banna's editorial direction.

Just over a decade later, another Muslim Brother, Sayyid Qutb, initiated a new era in Ikhwani propaganda efforts. After resigning his post with the Egyptian civil service, he became *Majallat al-Ikhwan al-Muslimin*'s editor-in-chief during the 1950s. At the same time in Egypt, another regularly published periodical called *al-Dawa* (*The Call*) had appeared. Owned and run by another member of the Brotherhood, Saleh Ashmawi (a man who had played a key role in recruiting Sayyid Qutb into the Brotherhood), the periodical firmly supported the Brotherhood's agenda of advancing social reform in Egypt. In 1953, however, Ashmawi fell out with the Brotherhood's "supreme guide," Hasan al-Hudaybi, which led to Ashmawi's expulsion from the organization.[5] Taking his magazine with him, *al-Dawa* was transformed into a free-standing Islamist periodical, which led to intra-Ikhwan dissent that came to the attention of the Egyptian President, Gamal Abd al-Nasser. As a result, when the government began its repression of the Brotherhood in November 1954, *al-Dawa* was allowed to continue publication largely unfettered.

In 1971, with the rise of Anwar al-Sadat, the Brotherhood finally found some breathing room, and with the death of Hudaybi in 1973, Ashmawi hoped that he and his magazine would once again have a role to play in the organization. Although no successor to Hudaybi was named, Umar Talmasani, an Egyptian attorney, became one of the primary public faces of the movement. In 1976, Ashmawi approached Talmasani about turning his journal back over to the Brotherhood. Talmasani agreed, a new format was designed and the magazine's accounts were placed under the direction of the Islamic Publication and Distribution Company, with Talmasani himself as chairman of the board.[6] Talmasani, alongside Mustafa Mashhour, released the new and improved *al-Dawa* in July 1976. It was dedicated to establishing *Sharia* law on Earth by providing "the voice of truth, strength and liberty," to the public. By the January 1977 issue, the magazine's auditor estimated a readership of 78,000. *Al-Dawa* appeared regularly until September 1981, when all non-government press in Egypt was banned. By this time, however, a variety of Jihadist media were already in place.

Afghan Jihadist propaganda

In his book *Chatter on the World's Rooftop*, Abu-al-Walid al-Masri, a member of the Arab Afghan brains-trust and brother-in-law of al-Qaida's military commander Sayf al-Adl, explains the similarities and dissimilarities between the Jihad of the Arab Afghans and that of the Islamists in Palestine.[7] Abu-al-Walid had a strong background working with Islamist and Jihadist groups. He began his writing career with the Muslim Brotherhood but ended sharply splitting with them, particularly because of their willingness to work with Arab regimes. He traveled to Abu Dhabi to work and studied the writings of the Islamic Preaching and Call Movement, better known as Harakat al-Tabligh wal Dawah, as well as the *fatwa* issued by clerics calling for all Muslims to rise up and wage violent Jihad. He then left for southern Lebanon in order to assist the Palestinian organizations in their Jihadist operations, but he grew frustrated with what he described as a "movement of emotion," rather than one that maintained a rigorous political vision or conceived strategy. Afghanistan was to be his next stop. Thanks to his razor-sharp writing skills and affable nature, Abu-al-Walid moved up the ranks, becoming a trusted confidant of the Taliban's senior leadership. He was placed in charge of the *al-Imarah* magazine, which was published in Kandahar as an official mouthpiece of Taliban commander Mullah Muhammad Umar. He spent much of his time writing about the struggle of Arab veterans of the Afghanistan war who returned to Peshawar in order to continue pushing Jihadist thought and action.[8] He also criticized the Arab Afghans throughout his books and propaganda literature, focusing on what he called a lack of a solid foundation, or baseline knowledge, among Jihadist youth, particularly with regard to world history. Such a foundation, he argued in his propaganda, is critical in order to understand better and respond to the challenges facing Islam in the contemporary environment.

Abu-al-Walid is but one of hundreds of figures active in the 1980s and 1990s who helped to develop "Jihadist journalism." Most of this writing emerged from Peshawar and Kandahar, all under the watchful eye of global Jihadism's godfather, Abdullah Azzam.

Azzam, The Lofty Mountain *and* al-Jihad

Abdullah Azzam is considered by many both inside and outside of the Jihadist movement to have made global Jihadism what it is today. He provided the first modern hybridization of deep Jihadist ideological thinking with unswerving commitment to fighting and spreading the call of Jihad around the world. Perhaps the most famous Jihadist periodical of the twentieth century was produced almost single-handedly at first by Azzam: *al-Jihad* magazine. Launched officially in 1984, it signaled a shift from the local focus of most groups then operating in such places as Egypt.

David Cook, a scholar of Islamic movements who has analyzed *al-Jihad* in depth, describes its first editions as "amateurish" and "basically mimeographed." However, although they were simplistic in their design, Cook notes, they were remarkably progressive in terms of their coverage of global news and presentation of a globalized Jihadist ideology. So what the magazine lacked in design flair was made up for in substance by its staff of earnest reporters. These correspondents were unique because they had first-hand experience of the war in Afghanistan. For instance, in December 1985, Abdul Samad, a 27-year-old journalist on the magazine, was killed when he decided to pick up a weapon and fight in Jalalabad while covering a story. The tenth issue of *al-Jihad* (January 1, 1986) commemorated his death.

In 1986, the quality of *al-Jihad* made a "huge leap" forward, according to Cook, particularly in terms of its aesthetic appeal. Glossy color pages replaced the black-and-white mimeographs. But perhaps more importantly, Cook observes, *al-Jihad* almost entirely stopped covering any stories not directly related to Afghanistan. The following year, Azzam expanded his staff of correspondents and began outsourcing more of the stories.[9] No matter what security challenges or logisticial hurdles he faced, he stayed committed to releasing an issue every month. The magazine's dramatic rise in popularity across the Jihadist community can be attributed to the fact that it reflected Azzam's own approach: it was inclusivist, not elitist. Its goal was to foment discussion among Jihadist groups in order to raise overall awareness about the need to establish a broader international movement.

One of Azzam's closest friends and associates in his propaganda efforts was Shaikh Tameem al-Adnani, whom Azzam eulogized in his last book, *The Lofty Mountain* (titled after Adnani's nickname, given to him because he was so overweight). Adnani was known for his dedication to waging Jihad, Azzam fondly recalled: he collected money for the Jihad, he prepared himself, he incited others, and he fought. He also served as Azzam's right-hand man, traveling extensively on the latter's behalf to lecture and promote global Jihadism. He went to Nigeria to open an exhibition there on the Afghan Jihad and he gave lectures in English, which he spoke fluently. He also traveled to Sweden, Jordan, Saudi Arabia, the United Arab Emirates, Qatar, Venezuela, and the United States. Wherever he went, he charmed the local media, ensuring that his speeches were covered in newspapers and on television.

According to Azzam, at one point Adnani's son, Yasir, wanted to take many issues of *al-Jihad* with him to Qatar. Father and son filled one suitcase with hundreds of copies and another with about 20. At Doha airport, the security officials opened only the second case. Given the small number of magazines, they did not think that Yasir was smuggling Jihadist literature, so they did not bother opening the full case.[10]

Adnani always carried stockpiles of cassettes, issues of *al-Jihad* and other promotional materials that he passed out generously wherever he traveled. Local Jihadists copied these materials and, according to Azzam, they "spread like wildfire." Adnani traveled to America in 1989 with two goals: to attend a series of talks and conferences in a variety of states; and to enroll in a weight-loss program. He visited Muslim communities in Tucson, San Francisco, and Orlando, but unexpectedly fell ill in Florida and died there. His death was a tragic blow for Azzam both personally and professionally. But he did not have long to grieve. On November 24, 1989, he and his two teenage sons were killed while driving on the main University Road in Peshawar by a bomb that had been planted on his vehicle. In 1990, a eulogy said: "we used to smell from you, oh shaikh of the *mujahidin* the smell of the righteous salaf. We could feel in you . . . Hasan al-Basri, the *Fiqh* of Abu Hanif, *Shahid* Ibn al-Mubarak, the bravery of Ibn Taymiyyah; see in your bright face, the vision of Ibn Badis, Hasan al-banna, Sayyid Qutb, Maududi."[11]

With Azzam's death, *al-Jihad* declined in terms of both quality and focus. By 1991, it had effectively devolved into little more than a news and information bulletin, barely resembling the vanguard of Jihadist journalism that it had once been. Other Jihadist publications, however, had emerged to take up the torch, one of them being *al-Bunyan al-Marsous*.

Al-Bunyan al-Marsous

Al-Bunyan al-Marsous (*The Solid Edifice*) was published monthly in Arabic and Urdu in Peshawar. Like many other periodicals established during the Afghan Jihad, it was designed to cover various developments and provide Jihadist news for the fighters. And like *al-Jihad*, it had a cadre of professional and dedicated correspondents. One of them was Wadi al-Hage, who is now serving a life sentence in the United States for his role in the 1998 US Embassy bombings in East Africa. He was also at one time Usama Bin Laden's personal assistant. Hage worked for the periodical in Peshawar from 1989 to 1990, before traveling to the United States, where he distributed it from his home in Arlington, Texas, for another year.[12]

An even more notorious correspondent for the magazine was Abu Musab al-Zarqawi, who went on to become al-Qaida's emir in Iraq. According to his brother-in-law, Saleh al-Hami (who himself worked as a correspondent on *al-Jihad*):

> I got to know him [Zarqawi] while I was wounded [in Afghanistan]. He saw me when I was wounded and covered in blood. I had not known him before that. When I recovered, he introduced himself to me, saying, "I work with the *al-Bunyan al-Marsoùs* magazine, as a correspondent of course" . . . He offered to marry his sister to me. Actually, I admired this noble character and courage.[13]

Al-Bunyan, like other Jihadist magazines at the time, had its share of casualties. On March 16, 1989, for instance, a 33-year-old Syrian photojournalist working for the magazine, Abu Hussam, was photographing a battle near Jalalabad when a bomb dropped on the Jihadist fighters by the Soviet-backed Kabul forces killed him. In August the same year Abu Muaz Zakariyah, a 20-year-old Syrian journalist, was killed when fighting alongside Jihadist fighters. And in May 1990 *al-Bunyan* correspondent Abu Mohammad, a Libyan who had traveled to Afghanistan in 1988 in order both to fight and write about the conflict for Jihadist press outlets, was killed in Jalalabad.

Peshawar in the 1990s

Peshawar bustled with activity in the aftermath of the Afghan Jihad against the Soviets. With the Soviet troop withdrawal in 1989, many groups remained and continued operating in the region. Some were humanitarian and relief organizations, such as the Saudi Red Crescent, the Kuwait Red Crescent, the Saudi Relief Committee, the Islamic Dawa Committee, the Afghan Services Bureau, the Islamic Relief Agency, the Muslim World League, Muslim Aid, the Afghan Reconstruction Office, the Reviving Islamic Heritage Society, and so on. Others were propaganda or journalistic organizations, most of which were directly connected in some way to the *mujahidin* and published their output in Peshawar (although some maintained offices in Lahore as well). Besides Azzam's journals, these publications included: *al-Mauqif* (*The Stance*), a monthly military magazine produced by the Hezb-i-Islami group; *Sawt al-Jihad* (*Voice of Jihad*), a monthly political magazine produced by Jamiat Islami (Islamic Society) under the editorial direction of Abdul Ahhad Atarshi; *al-Nafir Alam*, a monthly produced by the Islamic Unity of the Afghan *mujahidin*; and a variety of others, some of which were produced by Egyptian terrorist leaders who had replaced to Peshawar.

Egyptian tensions in Peshawar

Two competing Egyptian Jihadist publications emerged in the late 1980s and early 1990s: Ayman al-Zawahiri's Egyptian Islamic Jihad published *al-Fath* (*Conquest*) while the Islamic Group launched *al-Murabitun* (*Steadfast Warriors*). The latter had a fractured but functional command and control structure.[14] Its Pakistan-based leadership included Talat Fuad Qasim, Abdel Akhr Hamad, and Muhammad Shawqi al-Islambouli (the brother of Khaled, Anwar al-Sadat's assassin). In Peshawar these senior figures held their own tribunals, determining the guilt of various Egyptian government officials.[15] Other leaders elsewhere, including Rifai Ahmed Taha, would attempt to serve as executioner by coordinating assassinations. All the while, Umar Abd al-Rahman, better known as the Blind Shaikh, provided spiritual and strategic guidance from his base in the United States. Qasim and Usama Rushdi also served as the co-directors of *al-Murabitun*. Eager to damage Zawahiri's reputation in Jihadist circles, the *al-Murabitun* editors began publicly accusing him of embezzling funds that his al-Jihad organization had raised to support the *mujahidin*. Zawahiri's burgeoning relationship with the wealthy Saudi financier Usama Bin Laden provided him with vast resources with which to hire correspondents, print his journal, and disseminate it broadly. Such accusations of financial impropriety were therefore easy to lob at him.

Another Egyptian reportedly involved with the publication of *al-Murabitun* was Muhammad Khalil al-Hakaymah, an Egyptian propagandist who later aligned himself with Zawahiri, eventually even appearing alongside his erstwhile rival in a video message.

The Islamic Group also distributed cassette tapes recorded by Umar Abd al-Rahman in which he called for the overthrow of the Egyptian regime and the return of the Islamic Caliphate. These cassettes, as well as books, magazines, and pamphlets, turned up in their thousands on street corners, in mosques, at bazaars. Most importantly, they made their way into the hands of Egyptian youth. In one security operation, a Sudanese man and an Afghani were stopped crossing into Egypt with over 2,000 cassettes in February 1993. The two confessed to having previously smuggled 100,000 cassettes into the country and spreading them to mosques and poorer neighborhoods. In 1997, the Islamic Group began publishing political writings that were banned in Egypt at the time on the internet at *http://www.almurabeton.org*. This website became instantly popular with Egyptian students, both as an anti-establishment novelty and as a new and easily accessible repository for oppositional writing.

Meanwhile, Zawahiri and his Egyptian Islamic Jihad group began publishing another magazine in the mid-1990s, *Majallat al-Mujahidun* (*The Mujahidin Magazine*). Over the course of more than 60 issues it featured such articles as

"The Road to Jerusalem Passes through Cairo," "Advising the Nation to Avoid the *Fatwa* of Bin Baz," and "Why Proceed with Jihad?" One of its correspondents was Abu Musab al-Suri, a legend in Jihadist propaganda. He is certainly one of the most energetic Jihadist propagandists of the past 50 years, although his activities have now been curtailed since he is allegedly in prison. A Syrian born Mustafa Setmariam Nassar, he is a career revolutionary who has spent much of his life fighting Jihad, training others to wage Jihad, and writing about how to conduct Jihad more effectively.[16] His arguments about the Jihadist movement shed important light on the future evolution of global Jihadism.

Suri's goal has been to make global Jihadism as a body of thought more accessible to more people in more ways. The establishment of the al-Qaida organization and its attacks around the world—particularly those on 9/11—were critical steps, but not sufficient in themselves to catalyze the global Islamic revolution that he envisions. Drawing upon the operational, tactical, and strategic lessons of past Jihadist movements, including his own experience in the Algerian civil war and several attempts to overthrow the Syrian government in the 1980s, Suri gained a sense of where Jihadism as an ideology needs to go in order to be successful.[17] The obvious next step, he says, is to cultivate an intellectual, cultural, and military guerrilla movement around the world. By building organizations, elaborating ideologies, socializing and mobilizing constituencies, and shaping collective identities, Suri himself has tried to be a catalyst for social change. In 1996, he established the Bureau for the Study of Islamic Conflicts in London.[18] This office is perhaps best known for facilitating two press interviews with Usama Bin Laden for the BBC and CNN. At that time, Suri reportedly planned to pursue university studies in journalism and political science in Britain, but due to pressure from the British security agencies he fled to Afghanistan in 1997, where he stayed until December 2001. During that time, with the help of the Taliban's Ministry of Defense, he established the al-Ghuraba terrorist training camp in the infamous Qarghah Military Base in Kabul. With the invasion of US and Coalition forces in 2001, however, he saw the decimation of the training camp network that he and many others had worked so hard to construct. This was not necessarily a negative development for him, though. Without the training camps, the proponents of Jihadism had to find new ways to educate, train, and inspire the next generation of Jihadist fighters.

Although Suri himself had only limited knowledge of the internet and new technology, he was acutely aware of their potential power as instruments for empowering the masses to conduct their own research, communicate with one another, and identify with broad concepts. In his most recent work, *The Call to Global Islamic Resistance*, he frequently discusses the internet and new media technologies, recognizing them as critical vehicles for inciting global resistance.[19] If Muslims can no longer come to the training camps, Suri argues, then the Jihadist movement must send the camps to the people. But this will be effective, he argues, only once the masses understand both the problems they face and why their help is needed to overcome them. And he claims that the only way they will fully understand the political repression and economic exploitation they face is by participating in resistance activities, which could include anything from accessing and distributing Jihadist propaganda to actively fighting against the West.

He says that if the Jihadist movement is to evolve, it must do so as an organic, grassroots social movement. A truly effective grassroots campaign, he argues, relies on technology exploited in small-scale, directed operations by a large number of people. Propaganda, for instance, should be sent to email contact lists. Jihadists should also use computers, CD-ROMs and DVDs to circulate large quantities of Jihadist information—in the form of books, essays, brochures, photographs, and videos—around the world. Those who recognize the need to participate in the global Islamic resistance movement should work within small propaganda cells in order to:

- call on Muslims worldwide to join the resistance in every publication;
- publish works on military tactics and training to inform the popular resistance;
- translate those works into Turkish, Urdu, Indonesian and any other languages spoken in Muslim-majority countries;
- disseminate any scholarly writing that supports the spirit of resistance, including opinions regarding the enemies of Jihad and writings identifying unbelievers.

For Suri, a global problem requires global solutions. The key to long-term success for the Jihadist movement, he feels, can be found in the comprehensive education and indoctrination of a new generation of Jihadist-minded youth who are willing to kill and die for what they believe.

Suri launched his own propaganda cell while at the al-Ghuraba camp. Its primary function was to publish a periodical entitled *Qadaya al-Zahirin ala al-Haqq*, but it also produced radio addresses (for Radio Kabul) and other forms of propaganda for the Taliban as well as more general global Jihadist propaganda, including hundreds of audio cassettes and videotapes, brochures, and essays on political science, military strategy, and the *Sharia* aspects of Jihad. With the destruction of the Qarghah neighborhood by Coalition airstrikes on October 11, 2001, though, Suri was forced to continue his ideological labors elsewhere. Very little is known of his activities since then. He likely remained in hiding in Pakistan and perhaps travelled to Iran. Reports surfaced in November 2005 that he had been captured somewhere in Pakistan but he was never presented to the public and his current condition and location are unknown.

Global Jihadist propaganda

In the years that followed the Afghan Jihad, the Jordanian government began to see the problems that could be posed to its security and stability by returning Afghan Arabs. These men possessed the deadly combination of total disregard for secular laws, an axe to grind against the Jordanian ruling regime and those who supported it, and the capability to transform grievances into violence. For the most part, though, the Jordanian intelligence and security services kept the spread of radical literature to a minimum during the 1990s, with ultra-conservative strands of Islamic propaganda banned.

Al-Asalah

One magazine that was published during this time was *al-Asalah*. It was an Arabic publication launched in Jordan by several of Shaikh Albani's students. The first issues appeared in the early 1990s in order to promote more mainstream version of Salafism. They sought to connect the Muslim masses to the major Salafist scholars and their students.

Al-Asalah became widely distributed and read by followers of Salafism around the world, and its popularity irritated Jihadist critics of the Albani school. One of the most popular sections of the magazine was the "*Fatwa* Section," in which Shaikh Albani answered letters sent in by students and followers. The submitted questions spanned subjects ranging from the mundane to the esoteric. But answering them gave Albani something which few clerics possessed at the time: the ability to make Salafists, regardless of geography or ethnicity, feel as if they were speaking directly with a heralded shaikh.

Majallat at-Tawhid

Other publications tended to be more Jihadist in nature. While imprisoned in Jordan, the Islamic scholar Abu Muhammad al-Maqdisi and his small group of followers began publishing a magazine called *Majallat at-Tawhid* (*The Unity Magazine*). Maqdisi's prison congregants wrote the articles to hone their ideological approach. They secretly produced the magazine and then quietly distributed it throughout the prison.

Sometimes, members of Jordan's parliament or other government officials would visit the jail. With those men in mind, Maqdisi wrote *Unveiling the Falsehood in the Provisions of the Constitution*, a book that scrutinizes the Jordanian constitution and attempts to show its contradiction of *Sharia*. Maqdisi and his followers subsequently offered the book to any government official who visited the jail. He also wrote a number of essays aimed at youngsters. When public visits were allowed, Maqdisi and his followers invariably had long lines of young men from all over the country waiting to speak with them. Many of these visitors had read the magazines or Maqdisi's books, or at least heard about his prison teachings. Maqdisi used such opportunities to pass his prison writings to them with the understanding that they would aggressively publish them outside the jail. His ability to disseminate new writings while imprisoned in this way enraged the Jordanian security forces.[20]

London in the 1990s

London during the 1990s was nothing short of a Jihadist playground. It became a central hub for global Jihadist thought, planning, and propaganda: many individuals facing security pressure in their home countries of Egypt, Saudi Arabia, Jordan, Kuwait, and Pakistan found that the United Kingdom offered them respite. There are at least three reasons why London became so important in the evolution of the global Jihadist movement. First, some of the leading Jihadist intellectuals in the world lived there, including Abu Qatada, Abu Basir al-Tartusi, Abu Musab al-Suri and Abu Hamza al-Masri. Second, a broad second-tier support network existed to help print, disseminate and explain the works of these men to the broader Muslim audience. In this group were Muhammad al-Masari, Saàd al-Faqih, Yassir al-Sirri, Omar Bakri Muhammad and others. Third, the British government allowed a high level of Jihadist activity to occur before it began to exert some control over the situation in the late 1990s. The propaganda efforts taking place in London during that decade served as a means for Jihadists around the world—many of whom were floating between Peshawar, their home countries and Jihadist conflict areas such as Somalia, Bosnia, Kosovo and Chechnya, as well as safe-havens like Sudan and Afghanistan—to stay connected with one another. In short, London allowed the "global" to be put into "global Jihadism."

Al-Fajr

In the mid-1990s, remnants of the Libyan Islamic Fighting Group (LIFG) working in and out of London began publishing their *al-Fajr* magazine under managing editor Said Mansour. Contributors included Abu Musab al-Suri, Abu Laith al-Libi and the rising star in the field, Abu Yahya al-Libi. Articles were also penned by Abu Munder al-Saidi, the spiritual leader of the LIFG, who had been one of the founding members of the group, alongside Awatha al-Zuwawi.

Said Mansour, a Moroccan-born Jihad propagandist who holds Danish citizenship, is now serving time in prison. After *al-Fajr* ceased publication in the late 1990s, he continued to produce global Jihadist propaganda, but he was arrested in September 2005 on charges of incitement to terrorist acts. He was accused of producing and distributing CDs, DVDs, and videos containing speeches and chants in which people linked to terrorist organizations called for Jihad and praised terrorists.[21] This material was distributed widely. CDs bearing the logo of Mansour's publishing company were found in Spain, among those with possible connections to the 2003 Madrid train-bombing cell; in Italy, in the possession of a radical imam who is now serving time himself for planning a terrorist attack on Milan's subway system; and in Germany, in the home of a man who is believed to be involved in the so-called "Hamburg cell," the terrorist group that provided four of the plane hijackers who attacked the World Trade Center in 2001.

Al-Ansar

In mid-1993, a group of Algerian Jihadists arrived in London after fleeing Peshawar. Together with Abu Qatada, they would seek to continue the legacy of their Peshawar-based *as-Shahadah* magazine, which had been funded with the help of Egyptian Islamic Jihad in order to promote the insurgency in Algeria. They established the Algerian Armed Islamic Group's (GIA) primary propaganda magazine, *Usrat al-Ansar*. While Abu Qatada provided the intellectual and ideological firepower for this weekly journal, it also published regular contributions from a variety of global Jihadist thinkers, including such members of its editorial board as Abu Musab al-Suri, Abu Hamza al-Masri, and Abu Munder Saidi, the spiritual leader of the LIFG. *Usrat al-Ansar* would become a trusted source of news and information about the GIA for Islamists around the world.

However, as the GIA began advocating increasingly lethal and indiscriminate operations, and more Muslim blood was shed in Algeria, support for the organization began to ebb, even among *Usrat al-Ansar*'s editorial board. Nevertheless, even though the Jihadist movement's popularity around the world was being seriously eroded *Usrat al-Ansar* waited nearly eight months before issuing a public statement about the recent events in Algeria. Belatedly, its editorial board began pressurizing the GIA's leadership to mend its ways and try to restore some of its squandered global support. This tension eventually fractured the relationship between Abu Qatada and two of his most influential correspondents, Abu Musab al-Suri and Abu Hamza al-Masri. Suri had been quick to withdraw his support for the GIA, viewing their activities early on as a public relations disaster in the battle to win the hearts and minds of Muslims around the world. Abu Hamza too saw the futility of the GIA's campaign. Despite their arguments, though, Abu Qatada insisted on continuing to support the GIA, even issuing a *fatwa* in favour of its violent actions and indiscriminate killings.

As a result of the overwhelming internal pressure and factionalization occurring across its ranks, the GIA's commander, Antar Zouabri, released a short statement in which he expressed some sympathy for the Algerian population and promised to be their guardians and to protect their religion, honor and property. Nevertheless, he defended all of his attacks, even those in which he knew innocent Algerian civilians would be killed. All he offered was an apology to any person who had been killed in the process of "defending Islam." *Usrat al-Ansar*'s editorial board immediately issued a denouncement of Zouabri, the GIA and all of its activities in Algeria, which it published in both Arabic and English newspapers. The statement referred to the GIA as "*Khwarij*," or those who have left the community of Islamic believers. After this statement, members of the board began receiving death threats and hate mail. The GIA continued to flounder for several more years until Zouabri was killed in a shootout, the remaining senior leadership further factionalized, and the group lost all momentum. Both Suri and Abu Hamza wrote scathing books criticizing the GIA leadership in subsequent years.[22]

Suri's personal propaganda machine

While still in London, in 1997 Abu Musab al-Suri established a quasi-Islamic media organization called the Stranger's Center for Islamic Conflict Studies (Markaz al-Ghuraba). The Center thrust Suri into the Jihadist propaganda limelight as he used it to publish writings on the hot topics within the Jihadist community, including the plight of Muslims in Afghanistan and the Taliban (1998), in Central

Asia (1999) and in Yemen (1999). In 1997, he told CNN correspondent Peter Bergen, while they were in transit to meet Usama Bin Laden, that his Center was an independent journalist group sponsoring correspondents in Kashmir, Bosnia and Pakistan. He also maintained a branch office in Kabul, Afghanistan, and used the copy filed by his reporters to inform his numerous publications on the status of Islamic conflicts around the world.[23]

Suri then returned to Afghanistan and reestablished his Ghuraba Center (generally referred to at this point as the "Center for Islamic Studies and Information")[24] under the direction of Mullah Muhammad Umar in Kandahar. Suri wholeheartedly supported the Taliban's propaganda efforts, working with the Ministry of Information, writing in the official newspaper, *Sharia*, and helping to set up the Arab Radio Kabul station. He also continued to release writings under the auspices of the Ghuraba Center, including his own reflections on *Sunnis in the Levant* (2000) and a compilation of letters and statements from Usama Bin Laden and Saàd al-Faqih to Saudi scholars (2001).[25]

In December 2000 the Ghuraba Center released the first issue of its *al-Dhahirin ala al-Haq* (*Upholders of the Truth*) bulletin.[26] This first issue concentrated on three key themes: increasing Muslim activism; helping readers to distinguish between "good" scholars and "bad" scholars; and opening the eyes of Muslims to Jihadist revolutionary movements around the world. On the first point, the issue opened with an article entitled "The Vastness, Magnanimity of a Quranic Verse," which discusses how "true believers" will sacrifice their material possessions and self for God and warns readers of the "dangers and seduction that they may face in life's journey." Suri's editorial called on Muslims to follow the path of the upholders of the truth. He placed special emphasis on calling Muslims to participate in the Ghuraba Center's activities but also outlined the acceptable nature of that participation.

In order to help its readers gain a better sense of the Jihadist movements waging violence in the name of Islam around the world, the magazine profiled several cases. The first was in Suri's own article, ''Palestine and the Struggle with the Jews and the Global Crusades.'' This focused on the "centrality" of the Palestinian issue to Muslims everywhere. According to Suri, this centrality is due to the holiness of the al-Aqsa Mosque in Palestine and the "close cooperation between the Jews, the Crusaders, the Shiites, and the hypocritical leaders in the occupation of Jerusalem all through history." The article also provided a review of how Palestine was occupied and how Israel was created.

The issue concluded with tactical training in a section called "Terrorist Education." This provided readers with a novel way to weaponize gas tanks simply by setting them on fire for 35 minutes. Suri explained, "If you want them to become anti-personnel weapons, put glass and nails around them."

In March 2001, Suri released the second issue of the magazine. His opening editorial provided a comprehensive analysis of the Muslim world's global crisis, arguing that infidelity has become pervasive and that the confrontation between good and evil, between Islam and disbelievers, is occurring everywhere, from China and Indonesia to North Africa, from Central Asia to the Caucasus, and from the Balkans to the Arabian Peninsula. It is a conflict above all else between the "new world order represented by its cunning and mean troika—the Jews, the Crusaders and the apostates—supported by their allies the hypocrites, who claim to belong to Islam."

Azzam.com

In late 1996, Babar Ahmad (or "Mr. B", or "mrbee42"), a 22-year-old undergraduate at Imperial College in London, launched a website dedicated to promoting Islamic fighters in Bosnia, Chechnya and Afghanistan that he named "azzam.com." In time, he and his colleagues would establish a network of sister websites, including azzam.co.uk, qoqaz.net, qoqaz.co.uk, webstorage.com/~azzam and waaqiah. com. Azzam.com and the other websites provided a stage for English-speaking Jihobbyists to discuss everything on their minds with regard to global Jihadism. More specifically, it was designed to recruit individuals to become Jihadist fighters as well as to solicit and raise funds and assistance for Jihad, including for the Taliban and Chechen *mujahidin*. Azzam.com was a breakthrough, allowing militant groups to spread their messages worldwide and recruit new followers.

Evan Kohlman described azzam.com in a *Washington Post* article as the "very first real al Qaida Web site." According to Kohlman, "It taught an entire generation about jihad. Even in its nascency, it was professional. It wasn't technically sophisticated, but it was professional looking, definitely more professional than any other jihadi Web sites out there." It made its reputation in part by selling some of the earliest English-language videotapes glorifying Islamic fighters. One of these, *Martyrs of Bosnia* (1997), featured a masked narrator—thought to be Ahmad—waving an automatic rifle and urging Muslims to go to the Balkans to kill nonbelievers.[27]

Two of Ahmad's closest associates, Syed Talha Ahsan and Ahsan Ahmad, helped create, operate and maintain the websites. These websites, and other forms of internet communication, disseminated material which was intended to recruit *mujahidin* for the Taliban and associated groups, raise funds for violent Jihad, provide instructions for travel to Pakistan and Afghanistan and for the surreptitious transfer of funds to the Taliban, and solicit military items, including gas masks and night-vision goggles. The men used various email accounts to communicate with other individuals also involved in the operation and administration of the websites as well as with members of the Taliban, the Chechen *mujahidin* and associated groups. They also contacted members of the public who wished to support the violent Jihad activities depicted on the websites through material support and donations. These supporters often purchased videotapes advertised on the website that depicted and promoted violent Jihad in Chechnya, Bosnia, Afghanistan and elsewhere, and the torture and killing of captured Russian troops.

Mazen Mokhtar, a computer professional who trained at Johns Hopkins University in Baltimore, is a familiar face to young activist Muslim men in New Jersey, often delivering what acquaintances describe as mild speeches extolling marriage and religious piety. His lawyer, Yasser Helal, confirmed in 2007 that

Mokhtar had been under investigation by US authorities since March of that year, when Homeland Security agents seized computer files and other records in a search of Mokhtar's North Brunswick home. Helal was not prepared to discuss the investigation or to comment on allegations that Mokhtar had worked with Babar Ahmad to create backup copies of azzam.com when administrators shut down the website after the 2001 terrorist attacks.

In court papers, an Immigration and Customs Enforcement agent claimed that "a concerted effort existed between the administrators of Azzam, including Ahmad, and individuals in the US . . . to further the goals of Azzam, that is, to solicit funds for blocked organizations, namely the Taliban and the Chechen Mujahideen, in an effort to support their goals." Although Mokhtar is not named in the complaint filed by US authorities against Ahmad, a website that he registered and administered, www.minna.com, is cited.

From at least August 21, 2000 through September 2, 2001, administrators of Azzam Publications used email accounts to communicate with one another. Around July 2001, Ahmad, using these email accounts, reportedly communicated with a US naval enlistee who was sympathetic to the views expressed on azzam.com and praised the attack on the USS *Cole* in March 2001. Ahmad encouraged the enlistee to "keep up the psychological warfare [*sic*]." In August 2004, Ahmad acquired a number of documents, including a drawing of the Empire State Building, literature supporting violent Jihadism around the world, guerrilla warfare manuals, and other documents describing operations such as waging attacks on commuter rail platforms and military aircraft.[28]

The popularity of Azzam Publications cannot be overstated: it provided an invaluable bridge between the British Jihadist commmunity and the global Jihadist movement. Its output can be divided into three main categories: eulogies of killed Jihadist fighters; interviews with Jihadist fighters and commanders; and new editions of some of the greatest Jihadist books, essays and articles. The group also used the internet to disseminate still photos, video captures and audio files detailing a variety of Jihadist activities, and thereby pioneered the Jihadist internet presence.

Nida ul-Islam

Nida ul-Islam described itself as a "Comprehensive Intellectual Islamic Magazine, published by the Islamic Youth Movement—Media Office, Sydney—Australia."[29] It was an online magazine released in both Arabic and English that began publishing as early as January 1994. Over its lifespan, it improved the quality of its articles, artwork and typesetting, moving to a full-color cover and expanded its contributor network significantly. It also continued to expand its distribution, tripling the number of printed issues it released in its first three years. The magazine was able to secure interviews with an impressive collection of Jihadists throughout the 1990s, including one in late 1996 with Usama Bin Laden, in which he enthusiastically stated that the Taliban "are committed to support the religion approved by Allah, and that country remains as the Muslims have known it, a strong fort for Islam, and its people are amongst the most protective of the religion approved by Allah, and the keenest to fulfill His laws and to establish an Islamic state." Other interviewees included: Saudi Jihadist clerics Salman al-Awdah and Safar al-Hawali; the preeminent Jordanian Jihadist ideologue Abu Muhammad al-Maqdisi; the renowned Pakistani Jihadist cleric Maulana Masood Azhar; the Egyptian leaders of the Islamic Group, Rifai Taha and Abu Talal al-Qassimi; and official spokesmen for the Libyan Islamic Fighting Group.

According to its website at the time, *Nida ul-Islam*'s goals included:

1   Originating subjective Islamic media which adheres to the pure teachings of Islam.
2   Clarifying and presenting the Truth in a direct uncompromising way.
3   Reflecting the views of the Jihad stream amongst the Islamic movements.
4   Safeguarding and standing up to the Zionist–Crusader assaults against Islam and Muslims.
5   Planting and promoting the authentic Islamic teachings and principles, which are based on the Qur'an and the Sunnah as understood by our Salaf Salih— the first three guided generations, our righteous predecessors, may Allah be pleased with them all.
6   Presenting the Islamic alternative since Islam is a complete system of life, and supplying the Islamic rulings with regards to the modern inventions, especially on the economical side.
7   Striving towards producing a section in the society which understands Islam to its true reality, and which realizes that Jihad is the only path to establish the Islamic State, and which therefore acts accordingly.
8   Confronting and responding to the misguidance and misconceptions promoted by the deviated sects, and which are directly supported by the international Jewish movements and the Free Masons.
9   Clarifying the important and controversial Islamic concepts to the sons of the Islamic movements.
10 Maintaining the Islamic identity in the Western societies and bidding to strengthen their ties with the Muslim Ummah, so that they may share its sorrows and happiness.
11 Giving the youth generation the attention it requires, since it forms the fuel for the Islamic movement in general and the Jihad stream in specific.

The magazine ran articles on a variety of topics directly related to the Jihadist movement, ideological discussions about *al-Wala wal-Bara*, historical essays about Islamic conquests and discussions about contemporary Jihadist military challenges in places like Eritrea. It was finally removed from its server in late August 2005 and at the time of writing had not reappeared.

Saudi Jihadist propaganda

Al-Qaida's propaganda machine in Saudi Arabia emerged in the mid-1990s with the establishment of the Center for Islamic Studies and Research (Markaz al-dirasat wal-buhuth al-Islamiyyah). The Center originally served as more of a mouthpiece for the organization out of the kingdom, a vehicle to transmit the messages of al-Qaida's leadership and spokesmen. It set up its website, al-Neda.com, in order to help broadcast those messages more broadly. Yousef al-Ayiri was the Center's supervisor and its website administrator until his death in May 2003.[30] Some reports suggest that Bin Laden himself had called for the establishment of the Center in 1995 and that he had established offices in London (likely referring to Khalid al-Fawwaz's London-based Advice and Reformation Committee) and New York.[31]

An especially productive year for the Center was 2002. In March it released an article entitled "A Call for Supremacy and Happiness." In April it published "Appeal to Muslims to Rescue Their Brethren in Palestine," by Shaikh Safar al-Hawali. In May it released "To the Head of the Infidel: God Has Kept for You What Harms You" and a series of articles by al-Qaida spokesman Sulayman Abu Ghayth. And in June, it published "Do Not Lie: The Prisoners Do Not Know What You Are Claiming." However, on July 3 the website abruptly closed. The London-based azzam.com published a statement on the matter on the same day:

> In breathtaking arrogance, typical of the Americans—the US has directed that all web hosting countries around the world not to allow any website having contents and news related to Jihad, Al-Qaida and the Taliban. Censorship of alternative world views being acceptable under Bush's "War Against Terrorism." The US government claims that "alneda" is the main website of Al-Qaida. US sources stated that Al-Qaida spokesman Suleiman Abu-Ghaith's audio cassette was advertised through this website. The Telecommunication and Internet Tracing unit of the CIA have said that the US government intends to shut down all websites of extremist Islamic groups . . . The "alneda" website has been uploaded to a new domain "darasat.com." We recommend that as many people as possible mirror the contents of this site—to foil the US's concerted attack on free speech.

In fact, the Center launched several new websites in order to continue making its resources available to the Jihadist public. On September 11 of that year, it posted an official statement from the political bureau of al-Qaida, which stated: "we are constant and we resolve to carry on; we are determined to hit the structure of this nation."

One month later, it released a statement updating its readers about its ongoing struggle to maintain a web presence:

> We would like through this statement to inform our brother Muslims and the world about the new developments in our current war with the Americans on the Internet . . . FBI used to force the companies hosting our website to immediately delete the site in violation of all publication laws on the network, as well as its own old laws. The Americans' behavior in forcing host companies to delete the website happened to most of our 19 websites, which were hit.

In the fall of 2003, the Center began publishing two online magazines: *Sawt al-Jihad* (*Voice of Jihad*), which focused on Jihadist ideology and thought; and *Muaskar al-Battar* (*Camp al-Battar*), which provided operational-level advice to the Jihadist community. After disappearing for a month, the Center's official website reappeared on December 16 as part of a German travel agency's website, but it disappeared again three days later. It would be back up by the following March, when it posted the full 45-minute tape and transcript of an audio message Bin Laden had recorded on January 4. That spring, the Center continued to publish statements by Taliban officials and leading al-Qaida commanders in Saudi Arabia.

In late 2003, the London-based Arabic newspaper *al-Sharq al-Awsat* had reported on the previously unheralded Global Islamic Media Center, and interviewed its spokesman Ahmad al-Wathiq Billah. He said, "Do you remember how Al-Qaida was born in Afghanistan? It began with a 'Services' office, 'Bayt al-Ansar' [hostel], 'Al-Faruq Camp' and other phases everybody knows, until it reached the present stage of Al-Qaida University for Jihad Sciences." This university, Billah claimed, "comprises colleges for 'electronic Jihad', practice on arms, car bombs and the use of ammunition." Its students included the "zealous among the sons of Islam and those sincere to their nation and religion," and its dean was Usama Bin Laden.[32]

In early 2004 the Global Islamic Media Center itself began to raise its public profile. In January, for instance, it posted a book entitled *Stories from History Presented to the Wanted—A Gift to the 26*, by Abu-Jandal al-Azdi, a chief scholar and propagandist for al-Qaida's Saudi group. In March, it followed up by posting another of Azdi's works, the highly anticipated *God is Great! America Has Been Destroyed*.

Toward a global media front

As can be gathered from the above examples, the global Jihadist internet world is perpetually in flux. The main originators of Jihadist propaganda are either virtually or physically attached to al-Qaida's regional commands, including:

*   Islamic State of Iraq (al-Furqan Media);
*   Al-Qaida High Command in Afghanistan (as-Sahab Media);
*   Ansar al-Sunnah Group;
*   Al-Qaida in the Land of the Islamic Maghreb (Media Commission);
*   Al-Qaida in the Arabian Peninsula (*Sawt al-Jihad*).

These groups film, edit and produce their own media, which includes audio, video and print. Their topics include attack footage, recorded statements, news updates, propaganda material and so on. Although these groups could post their works directly on the numerous websites in the global Jihadist world, al-Qaida has created a more regularized mechanism for conducting the distribution process, which serves to ensure authenticity and brand management, facilitating the rapid, efficient and untainted dissemination of new releases. In recent years, there have been two primary dissemination conduits: the Global Islamic Media Front (GIMF) and the al-Fajr Media Center. The latter has become the dominant force of late, as GIMF seems to have moved entirely away from dissemination and into generating its own original products, including video games, technical manuals and anthologies.

The GIMF

As early as December 2002, two propaganda outlets—the Global Islamic Media Center and its sister organization the Abu Banan Global Islamic Media Group— were generating violent Jihadist content. They published increasingly important statements, and by 2004 were the primary sources of major Jihadist publications. Two names became closely associated with these organizations' websites: Abu-Abd-al-Rahman al-Turkumani and Ahmad al-Wathiq Billah. The latter published *The Nation of al-Qaida and Its Promising Strikes*, a series of studies on the al-Qaida movement, while the former wrote several essays that were widely read and disseminated among Jihobbyists.

On August 8, 2004, Billah and his Global Islamic Media Center publicly called for the creation of a "unified Islamic Media Network of international scope with a coordinating body," intended to "exploit the internet" for the "benefit of the Islamic Ummah." He then itemized the qualities and types of people that would be necessary for such an enterprise to succeed:

1 Sincerity, dedication, reliance on God, using available means, but taking the necessary security precautions.
2 A commitment to not reviling or insulting Muslims, especially scholars, preachers, *mujahidin*, and reformers.
3 People who are experienced in the media business who are willing to help the Jihadist movement formulate and publish better reports and teach them how to depict events and developments.
4 Those willing to cooperate, coordinate, and communicate with the information wings of the front-line and battlefield resistance and Jihadist groups.
5 Those interested in publishing on economic, medical, and scientific news of benefit to the Ummah.
6 Those who believe that America is a country of interests, not one of values and principles, and that the so-called state of Israel is a cancer on the body of the Ummah, one that must be eradicated by all possible means.
7 Those who believe that peoples and individuals have the right to defend their nation, dignity, and property and that if they are threatened by force, they have the right to use force.
8 Those who are willing to leave open the door for dialogue with those Westerners and non-Muslims who are at peace with the Jihadist movement, who are sympathetic to the Palestinian, Iraqi, and Afghan people and to the cause of Kashmir and Chechnya.
9 Those with language skills who can form Jihadist translation teams and help the Global Islamic Media Front to reach more people in more languages.
10 Those who are patient and steadfast, whatever trials and problems obstruct the course of the Islamic media.[33]

In the immediate aftermath of this call the Global Islamic Media Front launched its first website. Although it was devoid of any original content, its appearance started a trend that would rapidly become the standard operating procedure for global Jihadists. On October 5, 2004, Billah officially marked the establishment of this new umbrella media front by calling for Jihadists' help in the following:

- designing a logo for the front;
- forming detachments that are offshoots from the front. Each detachment would have a particular role or roles—for example, a detachment to transmit statements by *mujahidin* and news reports, a detachment specializing in matters of indoctrination, a detachment for scientific and research matters and various studies, a detachment for economic matters, and so on;
- facilitating cooperation with experienced media people.

The London-based *al-Sharq al-Awsat* highlighted how this Global Islamic Media Front idea was the media equivalent to Bin Laden's February 1998 announcement of the "World Front for Fighting the Jews and Crusaders." The newspaper asked Dr. Hani al-Siba'i, director of the London-based al-Maqrizi Studies Center, about Billah's speech. He replied, "The new international media front is one of the fruits of the ideological unity that Al-Qaida is calling for and is not necessarily linked organically to Bin Laden's organization." The front, he suggested, "will attract small groups from all over the world and this will strengthen it so that if the media section of any group is hit, this will not impede the overall media process because each one of these groups will comply with Bin Laden's principles."[34]

Just two weeks later, the Global Islamic Media Front released its first publication, an electronic analysis of Abu Musab al-Zarqawi's group in Iraq. A statement about the e-book indicated that it had been prepared by "Qa'qa" of al-Ansar forum, who wrote:

I have gathered in it [the book] everything that was issued by the group under the leadership of Shaykh Abu Musab al-Zarqawi, including statements, news, or announcements. I have taken some of the military operations and some of Shaikh Abu Musab's statements that reflect Salafi ideology and their jihad tactics so that the Muslim nation is aware that there are men in this age who are fighting for religion and the elevation of God's words.

The compilation and distribution of this work represented everything that the new GIMF hoped to be.

By the fall of 2005, the GIMF had advanced significantly in terms of sophistication and creativity. For instance, it released several videotaped news productions entitled *Sawt al-Khilifa* (*Voice of the Caliphate*). Each was approximately 20 minutes long and contained news, commentary and video footage on a variety of topics, such as the fighting in Iraq, a profile of the Muslim experience in Niger, Jihadist assaults on Israel, Taliban suicide bombings in Afghanistan, political prisoners in Egypt and the state of Muslims in Algeria, among other themes. During this time, the GIMF announced that it was a globally networked media organization whose goal was to "clarify the truth" through "logical and legitimate methods," to support Islam and Muslims, and to defend Islam and attract people to the religion. It reportedly encompassed multiple Jihadist media outlets, such as "forums, sites, news groups, and a variety of media organizations," but was not owned by or affiliated to anyone other than "zealous Muslims." It relied on religious scholars in its activities, and opposed "division, prejudice, and discord."

On November 21, 2005, the world had the chance to meet the GIMF's public relations bureau director, Dr. Sayf al-Din al-Kananiy, in a videotaped interview he released as part of a series entitled *And the Discussion Continues*. This short video featured Kananiy masked and sitting on a couch. The presenter began the interview by asking what message Kananiy had for the youth of the Islamic world. Kananiy asked them, "What are your capabilities?" before continuing, "For you, my brother, decide your capabilities. Yes, you, not us. Our messages relating [to this] are available in the forums and a simple press of a key will let us know what you have [to offer] and we will place you in your appropriate position that you deserve." The GIMF, he reported, had recently opened the door for people to join it by means of the internet, and he explained how this was a new and effective method of enlisting fresh cadres to assist in bringing out "the hidden capabilities of the youth in the Jihadist forums." When asked if he worked directly for al-Qaida, he emphasized that the GIMF stood neutrally behind the Jihadist movement, not preferencing one group over another.

By September 2006, the GIMF had taken its productions to new heights, releasing what would become the most popular Jihadist video game to date: *Night of Bush Capturing*. The game's title is a play on the title of a famous Arab television series and movie: *Night of Fatima Capturing*. The GIMF also began to release its own online periodical, entitled *Sada al-Rafidayn*. This encourages

> the brothers and the sisters to distribute this material to relatives, friends and the general public in mosques, and anyone who does not have access to the Internet, by printing and distributing them, or reading them in gatherings, as well as forwarding them through electronic mail, various electronic groups, chat rooms, and any other venues of distributing the news of your *mujahidin* brothers in the Land of the Two Rivers, that will give good results.[35]

Majallat al-Ansar, Sawt al-Jihad *and* Muaskar al-Battar

Beginning in 2002, the global Jihadist movement launched a new generation of online magazines. These e-publications were available in multiple formats, could be quickly distributed, and discussed matters of serious concern for Jihobbyists. They contained hard-hitting insights, articles and updates, and came in aesthetically appealing formats.

Early in 2002, senior al-Qaida figures began posting a new bulletin entitled *al-Ansar: For the Struggle against the Crusader War* on the website *http://www. geocites.com/al_anssar/*. Little more is known about the publication other than that it represented the most advanced strategic thinking from the global Jihadist movement up to that point. Its major contributors included men about whom little is still known today, including: Abu Ayman al-Hilali, Abu Ubayd al-Qurashi, Saif al-Din al-Ansari, and Abu Sad al-Amali. These strategists wrote a variety of pointed and rigorously researched articles under *al-Ansar*'s topical headings, such as: "A Vision of Faith," "Strategic Studies," "Political Analyses," and "Educational Pause." Nothing has been heard from this publication since April 2003, however.

In mid-October 2003, the *Sawt al-Jihad* (*Voice of Jihad*) and *Muaskar al-Battar* (*Severer's Camp*) online magazines picked up where *al-Ansar* had left off. Published out of Yousef al-Ayiri's Center for Islamic Studies and Research, *Sawt al-Jihad* provided readers with cutting-edge discussions of Jihadist ideology and strategy. *Battar*, on the other hand, offered hard-nosed practical advice. The Center made both publicly available on a number of websites, and the magazines were immediately a huge hit within the global Jihadist world.

Sawt al-Jihad provided some of the brightest minds within the global Jihadist movement with a popular forum in which to speak about matters on an intellectual level. It followed the same general structure from issue to issue, usually opening with an unsigned editorial piece and then moving to:

- in-depth discussion of recent Jihadist happenings in Saudi Arabia;
- a featured interview with a prominent commander or scholar;
- eulogies for dead al-Qaida fighters;
- several articles about applying Jihadist ideology to the world;
- eyewitness news as seen through the eyes of the *mujahidin*;
- a question-and-answer section;
- excerpts from upcoming Jihadist books;
- Jihadist poetry.

The magazine ran, in fits and starts, for 30 issues. The vigorous Saudi campaign to crush al-Qaida in the peninsula seems to have quietened it for the time being.

Muaskar al-Battar was published by the Committee of Jihadists in the Arabian Peninsula. It contained some longer articles discussing current events but mostly focused on informing its readers about tactical and operational-level advice. Among its articles were "Survival Kit," "Principles of Security," "Guerrilla Warfare," "Small Arms," "Physical Training," "PK 2," "Kidnapping Crew or Group," " Anti-Armor Weapons," "Disguises" and "Assasinations," to name just a few. It published 22 issues before closing.

By 2004, the Saudi al-Qaida propaganda group was being run by Isa Sa'd Muhammad Awshan, a native of Riyadh. Information about him is sketchy, at best. The story released by the Saudi government is that he had financial troubles in early adulthood and was unable even to keep up with his car payments. According to the Saudis, he moved to the Jazan area in order to look for work and somehow got swept up into Jihadist activity. However, he likely knew Yousef al-Ayiri from early in his life, and given his family's links to violent Jihadist activity, he probably did not simply stumble into the movement. He had two younger brothers who fought in Afghanistan before 2001 with the Taliban, stationed on the northern front. They both died in combat. He also had a cousin who was killed during the first Afghan Jihad against the Soviets. Later, another cousin was held at Guantanamo Bay, while two more were detained by the Saudi government.

Awshan assumed control over the propaganda group after Saudi security forces killed Ayiri in May 2003. Awshan had been deeply influenced by Ayiri's style and flair for propaganda, even penning an account of the latter's life under the pseudonym Muhammad Bin-Ahmad al-Salim. He also used the pen-name Salim in order to publish what has become one of the more popular Jihadist books: *39 Ways to Serve and Participate in Jihad*. He was obsessive in writing statements, designing formats, printing and passing on his craft to others. If he was not working at his laptop, his colleagues would later reflect, he was training someone in a particular task. By writing, supervising and revising material, he participated actively in the production of the group's magazines from their first issues until his death. He was adroitly aided in this by Mujab Abu Ras al-Dosari, who was killed alongside Awshan by Saudi security forces in July 2004.

Abu Usayd al-Falluji and Abu Abdallah al-Najdi then assumed the role of media emirs for the Saudi al-Qaida cell. According to al-Qaida's own reports, they supervised over a dozen websites and were part of Ahmad al-Wathiq Billah's efforts to develop an online university. Another major player in the Saudi propaganda world also emerged at this time. Abi Thabit al-Najdi became the new editor of *muaskar al-Battar*. However, al-Qaida's propaganda machine in Saudi Arabia today seems to have been decimated by Saudi counter-terrorism initiatives.

As-Sahab

Al-Qaida's official media production group is the as-Sahab [Clouds] Establishment for Media Productions. Although it is al-Qaida's most public arm, very little is known about this highly secretive organization. Its headquarters are likely co-located with the organization's High Command, which is thought to be based in the tribal regions on the Afghanistan–Pakistan border. Ayman al-Zawahiri likely oversees the general direction and operations of as-Sahab and he frequently appears in its video productions. Since 2003, as-Sahab has become a Jihadist media powerhouse. It releases several major video productions each month, including highly polished, hour-long statements by senior al-Qaida figures, documentaries and a variety of attack videos. It is an intensely visual organization. Most as-Sahab videos begin with flashy introductions, often centered on the group's shimmering golden logo. This logo, which is emblazoned on a bottom corner for the remainder of the video, carries deep significance as it signals that the video is an official and authentic al-Qaida production. The group has therefore become an integral part of al-Qaida's brand-name management efforts. A brand refers to an organization's name and logo. An organization is generally able to develop strong brand recognition with an audience if its name is easy to pronounce and remember, its logo is instantly recognizable, and it is able to attract attention and communicate its unique features.

An al-Qaida member who intimately understands the need for an organization to brand itself effectively is Khalid Shaikh Mohammed, or KSM as he is known across the counter-terrorism community. He looked to brand al-Qaida through massive, high-profile attacks, including an assassination plot against US President Bill Clinton, another against Pope John Paul II, a plot to destroy airliners simultaneously in the air (known as Operation Bojinka), and the attacks of 9/11. After his arrest, in his 2007 Combatant Status Review Tribunal, he told Defense officials that he "was the Media Operations Director for As-Sahab under Dr. Ayman al-Zawahiri. As-Sahab is the media outlet that provided Al-Qaida-sponsored information to Al-Jazira."[36] There is no way of knowing how influential KSM was in building up as-Sahab during its formative years.

One of KSM's media protégés was an American named Adam Gadahn (also known as Azzam al-Amriki). He acted as a translator early in as-Sahab's existence. According to an intelligence official, KSM criticized Gadahn under interrogation, saying that he had last seen him in Karachi, Pakistan, when he had asked him to join a plot to blow up gas stations in Maryland. Gadahn had declined, explaining that he had recently married and that his wife was pregnant. But the intelligence official added that Gadahn did participate in a number of "face-to-face brainstorming sessions" with KSM.[37] Instead of becoming an operative, Gadahn began to apply his promotional skills to his work for al-Qaida. He narrated his first al-Qaida production with an audio translation of a statement by Bin Laden in 2002. In October 2004, he released his first as-Sahab video as Azzam al-Amriki, with his face shrouded in a checkered scarf and sunglasses, his rhetoric awkward and stilted. Nevertheless, he has since become a regular feature on as-Sahab videos.

As-Sahab's production quality increased markedly in 2006 and 2007 as its staff grew more technologically adept. In 2006, for instance, the first anniversary of the London bombings and the fifth anniversary of the 9/11 attacks were both commemorated with documentary-style videos using a graphically compelling blend of still imagery, animation, Western news footage, subtitles, logos and more. But beyond sophistication, the sheer number of videos that as-Sahab releases each month is impressive. Consider, for instance, the releases issued in a recent representative 30-day period:

- *October 21, 2007*: an 85-minute video featuring the first interview with senior Taliban figure Shaikh Muhammad Yasir.
- *October 23, 2007*: a 33-minute video featuring Usama Bin Laden's "Message to the People of Iraq" in which Bin Laden discusses negligence during combat operations.
- *October 31, 2007*: a 15-minute video featuring Mansour Dadullah answering questions and responding to allegations against the Taliban.
- *November 3, 2007*: a 28-minute video entitled *Unity of Ranks* featuring new statements from Ayman al-Zawahiri and Abu Laith al-Libi.
- *November 7, 2007*: a 16-minute video statement by Abu Yahya al-Libi entitled "Closing Statement for the Religious Training that Was Held at One of the *Mujahidin* Centers."

- *November 11, 2007*: a 3-minute video containing footage of Jihadist fighters "liberating" a center from the "apostates" in Kandahar. (Part of the *Hell of the Americans in the Land of Khorasan* series.)
- *November 13, 2007*: a 2-minute video of Jihadist fighters ambushing an "apostate" convoy in Khost, Afghanistan. (Part of the *Hell of the Americans in the Land of Khorasan* series.)
- *November 17, 2007*: a 3-minute video of *mujahidin* ambushing a Coalition convoy in Kandahar. (Part of the *Hell of the Americans in the Land of Khorasan* series.)

In 2006, as-Sahab released an average of one video every six days, or 58 that year. In the following year, it was up to just over one video every three days, and there is no reason to suspect that production will decrease in the foreseeable future.

Al-Furqan

On October 31, 2006, the Islamic State of Iraq announced across the Jihadist web community the establishment of the al-Furqan Media Production Agency:

> It pleases the Ministry of Information of the Islamic State of Iraq to announce the establishment of a media agency that is dedicated to producing audio-video productions and any informational material put out by the Islamic State of Iraq's Ministry of Information, may God protect and strengthen it. This agency, God willing, is intended to become a unique guide on the road to an outstanding Jihadist media, which occupies a great position in managing the struggle with the Crusaders . . . and to expose the lies and deficiencies of the Crusaders' media. God willing, you can expect from this agency all that will please the believers and upset the infidels and hypocrites.

Al-Furqan started its work slowly, publishing a new audio message issued by Shaikh Abu Hamza al-Muhajir on November 10, wherein he pledges allegiance to Abu Umar al-Baghdadi, the emir of the Islamic State of Iraq, announcing that all groups, including the Mujahidin Shura Council and twelve thousand al-Qaida fighters, will accept the authority of the state. He also calls on the Ansar al-Sunnah and al-Mujahidin Army groups to declare allegiance to al-Baghdadi. Within several days, the transcript had been translated into English and French on Jihadist websites.

On November 14, al-Furqan issued its "*Mujahidin* Harvest in the Land of the Two Rivers" video bulletin, in which the Islamic State of Iraq boasts of having killed 499 Crusaders, 332 Iraqi policemen, 16 Interior Ministry commandos, 759 al-Mahdi Army soldiers, 236 National Guardsmen, 51 Badr Corps soldiers, 14 Peshmerga, 37 spies and 49 Israeli Mosad agents. In terms of equipment damage, it brags about destroying: 210 Hummers, 16 minesweepers, 38 armored vehicles, 22 transport trucks, 1 water/land vehicle, 8 tanks, 5 troop transporters, 119 sedans,

27 four-wheel-drive vehicles, 1 tanker, 1 trailer, 27 robots, 1 Black Hawk heli-copter, 1 spy plane, and more. One week later, al-Furqan released a 57-minute video compilation of previously released attack footage, commentary and war music entitled *Free the Prisoners*. The next week it released *American Intelligence in Baghdad's Streets*, a nine-minute video depicting three separate ambush operations against US vehicles. In all three operations, the fighters, who are armed with machine-guns and mortars, sit atop a bridge overlooking the highway and as soon as the American vehicles approach the bridge, they get to their feet and start firing.

From this point forward, al-Furqan began releasing videos at an ever-increasing tempo, up to several each day in the first half of 2007. It came under tremendous pressure, however, in the summer of that year when Multinational Forces Iraq (MNF-I) began a major offensive against the Islamic State of Iraq's media apparatus. Beginning in June, Coalition forces uncovered an al-Qaida media center near Samarra. This was equipped with a film studio and had been used to produce and distribute videos featuring recent terrorist attacks. Inside the building, MNF-I forces found 65 hard drives, 18 thumb drives, more than 500 CDs, and 12 personal computers containing recruitment and other terrorism-related materials.

In July, MNF-I captured Khalid Abdul Fatah Da'ud Mahmud al-Mashadani, also known as Abu Shahed, the ISI's Minister of Information, who served as the primary liaison between al-Qaida in Iraq's senior leadership and al-Qaida's High Command. This high-level capture started a chain reaction at al-Furqan and in the Islamic State of Iraq more generally. Between July and October, MNF-I killed or captured a total of 24 propaganda operatives from eight different media cells in Baghdad, Diyala, Tarmiyah, Samarra, Karma and Mosul, seizing over 23 terabytes of information in the process.[38] Al-Furqan was severely com-promised and managed to release only a handful of products during this period.

Al-Fajr

Since February 2006, all official al-Qaida media efforts today have been coordinated by the al-Fajr (Dawn) media network. Little is known about the organization other than it is a highly efficient disseminator of al-Qaida propaganda materials and allows the organization to maintain the integrity and authenticity of its productions. It is therefore now the best source of reliable information about al-Qaida on the internet.

Regional commands, including the Islamic State of Iraq, al-Qaida in the Land of the Islamic Maghreb and al-Qaida's High Command, all use al-Fajr to distribute their products. Al-Qaida in the Arabian Peninsula (Saudi Arabia) switched to al-Fajr after originally using the GIMF as its primary dissemination vehicle. These regional commands each use their affiliated media groups, like al-Furqan and as-Sahab, among others, in order to transmit their new media products to al-Fajr, which is connected with the affiliates via the internet. Once approved for dissemination, al-Fajr's correspondents coordinate their release plans and move material to pre-approved web forums, which al-Fajr has already publicly identified. This mechanism ensures that those websites receive the first look at any fresh media products from the regional groups.

Al-Fajr has created a trusted network of contacts, including Jihadist forum administrators, correspondents, editors and other technical support staff. Its correspondents all have a number of screen-names which they use when posting material on their Jihadist websites of choice. In June 2006, al-Fajr's leadership felt compelled to clarify who they were in order to limit the activities of impostors:

> A number of statements attributed to al-Fajr Media Center have surfaced recently. Al-Fajr Media Center hereby declares that the sites it uses (at this time) for publication and its reporters are as follows:
>
> - Mufakkirat Al-Hizbah, Al-Hisbah Islamic Network
> - Murasil Al-Ikhlas in Al-Ikhlas Islamic Network
> - Murasil Al-Buraq, Al-Buraq Islamic Network
> - Mufakkirat Al-Jihad, Al-Firdaws Islamic Network
> - Murasil Akhbar, Global News Network
> - Al-Ansar Jihad (Yahoo) Group
> - Statements Blog—Arabic and English
>
> We disclaim any [other] participant who posts a statement and attributes it to Al-Fajr Media Center. Such a person will be subject to termination from all websites.[39]

Global Jihadist media tomorrow

A Jihadist internet participant using the alias Gharib al-Diyar, who is likely a German media official for the Global Islamic Media Front, composed an essay that has recently featured on global Jihadist websites entitled "The Media Sword Campaign: How Can I Participate? What Can I Do? And What Is My Role?" Diyar's goal in writing this essay was to use the lessons he had learned from the legendary Jihadist propagandists, including Ayiri, Muqrin, Awshan, Kananiy and Dadullah, in order to inspire a new cadre of Jihadist propagandists.

He appeals to the Jihobbyist community, explaining that some of the current propagandists and media operatives of the global Jihadist movement are "students at schools, universities and institutes, teachers in classes and doctors in clinics and hospitals. Some of them are married and others are single. All of them have responsibilities. Just like you! However, all these life responsibilities couldn't inhibit their enthusiasm and their determination to work and support our religion." He explains that the movement is currently in need of assistance in several spheres. First, it needs more Jihadist forum administrators. These people create opportunities for Muslims to discuss matters that directly concern them, and they are important for organizing and coordinating the technical infrastructure and information necessary to keep the online Jihadist movement advancing.

Next, Diyar identifies the the moderators of Jihadist forums as being critical hubs in the online movement. They are the "unknown soldiers in the forums. No one remembers them in achievements, but they are the first to be blamed when trouble arises. And any mistake by them might collapse the whole forum, as they are the guards of the forums." Moderators are usually senior members who help administrators by ensuring people are posting and communicating with one another in appropriate ways. They are deputized by the administrators, even though they likely have never met one another, to help regulate interactions in the forums. Diyar explains that moderators must react strongly to anyone who tries to sow dissension between Jihadists in the forums. They must help to keep discussions on track, encouraging certain topics and themes. They also have the authority to remove and reject those postings that they view as counter-productive or irrelevant.

Diyar then points to the need for more Jihadist technical experts, including those knowledgeable about *Sharia* law and scholarship, and those who are skilled at video editing, graphic design and website creation. He also encourages anyone with language skills to help provide translation services and asks those who are adept with computer networks to join hackers' brigades or technical security teams.

Finally, for those who are not able to give such a commitment to the movement, he recommends a number of alternatives, including simply posting messages on the Jihadist forums to ensure that there is a continuously vibrant discussion. He also recommends that Jihobbyists should post messages in support of the movement on non-Jihadist and non-Islamic discussion websites, particularly in music, youth and sports forums, in order to broaden the dialogue and reach new potential recruits. Jihobbyists should write letters to editors, call in to news programs and "try to mention that you are defending the State of Islam after becoming on air, not before that." Diyar supports mass email campaigns to radio and television talkshows posing questions or making comments. And perhaps most importantly, he argues, as many people as possible should download the various publicity releases of the movement and share them with family and friends. They should burn videos to DVD and place them in their friends' backpacks, shopping carts or mailboxes.

Diyar is but one of numerous Jihadist propagandists who are trying to transform Jihobbyists from consumers of this material into producers of it.

6   Al-Qaida in Saudi Arabia

Oh you who offer prayer in the sacred mosque!

Had you witnessed us in the battlefield
You would know that, compared to our Jihaad,
Your worship is child's play.
For every tear you have shed upon your cheek,
We have shed in its place blood upon our chests.
You are playing with your worship,
While worshipers offer your worship
Mujahideen offer their blood and person.

Abumar, Jihadist internet forum participant

Between 2002 and 2005, al-Qaida in Saudi Arabia appeared unstoppable: armed sieges, kidnappings, coordinated truck bombings, targeted assassinations, speeding getaways in stolen vehicles. It set a new standard for applying the global Jihadist ideology, and it did so under the direct mandate of al-Qaida's High Command.

Al-Qaida's network within Saudi Arabia is still not well understood. Its operational structure in its period of greatest activity was cellular and highly fluid. Cells seemed to emerge quickly, morph under pressure, vanish and then reappear weeks or even months later, seemingly just as capable. Furthermore, in spite of this disaggregated network structure, the commander of al-Qaida in Saudi Arabia (whoever that may have been—there were at least six during this time) still managed to exert a high degree of hierarchical command over the network, particularly in regards to the strategic direction the group took and the operations it conducted while on that trajectory.

As spectacular as al-Qaida's operations in the peninsula were, however, their propaganda was even better. The group published extensive video documentaries of its training and attacks. It released a regular series of superbly illustrated magazines on strategy and ideology. And it even had a dedicated magazine designed to educate followers about the finer points of terrorist tradecraft.

Both inside and outside of the global Jihadist movement there were those who criticized al-Qaida for its decision to wage a bloody terrorist campaign inside the kingdom. Indeed, its attacks against Saudi targets caused a great deal of confusion inside the movement. Why was al-Qaida striking targets inside the Muslim world when that strategy had consistently failed in Egypt, Syria and Algeria, and when attacking the West had been so popular? Al-Qaida's Saudi arm responded that it was not attacking Muslims explicitly. It operated in the kingdom in order to drive out the Americans, Westerners and other non-Muslims who were in residence there. It claimed the idea was to create a hostile environment in which it could purge the kingdom of Western cultural influence and weaken the government's position domestically. But in reality, al-Qaida's Saudi leadership had few limits, few rules, and only spoke the language of violence.

Al-Qaida's campaign in the Arabian Peninsula served to provoke a massive state-led counter-terrorism campaign against it. Perhaps the final nail in al-Qaida's coffin, as will become clear by the end of this chapter, was that its actions had the opposite effect to what had been predicted: they convinced the Saudi intelligence and law enforcement agencies that they needed to cooperate even closer with their American counterparts. From 2003 onwards, the Saudi security services kept constant pressure on the organization, systematically killing and capturing its senior leaders, foot soldiers and religious backers. They launched what seemed like weekly raids on al-Qaida safe-houses and satellite channels and provided up-to-the-minute coverage of dramatic shootouts with al-Qaida operatives. But the attacks continued, in large part because Saudi al-Qaida had dug itself in deep. Under Ayiri's command it had always been prepared for a protracted and bloody war against the Saudi regime.

Roots of Saudi Jihadism

Jihadists generally avoided attacking targets in Saudi Arabia during the 1970s and 1980s. There were several reasons for this. First, the Saudi government's vicious reprisals against Juhayman al-Utaybi and his followers after they stormed the Grand Mosque in Mecca in 1979 made it clear that such behavior would not be tolerated. Second, Jihadists spent most of their time, energy and resources during the 1980s in Afghanistan, waging war against the Soviets. Radical Islamists in the kingdom were united in their campaign to defend Islam against an invading foreign power, not against regimes at home. Finally, the Saudi government effectively managed to quash nascent revolutionary movements by using its powerful religious establishment and massive oil revenues in ways that helped to silence oppositionist groups.

By 1990, however, the situation had started to change. As the Afghan War wound down and flocks of young Saudi men began to migrate home, the enthusiasm for spreading Jihadism that the kingdom had recently spent millions fomenting was beginning to look like a major domestic security threat. Things deteriorated further for the Saudi government in 1991 with the arrival of thousands of American soldiers in the kingdom. Hardline Salafists viewed the act of allowing foreign troops, Americans no less, on holy soil as nothing short of apostasy. This, when combined with the vibrant Jihadist scholarship emerging in the kingdom's university communities, led to a revival of militant Salafism.

The Saudi government acted swiftly, launching an aggressive campaign to silence Usama Bin Laden and the clerics who supported him: first they stripped him of his passport, and by 1994 they had frozen his financial assets and revoked his citizenship. Bin Laden was no longer welcome in the kingdom, and the al-Saud royal family also had little patience for the public protests and sit-ins organized by the followers of several influential Jihadist shaikhs in the mid-1990s. Widespread arrests, aggressive prosecutions and rigorous interrogation methods ensued. Through these methods the government was able to keep Jihadist-inspired activism relatively in check until several hundred Saudi youth, who had joined Bin Laden and the Taliban in Afghanistan in the late 1990s, began trickling home. Some of these returning Saudi militants came bearing direct orders from the High Command to open a new front in the global war against Jews, Crusaders and apostates. That front would be in Saudi Arabia itself. There would be no front lines: everything and everyone would be a potential target.

As early as May 2002, the Sudanese national Abu Huzifa, aided by a support network of Saudi operatives, reportedly tried to shoot down a US jet fighter taking off from the Prince Sultan Air Base with a Russian-made SA-7 surface-to-air missile. The attempt failed, and in fact drew no attention until Saudi security forces stumbled across the missile tube and other components inside a security fence at the base. The subsequent arrest of Abu Huzifa, 11 Saudis and an Iraqi led to the recovery of another surface-to-air missile system hidden in the desert near Riyadh. According to the Saudi Press Agency, the detainees were planning to carry out terrorist attacks against important installations throughout the kingdom using both explosives and the missiles.

The next month, on the morning of June 20, a 35-year-old British bank employee, Simon Veness, stepped into his Land Rover Discovery and started his commute to work. Several seconds later, the car exploded: a bomb had been stashed underneath it. Intelligence officials said that Veness was targeted by anti-Western extremists. The event was linked to the same group who several weeks earlier had fired five rounds at an Australian employee of BAE Systems as he left his compound in Tabuk.[1]

In the aftermath of these attacks against Western targets, the Saudi government acknowledged that it had detained more than one hundred people and questioned over seven hundred.[2] Most of the detainees were Saudi citizens who had recently returned from Afghanistan. Nevertheless, Jihadists continued their campaign against foreign businessmen.[3] Another BAE Systems employee, this one in Khamis Mushayt, was targeted unsuccessfully. One week later, Robert Dent, a commercial officer at BAE, was shot dead at close range by a Saudi gunman as Dent was waiting at a traffic light on his way home from a shopping trip in eastern Riyadh. His assassin, Saùd ibn Ali ibn Nasser, a 30-year-old Yemeni-born naturalized Saudi, had just returned from a trip to Pakistan, had named his newborn son Usama, and had suspected ties to al-Qaida.[4]

Al-Qaida's goals in Saudi Arabia came into clearer relief on March 18, 2003, when 29-year-old Fahd Simran al-Saidi inadvertently killed himself in an explosion in the al-Jazirah neighborhood, east of the capital, where he was putting the final touches to a bomb. Saudi security forces found explosives, ammunition, 12 machine-guns, two rifles and three bombs in his home.[5] Al-Qaida memorialized him and other operatives killed in action in a 38-minute video entitled *The Martyrs of the Confrontations in Bilad al-Haramayn*. Fahd al-Saidi, the narrator, says, "had a tender heart. He performed worship and fasted a lot. He was known for his gentle attitude toward the believers and tough attitude toward the unbelievers. He acquired extensive experience in manufacturing weapons and explosives. He then won martyrdom."

Saudi security forces were under pressure to locate the cell for which Fahd al-Saidi was building explosives before it went operational. Following leads found in the debris of his home, they identified an apartment in the Ishbiliyah neighborhood of Riyadh. On May 6, they raided it, finding forged identity cards and passports, a variety of weapons and over three hundred pounds of explosives. As a result of this raid, the Saudi Interior Ministry had enough evidence to announce a list of the 19 most wanted terrorists in the kingdom. This included the names of men who would go on to become legends in al-Qaida's history: Yousef al-Ayiri, Turki al-Dandani, Khalid Ali al-Hajj, and Abd-al-Aziz al-Muqrin.

Establishing a new front

Yousef Saleh al-Ayiri stood out as one of the most qualified Jihadists in the kingdom at the time. His background fighting in Afghanistan, Somalia, Bosnia and Kosovo, allied to his personal relationship with Usama Bin Laden, Abu Hafs al-Masri and other senior al-Qaida commanders, gave him invaluable insights into how to open a new front of the global campaign on the peninsula. Ayiri did not single-handedly build al-Qaida's Saudi network, however. He relied heavily on a number of senior deputies, perhaps none more important than Turki bin Nasir bin Mish'al al-Dandani (also known as Hamzah and as Abu Idah). Together, Ayiri, Dandani and a core group of well-trained and highly motivated Afghan veterans would rapidly boost al-Qaida's presence in Saudi Arabia.

Dandani grew up in the town of Skaka in the northern al-Jawf Province, a hotbed of Islamic radicalism. He was a bright student and had a number of childhood friends. However, while still at school he was convicted of possessing weapons and imprisoned. In early 2001, he travelled to Afghanistan and entered the al-Faruq training camp, an al-Qaida-sponsored facility, where he completed advanced courses in military training. He would later fight against Coalition forces in the treacherous mountain terrain of the country. Using forged identity papers, by 2003 he had made his way back to the Arabian Peninsula, where he and Ayiri would begin to forge a vast underground network of al-Qaida training camps, recruiting posts and propaganda centers.[6] They began actively recruiting university students and national guardsmen. They talked with their friends and exploited their kinship networks. And they began establishing weapons caches around Saudi Arabia in a network of safe-houses.

Ayiri's burgeoning paramilitary force trained both outdoors, in the desert, and in urban indoor facilities. Video footage demonstrates that these facilities were strikingly similar to the Afghan training camps that many of the group's senior leaders had attended. It also shows how they trained with rocket-propelled grenades, anti-tank missiles, cellphone-activated explosive devices, and a large cache of mobile surface-to-air missile launchers.[7] The stage was set.

May 12, 2003

The push was now on from al-Qaida's High Command to throw down the gauntlet and strike a major blow against the Saudi regime. Ayiri resisted, arguing that his group was not yet ready to launch a campaign. Al-Qaida's number two, Ayman al-Zawahiri, kept pushing, however, arguing that it was the only way to start the process of driving the American military and corporations out of the peninsula. Ayiri, the dutiful soldier, conceded, launching al-Qaida in Saudi Arabia on a trajectory that would eventually end in carnage and his own death.[8]

On May 6, 2003, 10-year-old Rayan Fahd was playing outside his house near the Jadawil housing compound in Riyadh when a group of about ten men in three cars pulled up beside him and asked for directions to a house that a bearded man had rented a couple of weeks earlier. Rayan pointed out the house, two doors down from his own. His mother, Munira Fahd, was returning home from a doctor's appointment several minutes later and watched as the men loaded black suitcases from the house into their cars. But she was not the only one watching the group. Saudi security forces had a surveillance team monitoring the safe-house, which the group quickly realized as they loaded their cars. They rapidly packed the rest of their mysterious suitcases and sped off, shooting out of their cars' back windows at the surveillance team as they went.

At 11:15 p.m. six days after the suspicious safe-house visit, the al-Hamra, Jadawil and Vinnell housing compounds all bustled with the usual family activity. The desert sun had gone down and people were out enjoying the cool evening: families were grilling, children were playing. No one could know that just outside the compounds' seemingly impenetrable 20-foot walls at least two vehicles sat parked, loaded with explosives, waiting for the guards to raise the barrier.

As a resident of the compound pulled his car up to the al-Hamra gate and the guards lifted the heavy iron security barrier, a team of al-Qaida operatives drove their vehicle through, launching a hail of machine-gunfire out of the windows. They proceeded directly to the compound's recreation center, which housed a gym, swimming pools, a restaurant and a disco, and turned their car into a ball of flames and shrapnel. Another team of operatives strolled through the compound, shooting at residents outside. Explosions and gunfire could also be heard at the Vinnell and Jadawil compounds. At Vinnell, gunmen killed the guards before they could lower the security barrier. Within a minute, the al-Qaida cell had driven their vehicle up to the housing complex and detonated their bomb.

As al-Qaida later explained, the May 12 attacks were part of a broader strategy to "widen the battlefield. The entire world has become a battlefield in practice and not in theory. They cannot ensure that another operation will not take place in a country where an operation had taken place against the Americans before." On June 7, Riyadh's Kingdom of Saudi Arabia TV1 showed pictures of the attackers and listed the following names:

- Khalid Muhammad Bin-Musallam al-Urawi al-Juhani
- Muhammad Uthman Abdallah al-Walidi al-Shihri
- Hani Said Ahmad Al Abd-al-Karim al-Ghamidi
- Jubran Ali Ahmad Hakami Khabarani
- Khalid Bin-Ibrahim Mahmud Baghdadi
- Mihmas Bin-Muhammad Mihmas al-Hawashilah al-Dawsari
- Muhammad Bin-Jazzaf Ali Al Mahzum al-Shihri
- Hazim Muhammad Said Kashmiri
- Majid Abdallah Sad Bin-Ukayl
- Bandar Bin-Abd-al-Rahman Minwir al-Ruhaymi al-Mutayri
- Abd-al-Karim Muhammad Jubran Yaziji
- Abdallah Faris Bin-Jafin al-Ruhaymi al-Mutayri.

The cell was said to have been led by Juhani, a Saudi who had left Afghanistan after the US invasion for Yemen before returning to the kingdom, and Turki al-Dandani. Juhani's videotaped will had been found the year before, along with wills from four other al-Qaida operatives, in the rubble of the house used by the organization's primary operational lieutenant, Muhammad Atef, in Afghanistan.[9]

Al-Qaida in the Arabian Peninsula claimed official responsibility for the attacks, and even went so far as to publish a scholarly assessment of them through Ayiri's Center for Islamic Research and Studies, which released a 76-page study entitled *The 11 Rabi al-Awwal Conquest: The East of Riyadh Operation and Our War with the United States and Its Agents* about the attacks. Key insights from the book included information that the operatives involved had previously taken part in the Tora Bora battles in Afghanistan, and that those who had not been killed had fled to Iraq, where they were involved in new operations.

The legitimacy of the highly controversial attack was significantly bolstered shortly thereafter when three of the most highly regarded Jihadist clerics in the kingdom, Ali Bin Khudair al-Khudair, Nasir al-Fahd and Ahmad Bin Hammud al-Khalidi, released a public statement in support of al-Qaida's actions. These clerics—known as the "*Takfiri* Troika" because of their support for the Jihadist concept of *Takfir*, or declaring other Muslims apostates—wielded massive influence both inside and beyond Saudi's borders. In their statement, they claimed that the operatives "are excellent *mujahidin* in the Way of God, God-fearing, righteous men. Thus we deem them, and we vindicate no one against God. They are men who have given of themselves, their property, and their blood for God the Exalted." The clerics also clarified the hostile religious environment in which these soldiers of Islam's vanguard were forced to operate, arguing that:

> They engaged in the Jihad against the malevolent Crusaders in Afghanistan and scored noteworthy deeds of bravery and heroism in the battles of the Tora Bora Mountains . . . The sad fact is that when they returned from the land of Jihad, the world shut its heart to them. They were greeted with frowns. Prison camps were opened for them. They were subjected to terrible torture. They

were killed, imprisoned, made fugitives, or persecuted. Jihad became a crime; the *mujahid* became a terrorist.

This announcement was so significant because three highly regarded conservative clerics declared it religiously "forbidden" for any Muslim in Saudi Arabia to "abandon these *mujahidin*, take a stand against them, mar their reputation, give aid against them, report them, publish their pictures, or pursue them." Doing any of these things, the clerics explained, provided the Americans with aid. People were supposed to adhere to this religious edict and to "distribute this statement in all gathering places, to print it, duplicate it, and publish it in homes, mosques, markets, and everywhere in order to come to the aid of the victims of injustice and uphold their rights."[10]

Saudi security forces responded by arresting the three clerics on May 27 and nearly six hundred others in a nationwide crackdown. Of those, Prince Turki al-Faisal told reporters, "around 190 have already been released, between 70 and 90 are being sent to trial, and between 250 and 300 are still being interrogated." Most of those detained at this time were between 15 and 25 years old.[11]

Post-Ayiri al-Qaida

On May 31, 2003, the Saudi Ministry of the Interior announced that at 9:50 p.m. the previous day, about five miles northeast of the city of Turaba, security officers saw a suspicious Toyota jeep stopped at the side of the road. When the officers asked the driver for his identity card, he and his passenger fled. The officers were following along the desert road when a hand-grenade flew from the car, killing Private Dardah Bin-Waqqa al-Shammari and Private Saùd Bin-Abdallah al-Shammari. Two other security officers, Private Farhan Bin-Humud al-Shammari and Private Abdallah Bin Mishal al-Shammari, were wounded. After continuing chase, the security forces were able to stop the vehicle at a roadblock. They killed Ayiri in the subsequent shootout and captured his accomplice, Abdallah Bin-Ibrahim Bin-Abdallah al-Shabrami. Saudi security agents reportedly found a letter written and signed by Bin Laden dated "04/10/1423 hegira" (December 9, 2002) on the body of Ayiri. It was among the evidence examined by forensics and police departments when inspecting the body.[12]

At the time, few understood the significance of Ayiri's death because his role in the movement was hazy. However, we now know that Ayiri was the godfather of contemporary global Jihadist action in Saudi Arabia. His death therefore dealt a huge blow to the movement, but it did not paralyze al-Qaida. Command in the peninsula passed to Khalid Ali al-Hajj, a Yemeni national although he was born in Jedda, Saudi Arabia. He had previously been deported from Saudi Arabia to Yemen and went on to fight in Afghanistan, where he became a bodyguard for Usama Bin Laden, a key stepping-stone for many ambitious al-Qaida operatives, and continued moving up the ranks before returning to the kingdom.

June 14, 2003

Ahmad al-Dakhil was the leader of al-Qaida's *Sharia* committee in the Mecca cell based in the al-Khalidiyah neighborhood. Abdallah al-Trawi, a Malian national, served as Dakhil's deputy and handled logistics, personnel and security issues. One such task was obtaining an apartment where some of the wanted al-Qaida operatives could stay. Trawi met with the landlord of a flat in al-Khalidiyah and explained that he was a newly-wed with no children. He then moved furniture into the apartment and began living there. Neighbors noticed that he and a woman (actually another al-Qaida operative dressed as a woman) came and went from the apartment, but they did not see anything suspicious, aside from the fact that the windows were permanently covered. The rest of the cell—Saudis, Egyptians, Chadians and others —were spread among several other apartments in the area. On any given day they debated the finer points of their ideology among one another, discussed attack plans and prepared weapons. Trawi had the idea of attacking the security checkpoint at al-Ruways prison, which the other members felt was ambitious.

On June 14, 2003, Saudi police surrounded the al-Attas building in al-Khalidiyah, where they believed the al-Qaida cell was hiding. "The place is besieged. Surrender yourself. Do not try to resist," they blared over the loudspeaker. Trawi frantically had all the men empty their wallets and identification into a bag. Then each of them was handed a weapon. For many of them it was their first sight of such equipment in the whole time they had been living there. As the security forces moved to storm the building, Trawi began firing. In the mêlée, more than 30 young men began scurrying around the apartment. Some sprinted down the hall and out of the backdoor into the courtyard. After the violence subsided, police had arrested 12 men and killed five others. One of the most prominent al-Qaida figures there was Dakhil, a prominent Jihadist cleric actively involved in supporting al-Qaida's operations in the peninsula, but he managed to escape after being wounded. He fled to the al-Qasim region in the middle of the country.

Police reported that they found a number of items in the apartment: 72 home-made pipe bombs; explosive-laden, booby-trapped copies of the Quran; 12 machine-guns and 50 magazines; 6 handguns with a large quantity of live ammunition; 11 bottles of battery acid; 40 butcher's knives; and several hand-held walkie-talkies.[13]

A surprising surrender

The Saudi authorities made another breakthrough on June 27 when the embattled Salafist cleric Safar al-Hawali, once a hero to Jihadists like Bin Laden but now seen by most as a sell-out, announced that a senior al-Qaida commander, Abu Bakr al-Azdi, had asked Hawali to help him surrender to Prince Muhammad Bin Nayif in person. The only stipulation that Azdi put on his surrender was that the Saudi government must release his wife, who had been detained in an effort to bait him. The prince readily agreed to this demand.[14]

Azdi was seized along with 709,782 riyals, two pistols, 34 rounds of ammunition, three magazines, and seven boxes containing jewelry and fake documents.

Hawali described the welcome given to Azdi by Prince Bin Nayif as "considerate and expressive. He embraced him." Hawali also stressed the need to refrain from calling suspects "terrorists" until they are convicted, saying: "One has to take into consideration the fact that they are suspects and that there is only one quarter that is entitled to make accusations." He accompanied Azdi in his private car as he drove to his first meeting with the Assistant Interior Minister.

Azdi's deputy, Sultan Jubran Sultan al-Qahtani, also known as Zubayr al-Rimi, was left to coordinate the cell's operations. He had earned a degree in physical education from the Teachers' College in Abha and then fought against the American-led Coalition in Afghanistan before returning to Saudi Arabia to join al-Qaida.[15] While he was well regarded among the network, his leadership did not last long.

July 2003

The Saudi authorities enjoyed more successes in 2003. At five in the morning on July 3, in the town of Zuhair, 560 miles north of Riyadh, security forces surrounded the home of Musaad Hamdam Faleh al-Ruwaily, the imam of a mosque, and ordered him and his house-guests to surrender. The imam and another suspect, Hassan Hadi al-Dossari, gave themselves up. Turki al-Dandani and others remained inside, prepared to die fighting. In a flurry of gunfire and exchange of hand-grenades, Dandani, Rajeh al-Ajami, Abd al-Rahman al-Jabarah, and Amaash al-Subaie were killed either by gunfire or by suicide detonations of grenades. Mohammed al-Suqabi, Nassir al-Ruwaily and Mahmoud Hazbar were caught trying to escape. The Saudi government hailed this as a major victory against al-Qaida and it provided new leads on the organization's Saudi-based network.

As a result of interrogations of the survivors, the security forces gained more information that enabled them to launch a counter-offensive later in July. Over the course of the next weeks, police arrested 16 members of a number of terrorist cells after searching their hide-outs in farms and homes in Riyadh, Qasim and the Eastern Province. They also recovered 20 tons of chemicals that could be used to make explosives; 72 kilograms of the explosive RDX; 981 meters of explosive match cord; 524 electric sparks; a number of machine-guns; 18 rocket-propelled grenades with five launchers; night-vision binoculars; communication devices; donation collection boxes; 300,000 riyals; and motorbikes and cars prepared to carry out terrorist operations.

On July 27, Dakhil was finally killed in a clash with security forces. Police had received information that a group of wanted men were hiding in a farm in the al-Mulayda of the al-Qasim region. Over one hundred officers from multiple security agencies encircled the farm and closed all the roads leading to it. As the officers began their search of the premises, machine-gunfire rained down on them and hand-grenades were lobbed in their direction. In the ensuing clash, five other al-Qaida operatives were killed alongside Dakhil. The al-Mulayda cell was an extension of the cell that had earlier been uncovered in al-Khalidiyah in Mecca. With the death of Dakhil, the Saudi security agencies had already made major progress toward killing or capturing all of the 19 men who had featured on their most-wanted list.

September 2003

At 3:00 a.m. on September 23, the Saudi security forces continued their assault on al-Qaida by raiding a farm that a cell was renting. It was located just behind the King Fahd Hospital's doctors' residence compound in Jizan. When the cell spotted the police, they fled, entering the hospital compound, where they were renting another apartment. Believing that the cell was planning to carry out a major operation against the non-Muslim residents at the hospital that day, Saudi Arabia's National Day, police were prepared to take whatever steps were necessary to stop them. They surrounded the three-story apartment building and began an 18-hour standoff with the suspects, who were armed with automatic rifles and hand-grenades. The cell had also taken several foreign doctors and nurses as hostages on to the roof of the hospital. Police eventually fired tear gas into the apartment and stormed the building, killing Sultan al-Qahtani and Turki ibn Saeed al-Thaqfan al-Bishri, the al-Qaida operative who had helped facilitate travel for Qahtani to Jizan.

Two days later, the Jizan police, in cooperation with the al-Darb police, raided a building near Abu Yahya village in al-Qiyas. According to the authorities, the building had been rented by a number of al-Qaida operatives, including Qahtani. The police found weapons, live ammunition, and two bags containing a highly explosive substance. Security forces also raided several houses in the Marbah area in Asir Province, which had also been rented by Qahtani. There too they found stockpiles of weapons, ammunition and explosives.[16]

However, in spite of these successes, al-Qaida persisted.

The al-Muhayya attack

The al-Muhayya complex—a collection of about two hundred homes not far from the main palaces of the Saudi royal family—houses mainly Arab foreigners working in the kingdom. At midnight on November 8, 2003, in the middle of the holy month of Ramadan, a white Toyota Maxima pulled up in front of the complex. Its occupants began tossing out hand-grenades and opened intensive gunfire on the guards at the gates. After subduing the guards, a Toyota jeep carrying over one hundred pounds of explosives entered the compound and burst into flames, killing 17 and wounding at least a hundred others.[17] In the jeep were al-Qaida operatives Nasir al-Yasari and Ali Bin-Hamid al-Ma'badi al-Harbi. Both had joined al-Qaida's Saudi operation after returning from Afghanistan, where they had fought alongside the Taliban against the Coalition forces. At least 13 of those killed were Arabs. Five were children.

Al-Qaida subsequently released a video detailing the training courses that the operatives had taken in preparation for the attack, including bomb-making. It also responded to criticism that they were desecrating Islam and their country: "If we wanted to destroy the country, then attacking institutions beneficial to the people is much easier than killing a single American," said Harbi in the video. The film also showed the operatives spray-painting the jeep dark blue with light blue stripes in order to resemble a Saudi security vehicle.[18]

In the aftermath, the authorities located a safe-house in the al-Dar al-Bayda neighborhood, where the operatives had used commercial automotive spraying equipment in order to disguise their vehicle.[19] After a shootout several weeks later in the northeast of Riyadh, the security services seized a car loaded with explosives that was being prepared for a similar attack. This time it was painted to resemble the vehicles used by the guards at most residential compounds. Several al-Qaida operatives escaped.

Turning the screw

It should be clear by now that clerics stand at the center of the Jihadist ideology. They illuminate the path on which the operational commanders tread. And they help to embolden foot soldiers who are prepared to die in the name of their ideology. When Jihadist ideologues speak, their followers listen. So when that power is turned against the movement, it can strike a deep blow to its membership. The Saudi government utilized the capture of three prominent Jihadist clerics to strike just such a blow in late 2003.

The arrest and imprisonment of the "*Takfiri* Troika" in May 2003, as we have seen, was a massive blow to al-Qaida in the Arabian Peninsula. But it was to get much worse for the movement six months later, when Saudi television's Channel One viewers heard the unthinkable: Shaikh Khudair distancing himself from his previous *fatwa* concerning *Takfir* and the shooting of Saudi security forces, characterizing them as "misguided" actions "that did not take into consideration reality and recent developments." He continued, "We never imagined that we would reach a situation that resembles what happened in Algeria. This bloodletting must be stopped." Khudair condemned the al-Muhayya compound bombings and explained that he was now actively re-educating young men who had adopted extremist *Takfiri* thinking.[20]

Khudair was joined in recanting previous *fatwa* by his colleague Ahmad al-Khalidi, who described his prior support of the Jihadist movement as "a grave mistake," in his interview on network television. Khalidi said that he was shocked by the suicide bombings being waged by al-Qaida in Saudi Arabia, calling them "sinful acts."

The bombers, he clarified, ought not to be thought of as martyrs because they had violated Islam by killing both Muslims and non-Muslims who were under the protection of the state, murdering women and children, harming security and property, distorting the images of Jihad and Islam. "Blowing oneself up in such operations is not martyrdom, it is suicide. How can they kill Muslims, innocent people, and destroy property in the home of Islam?" His interview was conducted by another Salafist cleric popular with the Saudi royal family, Dr. Ayed al-Qarni.[21]

Beyond leveraging al-Qaida's own clerics to condemn them, the Saudi government brought out six families of the remaining 19 wanted suspects—Salih

Muhammad al-Alawi al-Awfi, Abd-al-Aziz Bin-Isa Abd-al-Muhsin al-Muqrin, Rakan Muhsin Muhammad al-Saykhan, Hamad Fahd Abdallah al-Aslami, Faysal Abd-al-Rahman al-Dakhil, and Khalid al-Hajj—and had them publicly appeal to their relatives to turn themselves in to the authorities. In a telephone interview with the media outlet, al-Riyadh, for example, the mother of Muqrin said that she wished her son would give himself up immediately. If he were to come home, she said, she would hand him over to the authorities.

An al-Qaida resurgence

On December 6, 2003, the Saudi Interior Ministry announced a revised wanted list, this time featuring 26 men. Alongside the six from the original list were some names that would become more well known as the senior leaders were killed off: Karim al-Tihami al-Majati, Isa al-Awshan, Faris al-Zahrani, and Saùd al-Qutayni al-Utaybi. Just two days later, the police had a chance to start chipping away at the list when they received a tip-off about Ibrahim ibn Muhammad ibn Abdullah al-Rayyis's hide-out. They caught up with him at a gas station in southern Riyadh and killed him in a shootout. For his tip-off, the informer earned a reward of one million riyals. Police also killed another al-Qaida operative that day in a different clash, this time in Riyadh's southwestern al-Suwaydi neighborhood.

On January 29, 2004, the authorities received a tip-off that Khalid al-Juwaysir al-Farraj, an al-Qaida operative in his thirties, was living in the al-Fayha neighborhood in the al-Nasim area, east of Riyadh. Accordingly, a team went there to follow-up the lead, accompanied by the man's father. The team found two hand-grenades, two machine-guns, and five other guns at the residence. Suddenly, the agents came under heavy fire and Farraj's father was killed. The security forces did manage to arrest the younger Farraj in the course of the shootout, however. That same night, they raided a rest-stop in the same neighborhood and found a white pick-up truck loaded with weapons and computers.

New commanders, new strategies

Khalid al-Hajj's operating strategy at this time was to hit a major target and then lie low, observing the public reaction and engaging in carefully planned media relations. For him, targets had to be frequented or operated by foreigners, particularly Westerners. The al-Muhayya attack was a classic example of Hajj's approach.

At five in the evening on March 15, 2004, Hajj and his passenger, Ibrahim ibn Abd al-Aziz ibn Muhammad al-Muzayni, were spotted driving in a jeep in Riyadh. Saudi security forces pulled up behind them and ordered them to stop. Instead, the two men began shooting. The security men fired back, killing them both. In their search of the vehicle, they found hand-grenades, Kalashnikov rifles and ammunition, three revolvers, and 516,000 riyals.[22] With Hajj's death, command of al-Qaida in the Arabian Pensinsula shifted to Abd-al-Aziz al-Muqrin. For Muqrin, al-Qaida's strategy in the kingdom needed to be bolder, less discriminating. He therefore adopted a new policy of attacking Western individuals and targets without reservation. It would be a no-holds-barred war against the disbelievers, and it would be waged in the holiest of holy lands.

The renewed battle between the Saudi security forces and al-Qaida expanded several weeks later, on April 6, when the police tried to pull over another car in the Riyadh suburb of Rawdah. The driver, Abd al-Rahman ibn Nayif al-Sahli al-Harbi, refused to stop and his passenger began to open fire. The police killed Harbi but his passenger, Abdullah ibn Ghalib al-Sahli al-Harbi, managed to escape to a nearby house. However, after a seven-hour siege, the wounded man was arrested.

On April 12, a dramatic series of events unfolded. Saudi security forces engaged with an al-Qaida cell on a highway in Riyadh's eastern suburbs. During the course of the ensuing shootout, the al-Qaida operatives launched a rocket-propelled grenade at the police, killing one officer and wounding five others. Three of the operatives escaped by car, but early the next morning they were stopped at a checkpoint near Unayzah. Again, the al-Qaida cell opened fire, killing another four policemen. They then carjacked several of the police cars, drove to a nearby town and went into hiding. Two days later, several Saudi neighborhood patrol guards stumbled upon them, but they were shot and killed by the al-Qaida operatives. At the same time, Saudi police found three primed car bombs around Riyadh.

By this point, the United States government had seen enough and ordered all non-essential diplomats and all diplomatic families out of the kingdom. It also warned all other Americans that they should leave the country. Al-Qaida clearly was not prepared to give up without a fight.

April 21, 2004

In the mid-afternoon of April 21, 2004, Abdul Aziz bin Ali bin Abdul Aziz al-Mudaihesh drove a white GMC truck packed with more than 2,400 pounds of explosives into the five-story General Traffic Department in the al-Washm neighborhood of Riyadh, killing 6 and injuring 148. "The driver exploded the car 30 yards from the headquarters' gate," said an official from the Interior Ministry. A second car parked nearby exploded simultaneously, ripping off the entire façade of the building and littering the area with burned-out cars and concrete debris. The injured included the general director of the Traffic Department.[23] Muqrin's strategy was clear: hit them where it hurts.

Following up a lead, the security forces surrounded an apartment in the al-Safa neighborhood of Jedda the next day.[24] They immediately sealed off the area, asked citizens to evacuate, and ordered the al-Qaida cell that they believed to be hiding to surrender. Instead, the cell began shooting. The police returned fire, killing three of the cell members. While this was going on, though, two unidentified men came to the neighborhood and also began shooting at the security forces. After coming under heavy police fire, the newcomers carjacked a nearby vehicle and sped away. Some of the security forces chased after them, following them to an isolated area in the south of Jedda. After another shootout, one of the men lay dead, killed by police fire. The other blew himself up with a grenade.

Al-Qaida released a videotape featuring the wills of two of the operatives in the aftermath of all this, attributing the action to a previously unheard-of group calling itself the al-Haramayn Brigades. This implied that the group was independent of, and perhaps even in competition with, al-Qaida in the kingdom. Presumably the intention was to confuse the security establishment. In the video, the operatives, Mudaihesh and Fahd Farraj Mohammed Aljuwair (a 35-year-old Saudi national who was placed on the most-wanted list in June 2005 and was killed on February 27, 2006), were shown speaking separately, sometimes reading from prepared statements, other times talking informally. In some scenes they were shown surrounded by a collection of automatic rifles, rocket-propelled grenades, anti-armor missiles and explosive belts. Farraj claimed that he was willing to die to defend *Tawhid*, or the oneness of God. The video also included an extract from a sermon given by the Palestinian shaikh based in the UK Abu Qatada, wherein he justifies attacks in which innocent people, including children, are killed. Finally, pre-attack preparations were shown, including loading the GMC truck with explosives.[25]

May 1, 2004

Yanbu al-Bahr, which translates as "Spring by the Sea," is a major Red Sea port in western Saudi Arabia. It is also a key petroleum shipping terminal and home to three oil refineries and several petrochemical plants. On May 1, 2004, two separate incidents occurred there. At 7:00 a.m., four gunmen disguised in the khaki uniforms of the Saudi National Guard went on a shooting rampage in the part of the port controlled by ABB Lummus Global, a Houston-based subsidiary of the giant Swedish–Swiss construction firm ABB. They drove into a residential area, near a McDonald's restaurant and a hotel, and began shooting indiscriminately. As police chased them, they carjacked several vehicles after detonating their original vehicle, which had been packed with explosives, killing at least 19 security officers. They also killed two Americans, two Britons and an Australian. The other incident saw a bomb exploded and an exchange of gunfire between security forces and a Jihadist cell, who were also shooting at foreign workers.[26]

Muqrin claimed credit for the attacks on behalf of al-Qaida one week later, calling them a model for all Saudi youth to follow. The cell leader, according to Muqrin, was Abu-Ammar Mustafa al-Ansari, whom Muqrin called one of the best young *mujahidin*. Ansari had fought in Afghanistan and Somalia before returning to the peninsula, where he had contacted al-Qaida and expressed the desire to "martyr" himself. For Muqrin,

> [this] war is an urban war rather than a traditional one, which makes it hard and tough. The enemy's interests are many and are located everywhere, but he is trying to hide and cover them. It is so obvious that the enemy is trying to blend in and be neighbors with Muslims, but we will be looking for him and eventually destroy him, God willing, without causing harm to any Muslim by our actions. Our being so cautious not to shed Muslim blood makes us delay and slow down some of our operations. Our war is similar, in so many ways,

to the Palestinian war against the Zionist enemy. We are all witnessing how our enemy, relying on his full control of land, spies, and agents, kills symbolic figures and leaders, may God's mercy be upon them . . . This standing up against the enemy is the basis for success at the stage of attrition during the stages of guerrilla warfare.[27]

The Yanbu attacks served to shake foreign government confidence in the Saudi security situation despite the tremendous efforts put in by the Saudi government to minimize the damage. While the authorities downplayed the attacks publicly, they likely knew that al-Qaida under Muqrin was starting to concentrate its attacks on sensitive areas.

Al-Khobar compound siege

On May 29, 2004, Fawaz Bin Muhammad al-Nashmi, the reported commander of al-Qaida's al-Quds Brigade, and his three-man team left their safe-house and headed to the massive al-Khobar housing and corporate complex. Nashmi was driving a Nissan Maxima, which was packed with explosives. His passenger was Nimr al-Buqmi. Another al-Qaida operative, identified only as Husayn, drove a second vehicle behind Nashmi. Completing the team was a man called Nadir in a third car.

Muqrin had previously designated Nashmi to lead the assault team. Under his direction, the group had conducted reconnaissance of the targets, memorized all roads in and out of the compound and assigned the operatives their final roles. As Nashmi's vehicle headed for the al-Khobar compound's main gate, the other vehicles went to a secondary gate. Nashmi stepped out of his car and ordered the guard to open the main gate, but he refused to comply. Seeking an easier way, he and Nimr joined the others at the secondary gate and they all entered the compound there.

Making their way to the Petroleum Center Company, a complex inside the compound housing offices belonging to Royal Dutch/Shell Group, Aramco (Saudi) and Lukoil (Russia), the team pulled up at another security gate and exited their vehicles. As they walked into the area, they came upon some young Saudi men in the uniforms of the Aramco Company, who asked the crew, clad in military fatigues, what was happening. The operatives explained that they were al-Qaida operatives, and paused to lecture the men about their apostasy for supporting American imperialism. They then made for the complex's stairs and split up to search the offices for targets. First, they found an American, whom they shot immediately in the head. Next, a South African employee was shot and killed by Husayn.

The group then headed to another part of the compound, which housed the offices of the Arab Petroleum Investments Corporation, or Apicorp. As they went through Apicorp's main gates, they met the corporation's finance manager, Michael Hamilton, a British national, whom they shot and tied to the back of one of their vehicles. After also killing the two gate guards and firing their weapons at nearby vehicles and buildings, they proceeded to their final target, the most heavily fortified of the complexes within Khobar.

The Oasis Resort is a luxury residential site with 200 villas, 48 apartments, a hotel, restaurants, spas, an open courtyard and even an ice rink. According to al-Qaida's account, the explosives-laden vehicle driven by Nashmi was originally going to be detonated outside the resort's gates. When the team successfully penetrated the gates, however, they changed their plan, transforming a fiery suicide bombing into what would become a prolonged massacre. After parking and exiting their vehicles, Nimr forced open one of the hotel building's doors and the rest of the team followed, finding a group of people inside. The al-Qaida team began asking them for their identity cards and religion. While they took the opportunity to explain their mission and goals to the group, Nimr beheaded a Swedish employee and put his head at the entrance. At that point, a 45-year-old Iraqi-American engineer ran up to the al-Qaida operatives. Thinking that they were security officers, he began telling them about hearing gunfire and explosions. The cell then demanded to see his residency card, which indicates both nationality and religion. The group was torn about whether to kill him: he was American but a Muslim. "We are here because we want to promote Islam. We don't want non-Muslims to come to our country. We are promoting a Muslim cause," the engineer was told by the group. After several minutes of rational debate, one operative announced, "We are not going to shoot you." Instead, they gave him a lecture about Islam and their cause and then asked him to point out the houses of his non-Muslim neighbors.[28]

For nearly an hour, the team went door to door, searching for and killing non-Muslims. Although Saudi special forces began surrounding the hotel, they did not enter. As the team continued, they found a group of Christian Filipinos, whom they killed in honor of their al-Qaida brethren in the Philippines. They also killed Hindu Indian engineers. Then they made their way to the hotel's restaurant on the first floor, where they ate briefly and rested. They continued to the second floor, where they found another group of Indian contractors and killed them, dragging them into the stairwell for any storming team to see as they entered the hotel.

Then they held a Quranic discussion for their Muslim hostages, on how to read the al-Fatiha, or first verse, correctly. At some point they contacted the al-Jazirah television channel, which carried out an interview but did not broadcast it. They told the interviewer that they were calling from inside the compound and that they were targeting only non-Muslim employees. Five hours into the siege, Nashmi went into one of the rooms in order to watch the news, which was explaining that a SWAT team was preparing to break into the building. Nashmi ordered the team into defensive positions and waited for the assault. At 2 p.m., the SWAT team moved in. The al-Qaida cell, stationed above the entrance, threw hand-grenades and killed the SWAT team leader and injured some of the other soldiers. Nimr began taunting the soldiers, "Come closer, cowards!"

The soldiers outside fired at the hotel throughout the afternoon. The cell members remained defensively positioned on the lower levels but by this stage they had moved their Muslim hostages to the upper levels. During the shooting, Husayn realized that one of the hostages was Italian. Nashmi called al-Jazirah again so the man could deliver a warning to his country to stop supporting the Americans in Iraq. Since the Italian did not speak English, the team had to wait for al-Jazirah to find an Italian translator. After the man had spoken for about a minute, and Nashmi had confirmed that his message had been successfully recorded, Nimr executed him.

In spite of its ruthlessness, by now the team was growing anxious. They conducted their evening and late evening prayers but then exited out of an opening next to a gutter on a back wall. By 10:30 p.m. they were all out of the hotel and hiding in the trees around the perimeter. There they rested and prepared their escape plan before emerging from the trees, taking a group of Saudi soldiers by surprise. With these soldiers dispatched, they made their way to a group of three jeeps and shot and killed all the occupants. Then, however, they were in the middle of a fire-fight. Through a hail of bullets, all but Nimr escaped down a back alley, stole a car and continued to the next cordon of armored patrol and troop vehicles. Throwing their home-made grenades and firing their Kalishnikovs, they made it through this checkpoint and through six more before finally reaching the highway. After about six miles of driving, they entered a residential neighborhood, saw a parked Saudi National Guard pick-up truck and stole it. As they continued on their way, Saudi patrol vehicles sped past them in the opposite direction, heading to the compound they had just left. In their day's activities they had killed a total of 22 people.[29]

Back at the compound, the injured Nimr was airlifted to the Ministry of Interior medical complex in Riyadh, where he was treated and placed under armed guard. On June 8, three al-Qaida operatives dressed as women in head-to-foot veils entered through the main entrance, where the bomb-proof security gates had been left open. Witnesses said that once inside the hospital the gunmen threatened foreign staff and shouted Nimr's name, saying that they were willing to die to free him. But they fled before locating their colleague.[30]

Assassinations

June 2004 offered more bad news for foreign business investment in Saudi Arabia as al-Qaida under Muqrin continued its intimidation campaign through kidnappings and targeted assassinations.

According to al-Qaida's writings on the matter, they had received information from a source about several men whom they believed would make good targets for kidnapping and execution operations. On June 8, an al-Qaida cell shot and killed an American, Robert C. Jacobs, who was working as a contractor with the Vinnell Corporation in his home in the eastern al-Khalij suburb of Riyadh. The group released a video of the execution four days later on Jihadist websites to much celebration. The 58-second film opened with a title screen stating: "Robert Jacob" in English. Subtitled in Arabic was: "Killing of the American Jew Robert Jacob— Officer in the Vinnell Espionage Company." The video cut to images of wounded Arab children before switching back to footage of at least two men cornering Jacobs, who can be heard pleading for them to stop. The al-Qaida operatives fired at least ten gunshots into him at point-blank range and then decapitated him in the parking lot.

Four days later, al-Qaida struck again, shooting another American engineer, Kenneth Scroggs, who was also with the Vinnell Corporation, as he parked his car in front of his residence in Riyadh.

Al-Qaida had also received information about a third man, Paul Marshall Johnson, who was an engineer supervising electronic systems for the US-made Apache helicopters. He had served in the American military and had been based in the Arabian Peninsula for more than ten years. On June 12, an al-Qaida cell put its plan in motion. Posing as Saudi police officers, they set up a fake checkpoint on al-Khidmah Road, a route that they had previously observed Johnson taking to and from work. The cell claimed it obtained its official Saudi police uniforms and vehicles from sympathetic supporters working within the Saudi security services. When Johnson pulled up to the checkpoint, the al-Qaida operatives stopped him, removed him from his vehicle, forcibly subdued him and abducted him. Before leaving the area, they threw a home-made Molotov cocktail into his Toyota Camry, setting it ablaze.

Under Muqrin and Dakhil's watch, al-Qaida then proceeded to hold Johnson captive. The Saudi government was in a state of panic: it ordered fifteen thousand security officers to search more than a thousand homes in Riyadh. On June 15, Muqrin released a video offering a prisoner exchange: Johnson for all the detained al-Qaida operatives in Saudi jails. The authorities were told they had 72 hours to consider the offer after which Johnson would be executed. Three days later, Muqrin and Dakhil beheaded Johnson and posted the video of the execution online.

Within hours of this, however, Saudi security forces were able to use electronic surveillance technology to pinpoint Muqrin's exact location in the al-Malaz neighborhood of Riyadh. They immediately set up an ambush at a local convenience store. When Muqrin, Dakhil and their associates pulled up that night to get some supplies, security men stormed the area.[31] In the ensuing shootout, police killed Muqrin, Dakhil, and Turki al-Mutayri. Three others escaped.

Muqrin's loss was another massive blow to the organization and represented the start of a downturn for the group. Trying to show strength in the midst of chaos, al-Qaida's *Sawt al-Jihad* online magazine announced on June 20 that a former Saudi police sergeant and Jihadist veteran of Afghanistan and Bosnia, Salih ibn Muhammad al-Awfi, had succeeded Muqrin as field commander. For al-Qaida insiders, this was a strange choice, given that Muqrin had tapped Saùd al-Qutayni al-Utaybi to be his replacement, and after him Badr Mansur al-Subay'i. Awfi had not been mentioned. Nevertheless, the 38-year-old Awfi had been with the campaign since the beginning, and had appeared on the original list of 19 most-wanted operatives. He grew up in the holy city of Medina, and after his secondary education joined the Saudi national security defence training school. He later became a prison guard, rising to the rank of sergeant in 1989. He was eventually dismissed for "unbecoming" conduct, and in 1995 went to fight in Chechnya, but he returned home after receiving a serious head injury. According to relatives, he then went to Afghanistan and met Usama Bin Laden. After the fall of the Taliban regime, he returned again to Saudi Arabia, where he is said to have been in charge of al-Qaida's recruitment, logistics and training, including secret camps in the kingdom. Married with children, he owned a car dealership in al-Madinah al-Munawarah.[32]

Several weeks after Muqrin's death, on July 27, al-Qaida suffered another significant loss as a result of a gun battle between security forces and a cell holed up in a Riyadh residence. The officers killed Isa al-Awshan, editor of the *Sawt al-Jihad* website, and Mujab Abu Ra's al-Dawsari. In the middle of the fire-fight, a second group of al-Qaida opratives had appeared in an attempt to divert the attention of the security forces and rescue their colleagues. After a short time, though, this second group had fled. Initially, Saudi security forces believed that they had killed Awfi, who was in the house with Awshan and Dawsari, but later they learned that, although he had been wounded, he had escaped. Authorities took his wife and three children, who were also in the house, into custody. Upon conducting a search of the house, security officers discovered the head of Paul Johnson in a freezer. They also found a weapons cache, including a surface-to-air missile, bombs, machine-guns, and more than 30,000 bullets.

More surrenders

On June 24, Saudi Arabia's King Fahd issued a statement offering a one-month amnesty that would cover anyone who had committed a crime in the name of religion. It promised fair treatment for anyone who surrendered. Whether it was the pressure of being hunted, their consciences getting the better of them or that offer of amnesty, a slow trickle of al-Qaida operatives began to surrender to the security forces. On June 27, the first major figure to give up was Uthman al-Maqbul al-Amri. His capture was a public relations coup for the Saudis as he was the first operative on the list of 26 most wanted to surrender. Like Abu Bakr al-Azdi, he surrendered to the Salafist cleric Safar al-Hawali. On July 13, Khalid bin Awdah bin Muhammad al-Harbi (also known as Abu Sulayman al-Makki) surrendered to Saudi diplomats in Tehran, Iran. Harbi had been disabled during the original Afghanistan Jihad against the Soviets and had been a confidant to Usama Bin Laden. Three days later, Ibrahim al-Sadiq al-Qaidi surrendered under the amnesty offer to Saudi diplomats in Damascus, Syria. He had been living in Syria after fighting in Afghanistan and Bosnia. On July 22, facing the impending expiration of the amnesty offer, Fawzan al-Fawzan surrendered at the Saudi Embassy in Damascus. Fayiz al-Khashman al-Dawsari turned himself in to authorities in the Saudi city of al-Ta'if. Safar al-Hawali then appealed to the authorities to extend the amnesty deadline as he was in the middle of negotiations with Salih al-Awfi himself, but Prince Abdullah refused.

A key capture

Still celebrating their recent successes, the Saudis had another reason to cheer when, on August 25, they captured the chief religious scholar of al-Qaida's Saudi operation, Faris al-Zahrani. The authorities managed to arrest him in a park in the town of Abha even though he was carrying at least one hand-grenade, which he had planned to detonate in a theater where a famous Arab singer was due to perform.

Zahrani was the imam in one of the mosques in Abha's university neighborhood. Prior to his capture, he had penned a variety of texts legitimizing the killing of Saudi security forces. He had also publicly rejected the Saudi government's amnesty offer and was the man behind a 460-page book praising Usama Bin Laden entitled *Usama Bin Laden: Renewer of the Age and Conqueror of the Americans* as well as another popular text, *An Enquiry into the Ruling of Death upon the Soldiers and Officers of the Security Forces*. His claims to scholarly legitimacy were built on shaky foundations, though: his registration at the Imam Muhammad Bin-Saùd University in al-Qusaym had been cancelled because of his non-attendance at classes.

Utaybi takes over

The situation remained quiet during September and October 2004 as al-Qaida regrouped. While it was known that Awfi had been wounded, his current status was unknown. Then, on November 2, al-Qaida announced that Saùd al-Utaybi, the man whom Muqrin had originally chosen as his successor, was the new leader of al-Qaida in the Arabian Peninsula. The 33-year-old Utaybi had featured on the list of 26 most wanted. In a public statement that he released shortly thereafter, he accused the Saudi government of jailing highly respected clerics and forcing them to condemn Jihad and to call upon Jihadist fighters to repent. He was determined to revitalize the deteriorating al-Qaida organization.

US Consulate attack

On December 6, 2004, an armed cell of al-Qaida operatives brazenly attacked the American Consulate on the Red Sea beachfront in Jidda. In the lead-up to the attack, the cell conducted detailed reconnaissance of the building, photographing it from the Sulayman al-Faqih Hospital across the street. They took notes of the staffing, shift changes and guard protocols. The consulate's close proximity to private residences, the hospital and a mosque meant that al-Qaida would inevitably kill Muslim civilians, something they had made a point not to do, if they used vehicle-based bombs. So, instead, the team crafted a plan to storm through a primary gate as an official car was entering. The cell practiced this storming procedure at one of their training facilities and then conducted a dry run on-site three days prior to the operation. Muntasir al-Ghadadi led four other men in the attack.

The attack began around 11:00 a.m. as an official consulate car pulled up to the main gate. A lone car then attempted to follow it into the compound's secure area, but the main barrier descended before it was able to do so. The passengers of the car exited their vehicle and began to engage the local Saudi security staff at the gate in a fire-fight. They then pressed forward into the secure part of the compound and rushed toward the car that had just pulled in, which contained one of the vice-consuls, Monica Lemieux, among other passengers. Several of these passengers were shot as they fled for cover.

The cell pushed further into the compound, firing all the time. They rounded up 15 people and pulled down the American flag, then called the police to inform them that they had taken hostages and wanted to negotiate with the Americans over Muslim women being detained in Abu-Ghuraib prison. There were no negotiations, however, as Saudi security forces instead surrounded the consulate with snipers. The details of what happened next are unclear, but after a three-hour siege and a shootout, five staff members lay injured, while three of the operatives had been killed and the other two injured and arrested.[33]

The al-Rass stand-off

Saudi security forces began the new year with several minor operations, including one on January 9 in which they surrounded an encampment in the Najdi Desert between al-Zilfi and Buraidah in al-Qasim Province. Four al-Qaida operatives meeting inside a tent tried to escape in a car but were shot and killed in the process. The authorities found a cache of weapons, ammunition, explosives and false license plates in the camp.

The situation grew much worse for al-Qaida on April 3 when they initiated what would be the longest and bloodiest stand-off between their operatives and government forces to date. Saudi police had learned that an al-Qaida cell was hiding out in an apartment in the al-Rass district of al-Qasim (just over two hundred miles north of Riyadh). This cell contained a number of top operatives, including al-Qaida's Saudi commander, Utaybi, who had arrived the day before.

The security forces surrounded the hide-out and prepared to storm the building. Seeing what was happening, the cell tried to smuggle out Utaybi, but the authorities had already cordoned off every exit and they killed both the commander and his escorts.[34] The rest of the cell then unleashed a hail of bullets and rocket-propelled grenades. Intimidated by the sheer volume of firepower they were facing, the security forces called for assistance. Massive reinforcements from various Saudi security units, including several special forces detachments, began arriving at the scene. Once they were in place, the security forces began firing back with their own rocket-propelled grenades and machine-guns. The clashes continued throughout the night, abated in the small hours of the morning, but then erupted again at 11:00 a.m. The terrorists moved between several adjoining buildings by blasting holes in walls. As the stand-off continued, police shut down all electricity to the building, forcing the evacuation of about a thousand residents.

By the end of April 5, 15 al-Qaida operatives had been killed and three arrested. *Sawt al-Jihad* subsequently published the names of all those killed and arrested, together with their aliases. Among those who died was Karim al-Majati, a Moroccan suspected of masterminding the May 2003 Casablanca bombing and linked to the Madrid commuter-train bombings. *Sawt al-Jihad* also explained that the handicapped man whose identity was being discussed in the press coverage of the raid was not Salih al-Awfi but Hani al-Juaythin. He had previously received a bullet in the head which had left him in a wheelchair. That had not stopped him from being active in al-Qaida, however. After this confrontation, only four men from the authorities' list of 26 remained at large.[35]

Importantly, the arrests in the al-Rass operation led the Saudi police several days later to one of those four, Abd-al-Rahman al-Yaziji. Security forces surrounded the building where he was hiding, and in response Yaziji donned an explosive belt, fired off some rounds at the police, then blew himself up. With his death, only Salih al-Ufi, Abdallah al-Rushud, and Talib al-Talib from the most-wanted list remained alive.

Cat-and-mouse games

On May 29, 2005, after conducting close surveillance of three Cougar helicopters at the al-Qasim Regional Airport, the Martyr Shaikh Saùd al-Utaybi Brigade entered the airport on bicycles, disguised in airport workers' uniforms. They then headed for the helicopters, boarded them, doused them with gasoline and set them ablaze. Al-Qaida would later boast that the entire operation had cost just 331 riyals, its point being that victory would not be won by the side with the most money or the best equipment.

On June 28, the Saudi Ministry of the Interior struck back, announcing a new list of 36 wanted extremists. It comprised 29 Saudi nationals, three Chadians, and one each from Morocco, Kuwait, Yemen and Mauritania. Fifteen on the list were thought to be actively operating inside the kingdom, with most of the other 21 believed to be in Iraq. The three survivors from the previous list were, of course, on the new one, too. Prince Turki al-Faysal, Saudi Arabia's ambassador to the United Kingdom, also reported that extremist attacks had killed 91 foreigners and Saudi civilians and wounded 510. In addition, 41 members of security forces had been killed and 218 wounded, while 112 militants had been killed and 25 wounded. The attacks had cost about one billion riyals ($270 million).

It was not long before the authorities started making inroads into the new list. On July 1, Fayyiz Ayyub flew from Lebanon to Riyadh and promptly surrendered. At least two others on the list were confirmed in Iraq and another was found to be in detention in the north of that country. The next day, the man who headed the list, the Moroccan Yunis bin Muhammad bin Ibrahim al-Hayyari, was killed during a police raid on an al-Qaida safe-house in an eastern district of Riyadh. In the wake of his death, 35-year-old Fahd Farraj al-Juwayr, number two on the list, assumed control of the network in the Arabian Peninsula. He had personally recruited a number of al-Qaida's senior leaders, including a relative named Khalid al-Juwayr (number four on the list), who was captured by the security forces in al-Zulfi, Abd-al-Rahman al-Mut'ib, who was wanted for firing on a security patrol, and Ibrahim al-Mutayr (number 11 on the list).

Al-Qaida and the Saudi security forces played cat-and-mouse with one another throughout the remainder of the year. Minor clashes, shootouts at checkpoints, raids on safe-houses, uncovering of weapons caches and busts of arms warehouses continued for several months but there were no major incidents. On February 24,

2006, however, al-Qaida attempted another large-scale operation, this time against the world's largest oil-processing plant, the Buqayq oil facility in the Eastern Province. In a suicide attack, two pick-up trucks, painted to resemble Saudi ARAMCO vehicles and each loaded with a ton of explosives, were used to ram an outer gate of the facility. One truck collided with the gate, blowing a hole in the fence, and the second then drove through before detonating its load of explosives. Both attackers were killed and two security guards were wounded. Al-Qaida announced the following day that the attackers had been on the most-wanted list: Abdullah bin Abd al-Aziz al-Tuwayjiri and Muhammad Salih al-Ghayth.

Three days later, Saudi security forces surrounded a villa used as a safe-house in eastern Riyadh, killing five al-Qaida operatives in a fire-fight. The men had been tracked back to the villa through their vehicles, which had been captured on surveillance tape at the Buqayq plant just before the attack. Four of the five men killed—Fahd Farraj al-Juwayr, Jaffal Rafiah al-Shammari, Ibrahim Abdullah Ibrahim al-Mutayri and Abdullah Muhya Shulash al-Sulayti al-Shammari—had been on the list. Their deaths meant that nearly all of the 15 men thought to be operating in the kingdom had now been killed or arrested.

Al-Qaida released a video commemorating the attack on Buqayq and the subsequent shootout with police as part of the series *Blood that Will Not Be Wasted*. The video featured Juwayr's will, and this perhaps encapsulated what the Al-Qaida organization in Saudi Arabia had become: angry, loud and relatively incompetent compared to how it had appeared just one year previously. The will also helped to clarify al-Qaida in Saudi Arabia's overall strategy. In it, Juwayr identified several different categories of people and sent specific messages to each one. These messages indicated the thinking that had driven hundreds of young Saudi boys to support al-Qaida over the previous decade, both in the peninsula and elsewhere:

- *The Muslim people*: "How long will you remain silent and be ruled by the laws of the oppressors . . . how can you sleep well, when your brothers are getting killed and your sisters' honor is being violated?"
- "*The scholars of the Sultan*": Juwayr reminded them that they had given the present Saudi government its legitimacy, and asked them to return to God.
- "*Scholars who choose to remain silent instead of speaking the truth*": He assured them that they too will not be excused by God for not taking an honorable stand.
- *The Saudi police force*: "You astound me. If you are told to go out for Jihad, you hesitate and choose to cling to this life. But if [Saudi Prince] Nayif Ibn-Abd-al-Aziz told you to sell your souls for his government and to fight for his cause and that of the Americans in return for three thousand riyals and hell, you sacrifice your lives."
- *The Saudi government*: "I will only say to you what the Prophet, prayers and peace be upon him, said to the infidels of Quraysh, when he was alone: 'We come to slay you.' The *mujahidin* are going to defeat you. Do you know why?"
- *The Americans*: "Depart from the Peninsula of Muhammad, prayers and peace be upon him. Depart from all the lands of the Muslims. Desist from

helping the Jews in Palestine, and stop helping the Christians in Muslim countries. Otherwise you will face killing, destruction, and bombings."[36]

Al-Qaida "defeated"

On June 7, 2006, the Saudi government announced that it had defeated al-Qaida in the Arabian Peninsula. To this day, Saudi authorities continue to arrest new cells that appear within the kingdom, but the movement there now has almost nothing in common with its 2003–2005 incarnation.

On June 15, 2007, Saudi security forces arrested three of the last-remaining major online players in al-Qaida's Saudi network. Two had used the online aliases Abu Aseed al-Falluji and Abu Abdallah al-Najdi. The third, who was not identified, was a foreigner arrested in Medina. He was responsible for the publication of the internet Jihadist magazine *Sada al-Jihad* (*Echoes of Jihad*). Najdi was the publisher of *Sawt al-Jihad* while Falluji was an administrator of the Eklhaas forum, one of the most popular Jihadist discussion boards. These arrests were a death-blow to al-Qaida's propaganda efforts on the Arabian Peninsula.

Since then, the Saudi government has established an aggressive re-education program, implemented a variety of counter-radicalization programs across the kingdom, engaged in micro-level community outreach programs, and sought to educate its public through entertaining documentaries and reality television series about the dangers of the al-Qaida movement. All signs point to the enduring success of these initiatives so far.

7 Global Jihadism in the UK

Oh you Muslims who are defenders of the Tawagheet and their thrones, you must know you are blackening the memory of the Salaf you claim to follow. You blacken the names of these people, who were people of Kalimat ul-Haqq [words of truth], and those who took their understanding directly from the Sahaabah of our beloved Rasulullah.

Salafi_Jihadi, Jihadist internet moderator

On June 12, 2004, American CIA officers, working closely with FBI special agents, electronic surveillance specialists from the National Security Agency and Pakistani security officials, used telephone and internet intercepts to trace an al-Qaida operative named Musad Aruchi to an apartment building in a congested Karachi neighborhood.[1] For Aruchi, a nephew of 9/11 mastermind Khalid Shaikh Mohammad and a cousin of the 1993 World Trade Center bomb plot architect Ramzi Youssef, terrorism seemed to be in his genes.[2]

Storming the apartment, police found street maps of New York City, addresses of some important buildings, and other data on CDs. However troubling these findings were for security officials in both Pakistan and the United States, few could anticipate where information gained from Aruchi's capture would eventually lead. According to news reports, he revealed the locations of several of his colleagues during interrogations with police, including that of a young computer expert named Muhammad Naeem Noor Khan. Known to his friends as Abu Talha, Khan was born in Karachi and grew up in a professional middle-class neighborhood. His mother worked as an assistant professor of botany at St Joseph College in the city while his father served as the senior purser for the state-owned Pakistani International Airlines. In 2001, at the age of 22, Khan graduated as an engineer from Karachi's Nadir Eduljee Dinshaw Engineering University. "He was a little religious and had a short beard . . . but I never saw him engage in the activity of any student organization," one of his teachers told the Associated Press.[3]

A short time later, during a cousin's wedding reception in Pakistan, Khan was invited by a friend to attend an al-Qaida training camp in Afghanistan for several weeks. He agreed, but after undergoing the initial training exercises he decided that he could better support the organization from behind his computer keyboard.

Drawing on his electronics and engineering background, he became a key communications facilitator for the network, transmitting important information from al-Qaida members in Afghanistan and the Pakistani tribal areas to operatives around the world. In exchange for his services, al-Qaida paid his rent and provided him with a 90-dollar monthly stipend in order to cover additional expenses.

In this period, Khan used his father's connections to secure airline tickets for travel back and forth to London. On at least one of these trips, he reportedly met with Abu Hamza al-Masri, the now-imprisoned firebrand preacher at London's Finsbury Park mosque.[4] In January 2003, Khan enrolled in a human resource management course at City University in central London, but after attending just four of the ten lectures that he had paid for, he disappeared, most likely back to Pakistan.

On July 13, 2004, Khan walked into Lahore airport in order to pick up a package sent to him by his father, who was still living in Karachi, some six hundred miles to the south. But waiting for Khan was a team of Pakistani security officers, who took him into custody. Interrogations opened another lead in the joint effort between Pakistan and the United States to crack its al-Qaida problem. Pakistan's Inter-Services Intelligence Agency, working closely with CIA and FBI officials, prepared to capture another al-Qaida operative with whom Khan had been working—Ahmed Khalfan Ghailani. A Tanzanian, Ghailani had been indicted in 1998 for his lead role in the August 1998 bombings of the United States Embassies in Dar es Salaam, Tanzania, and Nairobi, Kenya, which killed more than two hundred people. Since then, he had been on the run, most likely in West Africa, while continuing to support al-Qaida.[5] His capture was a considerable victory for the international counter-terrorism community.

On July 24, nearly 450 officers, including local police and undercover Pakistani commando units, surrounded a two-story house in a middle-class neighborhood of Gujarat, a city 110 miles southeast of the Pakistani capital, Islamabad. A drawn-out siege ensued, concluding with Pakistani security forces setting fire to the back and sides of the house. Police recovered a treasure trove of computers, data disks, cellphones and documents, which they promptly turned over to the United States for analysis. As investigators combed through his computer files, they uncovered a cache of surveillance information. Although most of it was at least three years old, government officials in the United States decided to raise the threat level to "Orange," (high), particularly with regard to the financial districts of New York, Washington, DC, and Newark, New Jersey. Among the alleged targets were the Citigroup building, the New York Stock Exchange, the World Bank and International Monetary Fund in Washington, and the Prudential Plaza in Newark. Government officials told reporters that Ghailani was a computer expert and that investigators had found a long list of words used by him and Khan in their codes. In addition, al-Qaida seemed to have used Ghailani for document forgery: the authorities found more than 50 scanned Pakistani ID cards on his computer. Furthermore, as Pakistan's Information Minister, Shaikh Rashid Ahmed, told the Associated Press: "We got a few emails from Ghailani's computer about [plans for] attacks in the US and UK."[6] Although most of the reconnaissance data found dated back to before the 9/11 attacks, investigators could now cross-reference information from Khan's computers with that on Ghailani's. One file in particular, named "Eminem2.doc," stood out. It was a 39-page terrorist grant proposal for review by al-Qaida's High Command. In the proposal, the author described a fantastic plot full of simultaneous explosions and even the use of radioactive material. He explained that he had conducted extensive research and planning for the attacks, including thorough reconnaissance visits to the US, use of the internet and visits to public and specialist libraries. He described the possible effects of a bomb exploding on a tube train traveling under the Thames: "Imagine the chaos that would be caused if a powerful explosion were to rip through here and actually rupture the river itself . . . This would cause pandemonium, what with the explosions, flooding, drowning, etc. that would result."[7] Investigators now knew that they were dealing with a very serious problem.

British Jihadism

The United Kingdom still sits directly in the eye of the global Jihadist storm, as it has for nearly two decades. But it was only following the attacks of 9/11 that the Jihadist movement began turning its operational focus inward: Britain shifted from being a safe haven and recruiting ground to being a prime target.

In the early 1990s, a variety of Jihadist dissidents, oppositionists, recruiters and propagandists travelled to London, many of them seeking a respite from the pressure they were facing in their home countries like Jordan, Egypt, and Saudi Arabia. Bin Laden dispatched Khalid Abdul Rahman Hamad al-Fawwaz there in order to set up the Advice and Reform Committee (ARC), which began a fax pamphleteering operation aimed at Saudi Arabia, with special emphasis on propagating Bin Laden's ideas.[8] Fawwaz issued at least 17 separate statements from the ARC between 1994 and 1996 on a variety of topics, including Saudi corruption and the need for more true adherence to Islamic law. Beyond publicizing al-Qaida's message, the ARC helped support its methodology. Fawwaz used the committee as a front organization to recruit military trainees, disburse funds and procure equipment such as satellite telephones for al-Qaida. In addition, his office transmitted reports on military and security matters from various al-Qaida cells, including the Kenyan cell, to the organization's High Command in Afghanistan.

Abdul Hamed al-Raghie, better known as Anas al-Libi, was an al-Qaida computer expert who lived in the northern English city of Manchester, even after the US demanded his extradition on charges of participating in the bombing of the American Embassy in Kenya.[9] On May 10, 2000, the British police raided Libi's apartment in the depressed Moss Side area of the city. Although Libi had fled, and eventually had a $25 million bounty placed on his head by the United States, he left behind an al-Qaida training manual that spelled out the organization's tradecraft in 180 pages of chilling detail. The document became known across the counter-terrorism community as the *Manchester Manual*.[10]

Other British activists included the shoe-bombers Richard Reid and Sajid Badat. Reid was a British convert to Islam who tried to blow up a transatlantic flight by lighting a fuse in his shoes, which had been packed with plastic explosives, in December 2001.[11] Badat was a worshiper at the Finsbury Park mosque who went through the Afghan camps and was ordered to blow himself up on a plane around the same time as Reid. However, he testified that he changed his mind and dismantled his bomb instead.[12]

In 2002, British citizen Ahmed Omar Saeed Shaikh was arrested in connection with the murder of Daniel Pearl, the *Wall Street Journal* bureau chief in Pakistan.[13] Radicalized while attending the London School of Economics, he had hoped to fight in Bosnia in the 1990s but ended up instead with a Kashmiri militant group. He reportedly became a close associate of Maulana Masood Azhar, founder of the banned Jaish-e-Mohammad group and one of the most popular Pakistani Jihadist clerics today. A Pakistani court sentenced Omar Saeed to death for his role in organizing Pearl's kidnapping. This has yet to be carried out, however.

On April 30, 2003, two young British men of Pakistani descent traveled to Israel in order to conduct a suicide attack on a Tel Aviv hotspot.[14] Asif Muhammad Hanif blew himself up at Mike's Place, killing three other people. Two weeks later, the body of Omar Khan Sharif, whom Israeli investigators say fled the bar after the bomb that he was carrying failed to detonate, was found in the sea off Tel Aviv. The 27-year-old Sharif was married and a father of two from Derby. Hanif, from Hounslow, west London, was known as "Huggy Bear" by his friends and three brothers.

The attacks of 9/11 only confirmed that which many in the British counter-terrorism community had believed for several years: that they had to police their hardline Islamic community more aggressively.[15] But given that most of the British-born and -educated Jihadists were conducting attacks elsewhere, some British policy-makers continued to feel that the threat of home-grown Islamic-based terrorism was exaggerated. It was only the July 7, 2005 attacks on London's transport system that dispelled any lingering doubts about the seriousness of that threat. In hindsight, the evolution of global Jihadism in Britain over the 1990s and early 2000s shows a clear trajectory toward today's Jihadist security challenge.

Operation Challenge

Beginning in the early 1990s, a hodgepodge of preachers, propagandists and terrorist operatives started percolating Jihadist thought throughout the mosques and community centers of Britain. The Muslim youth there eagerly responded to their rage, competing with one another to spend time with their favorite mentors. Observers of Islamic radicalism in the United Kingdom tend to narrow their focus to several key individuals, groups or mosques. But the reality is that the Jihadist experience in the UK is messy. Among Jihadists, there are few rules and even fewer friends. The Jihadist leaders in the UK knew only that they needed to milk their freedom for as long as possible.

On September 28, 1998, British security services launched Operation Challenge, arresting seven men in the course raids on eight homes across London. These arrests were the culmination of a lengthy intelligence operation led by Special Branch and MI5, coordinating with law enforcement and intelligence officials from the United States.[16] The list of captured men, arrested under Section 14 of the Prevention of Terrorism Act 1989, is as good a thumbnail sketch as any of the spread of Egyptian Islamists in the 1980s and 1990s. For instance, there was Ibrahim al-Aydarusi, a former army officer who had been discharged in 1987 after being accused of fostering radical Islamic activities. In 1991, he left Egypt for Saudi Arabia, where he worked for a short time before arriving in London in 1995.[17] Sayyid Ajami, another Egyptian, was arrested several times during the 1980s for fomenting radical violence.[18] He was also accused of aiding three Jihadist leaders to escape from Turah prison in 1988, but was later acquitted. He also left Egypt for Saudi Arabia, travelled to Afghanistan, and then settled in London in 1995.

Then there was Abd al-Majid Abd al-Bari, an Egyptian Jihadist leader who had been sentenced to death *in absentia* in 1997 in connection with the attempt to blow up the Khan al-Khalili market in Cairo. He had entered Britain in 1991 and was granted political asylum in 1993. On August 4, 1998, Egyptian Islamic Jihad issued a statement threatening to retaliate against the United States for its involvement in the apprehension of EIJ members in Albania. That statement had been sent via fax to Bari in his Beethoven Street office before its release. Furthermore, Bari received an early morning fax transmission three days later from the "Islamic Army for the Liberation of the Holy Places," which claimed responsibility for the East Africa Embassy bombings. This was done even though those bombings had not yet occurred.

Sayyid Ahmad Abd al-Maqsud, a man who had been coordinating the movement of Egyptian Islamic Jihad members in Albania during the mid-1990s (and would later be sentenced to 15 years' hard labor by an Egyptian courts), also made the 1998 Operation Challenge list. As did two other Egyptians, Usamah Ahmad Husayn and Hani al-Sibai. The latter was born in Qaylubiyah some time between 1958 and 1961 and has spent the majority of his life living and working in Egypt. He served as legal counsel to the Supreme State Security courts and helped to found the country's Bar Association of Islamists. He also acted as the chief editor of two Islamist journals, *Criterion* and *The Architecture of Unity*,[19] and wrote for a number of other magazines, including the Australian *Nida'ul Islam* and the Algerian *al-Ansar*. Reports suggest that during this time he was active in the al-Jihad organization of Ayman al-Zawahiri. Before leaving his homeland and obtaining residency in the UK, Sibai worked for the well-known Egyptian attorney Muntasir al-Zayyat, defending Egyptian Jihadists at their trials. He was arrested in the aftermath of the assassination of President Anwar Sadat alongside hundreds of other Egyptian Islamists. Subsequently released and re-arrested several more times, he finally fled to the United Kingdom in 1994 and established the al-Maqrizi Centre for Historical Studies, which is dedicated disseminating to Jihadist-style news, translations and commentary with a distinctive Egyptian bias.[20] Following his seizure in Operation Challenge, Sibai spent nine months in high-security prison, where he went on hunger strike for 28 days in protest against his alleged ill-treatment. Now he is again actively involved in speaking, publishing and recording lectures on Jihadist matters out of the Center, and he has publicly praised insurgent fighters in Iraq on al-Jazirah.[21]

The Operation Challenge arrests sparked a violent reaction among British Islamists. Omar Bakri Mohammad, a Syrian-born Islamist and leader of the al-Muhajiroun organization at the time, argued that "The way the arrests were made proves that there is a campaign to persecute Muslims in Britain by arresting them and handing them over to the authorities in their countries on the pretext of fighting international terrorism, which means the assassination [*ightiyal*] of all aspects of human rights."[22] Islamist leaders in London set aside their differences and temporarily united in a demonstration outside 10 Downing Street on March 12, 1999, in protest against the continued detention without charge of five of the arrested fundamentalists in Belmarsh jail in southeast London. Collectively, this group of protestors also signed a statement arguing for the detainees' release. The signatories included: Abu Basir al-Tartusi, Muhammad Mustafa al-Muqri (Abu Ithar), Abd-al-Rahim Abu Muntasir, Muhammad al-Khalidi, Abu Qatada, Khalid Bin-Fathi (Abu-al-Walid al-Ansari), Yassir al-Sirri, Abu Hamza al-Masri, and Muhammad al-Masari. With the benefit of hindsight, this is a veritable who's who of British Jihadism. Many of these individuals brought their own unique skill-sets, reputations and social networks to bear on the British-based supporters of global Jihadism.

Yassir Tawfiq al-Sirri

Yassir Tawfiq al-Sirri, known in the Jihadist community as Abu Ammar, was one of the leading figures in the Vanguards of Conquest organization, an offshoot of Ayman al-Zawahiri's al-Jihad organization in Egypt.[23] Sirri's extensive rap sheet with Egyptian law enforcement strongly indicates a historical involvement in radical activities.[24] In 1994, he was convicted of participating with the group Vanguards of Conquest in an attempt to assassinate former Prime Minister Atif Sidqi and sentenced to death *in absentia*. (This was the attack that Zawahiri lamented soiled al-Jihad's domestic support base because a 12-year-old girl was inadvertently killed.)[25]

In an interview with the *al-Ahram al-Arabi* newspaper, Sirri disclosed a variety of details about his path toward Jihadism.[26] He attended primary school in al-Mansurah from 1967 to 1972, preparatory school in Suez from 1972 to 1975, secondary school in Suez from 1975 to 1982 and the Institute for Social Services in Port Said from 1982 to 1987. He began working for the al-Hidayah al-Islamiyah institution, providing assistance to families whose loved ones had been arrested in the crackdown on radical Islamists, fundraising for families whose husbands had been imprisoned, and organizing demonstrations. He delivered Friday sermons and took part in religious debates at the mosque and at the Lawyers Union. His goals were to establish *Sharia* in Egypt, enlighten people about what is right and wrong under that legal code, oppose civil law and eradicate the bad behavior of elements working against society.[27] Three of the demonstrations he organized protested against the government for its non-establishment of *Sharia* in Suez and for selling alcohol there. He also organized a demonstration in Cairo to call for the implementation of *Sharia*. Approximately a thousand people participated in each of these demonstrations, and in June 1985 he boasted that he had coordinated a protest in Cairo in which over ten times that number took part.[28]

In 1981, Sirri was one of hundreds of dissidents who were arrested and detained on charges of involvement in religious riots. He was released in February 1982, but re-arrested in 1984 and detained without charge for almost three weeks. The following year, he was imprisoned for participating in the large Cairo demonstration, and in 1986 he was again imprisoned, this time for one month on charges of distributing anti-government leaflets. He finally took the hint in 1988 and left for Jordan.[29] From there, he quickly continued on to Yemen, where he remained, working as a social services inspector, until November 1992. In that month he relocated to Sudan, which was his home until April 1994, but during that time he made upwards of ten trips to Saudi Arabia. He also traveled back and forth to Peshawar, Pakistan, in 1989, 1991 and late in 1992. A week before he left Sudan, he paid a Pakistani man three hundred dollars for a Yemini passport and seven hundred dollars for the attached visa. (His mother had to sell some of her land holdings in Egypt in order to pay for this.) Sirri presented the passport to British security officials upon his arrival in the United Kingdom.[30]

Once established in Britain, Sirri used his London-based Islamic Observation Centre to release statements against Egypt (which by this stage, of course, had sentenced him to death in his absence) and senior Egyptian officials and in support of Zawahiri's al-Jihad organization. He also began working alongside other Islamist leaders in the UK, speaking at the same conferences, preaching in the same mosques and recruiting among the same youth populations. One of the most senior these leaders in the UK at the time was Abu Hamza al-Masri.

Abu Hamza al-Masri

Familiar to many because of the hooks that he has in place of hands and the patch covering his left eye, Abu Hamza al-Masri has become a British Jihadist icon. Theories abound over what led to his disfigurement. He claims that an accident occurred while he was clearing Soviet landmines in Afghanistan. Others say that he lost them preparing explosive devices, while another theory is that both hands were removed as punishment for criminal offences.

Born Mustafa Kamil Mustafa on 15 April 1958 in Alexandria, Egypt, Abu Hamza al-Masri stands tall among the other towering figures in the United Kingdom's Jihadist community.[31] Although he is generally marginalized in Jihadist discussion of their top thinkers, if he is mentioned at all, there is no doubt that at one time he played a leading role in justifying and recruiting for the Jihadist movement globally.

Abu Hamza's father was in the Egyptian Navy and his mother worked as a headmistress for a local school. While in school, he worked part-time as a karate trainer and a nightclub bouncer. In 1977, he enrolled at the College of Engineering in Alexandria University for two years before relocating to Britain. Once there, he started a *halal* meat export company and married his first wife, Valerie, with whom he had his eldest son, Muhammad. Through his marriage, he was able to gain British citizenship, and he acquired his British passport in 1984. He divorced Valerie in 1986, his company folded and he enrolled at the College of Engineering, Brighton University, to restart his studies. It was during this time that he began to meet Jihadist fighters from Afghanistan who had come to Britain for prosthetic limbs. He took such a liking to them that he began translating their stories at the Harley Street mosque.

In 1987, during a pilgrimage to Saudi Arabia, he had a pivotal meeting with Shaikh Abdallah Azzam, who asked him to join the Jihad campaign in Afghanistan. But at that time he was opposed to the principle of fighting the Jihad in Afghanistan rather than in Palestine against Israel.[32] Back in Britain, and by now equipped with a degree in civil engineering, he worked as a contractor on a variety of engineering projects, including one at Sandhurst Military College in 1989 and 1990. (He would later admit that he held on to the engineering plans for the college.)[33] Soon thereafter, he decided to take his engineering skills to Afghanistan.

He claims to have been responsible for managing 28 different civil construction projects while in the region, working out of an office in Jalalabad and as the chief engineer in Kandahar. In 1991, following the assassination of former Egyptian People's Assembly Speaker Rifat al-Mahjub, he helped to broker a meeting between the two leading Egyptian terrorist organizations, Egyptian Islamic Jihad and the Islamic Group. It was the first successful act of reconciliation between these two organizations, attended by al-Jihad leader Ayman al-Zawahiri and Abu-Talal al-Qasimi.[34]

With support from al-Jihad, around this time Algerian militants began to publish their own magazine, *al-Shahadah*. Abu Hamza viewed these men as younger brothers and supported their efforts in their homeland and Afghanistan. He returned to London in 1993 and continued to network within the European Jihadist community, writing and editing articles for a variety of global Jihadist magazines and working with Muslim youth. He also initially remained committed to the Algerian Jihadists, particularly the Armed Islamic Group (GIA), helping British-based Jihadist thinkers to publish the *al-Ansar* bulletin, which covered news and events in Algeria and also dealt with a variety of ideological issues.[35] In the mid-1990s, however, as the GIA increasingly used indiscriminate violence and the civilian death toll began to climb, Abu Hamza grew ever more disillusioned with the Algerian cause. Before long, he and other leading Jihadist ideologues in London and elsewhere formally withdrew their support from the GIA.[36]

Abu Hamza's support for Jihadism remained undimmed, however. Beginning in 1994, he began traveling back and forth to Bosnia in order to support Jihadist activities there. And, in 1995, he founded the Jama'at Ansar al-Shari'a (Supporters of *Sharia*, SOS), organization in order to promote the establishment of *Sharia* law worldwide.[37] He envisaged using this organization to transfer new recruits and financial support to the Jihadists fighting in Kosovo under the banner of the Kosovo Liberation Army (KLA). However, KLA officials told Abu Hamza, much to his surprise, that his support was neither necessary nor welcome. In response, he published an article entitled "The KLA is not the Way."[38]

Somewhat demoralized by this snub, Abu Hamza began looking for other ways to engage the British Jihadist community. He found his platform at the Finsbury Park Mosque and a variety of youth centers around London, where he preached and met with young Muslim men daily. Abdul Wahid Majid was one of those men, and explained in an interview in 1999:

> After my basic training with swords and sticks at the [Finsbury Park] mosque, I then went on a number of courses where I was taught how to use real firearms and live ammunition . . . It is unlimited, the amount of things you can learn. Once in Pakistan I was introduced to a great range of military hardware including guns like Kalashnikovs and M16s.[39]

Abu Hamza continued vocalizing his fury after al-Qaida's attacks against the United States on 9/11. On January 20, 2003, police raided the Finsbury Park Mosque as part of a large-scale counter-terrorism investigation. Although he was not implicated in the investigation, Abu Hamza was ousted from the mosque, forcing him to give his weekly Friday sermons on the street just outside its gates. When fingered by the United States as a facilitator of terrorism, British police arrested him and subsequently charged him with 16 counts of encouraging murder, stirring up race hatred, recruiting for violence, possessing information that could be useful for someone preparing an act of terrorism and more.

In February 2007, he was sentenced to seven years in prison. One year later, the United States petitioned for, and was granted, the right to extradite him to the United States in order to stand trial for his alleged involvement in the 1998 abduction of 16 Western tourists in Yemen. Although he appealed against the ruling, the British Home Office denied his petition and at the time of writing he was still awaiting extradition.

Abu Hamza was not alone in teaching young men about the need to prepare for war. Abu Qatada al-Filistini was also busy preaching global Jihadism to British Muslim youth.

Abu Qatada al-Filistini

Omar Mahmud Abu Omar—or Abu Qatada al-Filistini, as he is better known—is among the most influential Jihadist thinkers in the world today. Since 1993 he has been in Britain, and he was granted political refugee status the following year. This security allowed him to expand his Jihadist networks and horizons from the mid-1990s onwards. He kept himself busy preaching at several mosques across London, including Finsbury Park, where both he and Abu Hamza met with a number of terrorism suspects. He also published several books that became bestsellers within the global Jihadist community and his writings appear on the most elite library websites within the global Jihadist movement.[40] Rarely is there a day when his name does not appear on at least one of the major Jihadist internet discussion forums.

In the 1990s, he served as chief editor of the Algerian Jihadist magazine *al-Ansar*. In this role, assisted by a senior council of contributors and editors including Abu Hamza and Abu Musab al-Suri, he provided the GIA in Algeria with the necessary Islamic credentials that it needed. Thanks in large part to his entrepreneurial spirit, *al-Ansar* grew quite popular in mosques throughout the UK and Western Europe, although it was closely monitored by security services.[41] The magazine, and Abu Qatada's support for the GIA's steadily increasing bloodletting in Algeria, eventually subsided, although Abu Qatada continued to support the GIA long after many of his contemporaries.

In 2000, his career began to take a noticeable downturn when a Jordanian court sentenced him to 15 years' prison and hard labor *in absentia* on charges of conspiring to attack US and Israeli tourists during the kingdom's millennium celebrations. This ruling was Abu Qatada's second *in absentia* conviction from a Jordanian court in two years, and enough to cause some concern within the British counter-terrorism community. According to the Jordanian government, Abu Qatada had provided funding to a cell of 13 terrorists led by Khader Abu Ghoshar, the former director of the Jordanian terrorist group Jaish Mohammed.[42] Although Abu Qatada adamantly denied the charge, his situation only deteriorated from there.

In the immediate aftermath of 9/11, investigators found 18 videotaped sermons given by Abu Qatada in the Hamburg apartment used by several of the hijackers, notably Mohamed Atta.[43] As a result, Abu Qatada was arrested under the Anti-Terrorism, Crime and Security Act 2001, which had been introduced soon after the 9/11 attacks. It permits the detention without trial of foreign terrorism suspects who are said to pose a threat to national security or have links to international terrorism but cannot be deported. Abu Qatada's response to being arrested was typically dismissive: "I was imprisoned for four days just because they found my name in the possession of someone who was arrested in Germany . . . They searched my house, they searched every single book. In fact they helped me. They found my national insurance card and they haven't given it back. Can you believe it?"[44] He was one of 38 individuals and organizations to have their assets frozen as the result of orders issued by Chancellor Gordon Brown and the US government. Investigators also found that Abu Qatada, who had reportedly been receiving social security payments for his wife and four children, was in possession of $260,000 at his home, which was seized by authorities. In an interview with *al-Hayat*, he denied that he had even one-tenth of that amount but admitted that he did keep money at his home because he did not trust British banks.[45] A judge initially rescinded his social security payments, but Abu Qatada appealed to have them reinstated as he had no personal savings with which to provide for his family. He won that case, but several weeks later he disappeared, and was presumed to have gone underground in order to avoid long-term imprisonment.

Unfortunately for Abu Qatada, his name thereafter became increasingly linked with known terrorists, including Richard Reid, Sajid Badat, Zaccharias Moussaoui and others, mostly because of the time he had spent preaching and meeting with such angry young men at the Finsbury Park mosque. As the evidence mounted of his involvement in directly supporting al-Qaida through recruitment and possibly in other ways, the British authorities realized that they had to find him.[46] On October 23, 2002, British anti-terrorist police and MI5 internal security agents had a lucky break when they conducted an armed raid on a house in Bermondsey, south London. There they found and arrested Abu Qatada.[47] According to Omar Bakri Mohammad, Abu Qatada was seized after family members had visited him at his hide-out and one of them had used a mobile phone that was being traced.[48]

Although arresting Abu Qatada helped to resource the British government that he was no longer actively involved in supporting terrorist operations at home or abroad, they still had to determine what to do with him. Under British anti-terrorism laws, he could be held indefinitely, giving officials a range of options, from trying him domestically to deporting him to any of the multiple countries that had outstanding convictions *in absentia* against him or warrants for his arrest. On August 10, 2005, the British government began the drawn-out process of deporting him to Jordan. This option had been resisted over the previous three years because, under international law, Britain cannot deport anyone to a country where they might face inhuman or degrading treatment. Furthermore, it has a domestic policy of not returning people to countries that employ the death penalty. To get around this, Jordan and Britain signed a memorandum of understanding under which both countries guaranteed the civil rights of Jordanian and British deportees. This ensured that a deportee would not be subject to mistreatment or torture, and would have the right to a lawyer, which was sufficient under British law to allow Abu Qatada to be deported legally. Since then, his lawyer has launched a series of appeals and protests in an attempt to block the deportation. All have so far been dismissed, but Abu Qatada still had not been deported at the time of writing, and European Court rulings in February 2008—in which the possibility of his torture was raised—seem to have stalled the process.

Omar Bakri Mohammad

Omar Bakri Mohammad offered British Muslims a third way for channeling their rage and religiosity: something between the violence of global Jihadism and the proselytization of Islamist activist groups. He knew all of the Islamist players on both sides of him doctrinally and worked with them regularly. His full role in fostering global Jihadism in the United Kingdom, across Europe and around the Islamic world is still being uncovered today.

Bakri was born in Syria. He has five children and, like his Jihadist colleagues Abu Hamza and Abu Qatada, claimed state income support and disability benefits while living in the UK. To be clear, Bakri should not be considered a global Jihadist in the same way as Abu Qatada might be. Bakri himself says he supports violent Jihad only in Muslim countries that are being illegally occupied.[49] He is what one might term a "Caliphatist," spending a significant amount of time discussing the need for Muslims to restore the Caliphate. He adamantly does not support the Muslim Brotherhood's policy of accommodation with Arab regimes, but also does not advocate the forcible overthrow of those regimes. There is a middle ground, he has historically argued.

For Bakri, the Caliphate was the basis of the thinking of the Hizb ut-Tahrir Party, which was founded in the 1950s by Shaikh Muhammad Taqiyy-al-Din al-Nabhani.[50] Following that organization's precedent of proselytization and social activism focused on establishing the Caliphate, Bakri founded his al-Muhajiroun movement when he was living in Jiddah, Saudi Arabia, in 1983. The Hizb ut-Tahrir leadership, however, did not approve of his approach, so he left Saudi Arabia for London, albeit with the intention of traveling on to Pakistan, in 1985. London, though, seemed to be a good place to operate, so he settled there instead and relaunched the al-Muhajiroun movement.

Under his watch, al-Muhajiroun organized British Muslims in political, social, religious, economic and ideological causes. It and its follow-on groups, al-Ghuraba and the Saved Sect, became well known for holding rallies, coordinating lectures, and promoting study groups, prayer sessions and youth organizations. Despite the distinctions that Bakri sought to make about his approach *vis-à-vis* that of global Jihadist groups, even a cursory examination of the messages and ideas promoted by these groups shows the virulent hatred for the West that he promoted.[51]

There can be no doubt that Bakri and his followers have had considerable influence throughout the Islamic world. One of the major reasons why his movement became so popular was because of his large-scale media initiatives and high-profile events. A good example of his flair for the extravagant can be seen in a mass rally that he co-organized with another Islamist activist in London at the time, Muhammad al-Masari. The International Islamic Conference Rally for Revival was scheduled to be held on September 8, 1996 at Wembley Arena. According to the advertisement that Bakri's group spread throughout the UK and beyond, it would feature as speakers: Shaikh Salman al-Husaini al-Nadwi, president of Jamiat-U-Shabab al-Islami (India); Maulana Zaahid-Ur-Raashdi, chairman of World Islamic Forum and chief editor of *al-Sharia* (Pakistan); Maulana Abdullah Patel, a prominent scholar from Gujarat; and Maulana Essa Mansuri, vice-president of World Islamic Forum (UK); and Bakri and Masari. The promotional material also provided information about messages by video, audio or letter that would be relayed during the rally. Those sending messages of support were said to include Shaikh Usama Bin Laden, Shaikh Omar Abdul-Rahman, Shaikh Muhammed Ubayd, Shaikh Muhammed Husain Fadhullah, Shaikh Ali Ballhaj, and Shaikh Abdullah Abou al-Farouq. Seating at the rally would be limited to the first 13,500 tickets, which could be purchased from al-Muhajiroun. Had Bakri and his associates been able to assemble even half of this global Jihadist line-up, it would have significantly bolstered his reputation across the Islamist world. Due to massive domestic and international pressure, however, he was forced to cancel the entire rally.

Thereafter, he continued to tread the line of acceptability with the British authorities through his work with al-Muhajiroun, al-Ghuraba and other initiatives. In the wake of the July 2005 London bombings, however, he saw the writing on the wall: he would either have to come out publicly in favour of British government policy objectives or he would have to leave. He chose the latter, relocating to Lebanon in late 2005, where he remains today. Meanwhile, several of his colleagues, including Masari, have tried to toe that tenuous line back in London.

Muhammad al-Masari and Saàd al-Faqih

Before 1991, few outside of King Saùd University in Riyadh had heard of Dr. Saàd al-Faqih or Dr. Muhammad al-Masari. The first was a professor of surgery, the second a physicist. What they had in common was deep animosity toward the Saudi regime for allowing American forces to be stationed on the Arabian Peninsula. Together they formed a small group that became a driving force in formulating the famous "Letter of Demands" in March 1991. This was a petition signed by senior religious figures in the kingdom demanding the establishment of an independent consultative council (*shura*) to that would rule in all internal and external matters. The Saudi regime viewed this petition as nothing short of mutiny by the younger generation of religious scholars and intellectuals. But since nothing in it violated the law, nor even contradicted anything that the House of Saùd had publicly promised, they let it pass.[52]

At this point, most oppositionists retreated, not wanting to press their luck any more than they had already.[53] The number of declared supporters of the petition's demands plummeted after 1992, and even those who continued to support the principle of reform significantly backed away from some of its recommendations, such as the establishment of a consultative council. Some scholars, including those in the burgeoning Sahwa movement, like Safar al-Hawali and Salman al-Awdah, however, argued that a second, more detailed petition was necessary. In 1992, the *Mudhakarat an-Nasiha* (Memorandum of Advice) began circulating, appealing for signatures. This effort generally failed, though, as it garnered less support, shied away from some of the more aggressive reforms that had previously been suggested, and was criticized heavily within the senior ranks of the Saudi religious community.[54]

In 1993, Faqih and Masari, both of whom had actively advocated both petitions, took things a step too far by establishing a human rights committee, which they called the Committee for Defense of Legitimate Rights (CDLR). The Saudi government responded by exiling both men from the kingdom. Reconnecting with each other in London, they vowed to make the CDLR an instrument for bringing the Saudi government to its knees. Faqih explained:

> When we came to Britain, our original mission consisted of four principles, which I felt Dr. Masari had later shifted from. The first principle was that CDLR should be focused on Saudi Arabia. It should not involve itself with any other country. The second was that CDLR should be a discreet and independent group. It would respect other groups and might even exchange ideas and experience, but it would not make an alliance or affiliate itself with any other group. The third principle was that decision-making in CDLR should be based on collective consultation. The fourth was we saw our role as ambassadors and messengers. We don't sell or promote ourselves as the future presidents or future leaders of the country. The real action is inside the country. We are only a media window or communications platform.[55]

Soon after Masari moved to the UK at the end of 1993, he announced that the CDLR would be based in London from that time forward. The organization immediately increased the pace and tone of its rhetorical campaign against the Saudi rulers. With Masari as official spokesman, the group relied heavily on the fax machine in order to broadcast its calls for reform in Saudi Arabia. Within a year, it had become fully integrated into the London Jihadist world. Faqih and Masari were coordinating public meetings, holding workshops, giving lectures and raising awareness for their cause. They became so effective that the Saudi government began to pressurize Britain to extradite the pair, something that British officials were unable to do, even if they had wanted to, because of the UK's prohibition of extradition to countries that employ the death penalty.

However, in 1996, Faqih and Masari fell out, leading to Faqih's resignation from the CDLR and his establishment of a rival group called the Movement for Islamic Reform in Arabia (MIRA). His goal in separating from Masari's organization was to concentrate exclusively on lobbying for reform in Saudi Arabia, as opposed to promoting the transnational Jihadist agenda that Masari was beginning to push.

Since then, the pair have managed to stay within the bounds of the law, although both have faced challenges. The United States officially considers MIRA to be a terrorist organization, and in 2004 charged Faqih with supplying financial and material support to al-Qaida, ordering MIRA's financial assets to be frozen. Oddly, though, America has had nothing to say about Masari's operation.[56] Conversely, Faqih has not greatly interested the British authorities, while Masari has given them a real headache in recent years. From his home on the northwest edge of London, he ran his Arabic-language *Tajdeed* (Revival) Jihadist internet discussion forum until 2007. In its prime, this website was visited by thousands of people each day, despite new UK laws aimed at inhibiting speech and publications that are deemed to incite others toward violence. The website is now defunct, however, and Masari has kept his head down, presumably in an attempt to avoid arrest and deportation.

Global Jihadism strikes back

Since 9/11, no Western state has faced the persistent threat of catastrophic Jihadist terrorism as much as the British. Since at least 2003, British counter-terrorism agencies have been forced to investigate multiple major plots by amorphously defined actors, most of whom best fit the Jihobbyist description: self-starting enthusiasts who eventually decide that they want to act. For instance, on March 30, 2004, 700 police officers descended on nearly two dozen locations, collapsing what they suspected was an al-Qaida-directed terrorist cell in an investigation codenamed "Operation Crevice." Arrested during this sweep, which was the culmination of over eight months of investigation, were seven young British men, six of whom had family ties to Pakistan. Five British citizens—Omar Khyam, Jawad Akbar, Salahuddin Amin, Waheed Mahmood, and Anthony Garcia —were jailed for life for their participation in the plot.

Operation Crevice

Salahuddin Amin was born in London but grew up in Pakistan. At the age of 16, he returned to Britain, where he lived a typical life in Luton, playing cricket for various local teams. He is reported to have drunk alcohol and dated occasionally, funding his social life with money earned as a part-time taxi driver. Although he was not deeply pious, he reportedly became increasingly attuned to the plight of Muslims in various conflict areas worldwide and began downloading battle videos he found on the internet from Jihadist hotspots like Bosnia and Chechnya (a common habit of those moving into the world of Jihobbyism).[57]

In 1999, Amin is said to have met two Jihadist recruiters who turned him on to the conflict in Kashmir. Feeling the urge to support the cause, Amin donated money toward helping Kashmiri fighters purchase weapons. The next year, he began attending lectures given by Abu Hamza al-Masri at the Finsbury Park mosque in London and his rage about the injustice and oppression that he saw Muslims facing around the world became more focused. He decided that he could no longer sit by while Muslim women and children were being raped and slaughtered: he had to fight.[58]

Amin had met those two Jihadist recruiters in a prayer center in his Luton neighborhood. One was a British Pakistani, Omar Khyam; the other an alleged al-Qaida operative, Abu Munthir, who was visiting London from Pakistan. Khyam was a young firebrand who had been radicalized at the age of 16 in the town of Crawley, just south of London, when he began spending time with members of the Islamist group al-Muhajiroun, the group headed by Omar Bakri. In 1999, Khyam joined his family on a visit to Pakistan, where he ran across an al-Badr *mujahidin*-sponsored rally for their Jihadist campaign in Kashmir.[59] He was struck by what he learned about Kashmir and it became a touchstone in his radicalization process.

At the age of 18, fueled with youthful rage and a sense of adventure, he told his parents he was going to France, but instead he returned to Pakistan, hoping to make his way to train and fight in Kashmir. "Linking up with [the Kashmiri terrorist group, Lashkar i-Toiba] was surprisingly easy. Khyam testified that on landing in Islamabad, knowing that Kashmiri militants 'had offices all over Pakistan in every major city,' he had simply told his taxi driver to 'take me to the office of the mujahideen.'"[60] Before long, he was training at a Lashkar camp in the rugged Kashmiri mountains, where he said he learned everything he needed to know for guerrilla warfare: AK47s, pistols, rocket-propelled grenades, sniper rifles, climbing and crawling techniques, reconnaissance, light machine-guns and more.

Khyam's family eventually tracked him down, brought him back to England and enrolled him in college. After no more than a few months, however, he began planning his next trip to Pakistan. In 2001, he departed ostensibly to attend a friend's wedding, but after arriving he ventured into Afghanistan in order to meet members of the Taliban. Like Amin, Khyam thought that fighting was the only way to commit himself fully to his religion. The two men traveled together between

Pakistan and the UK multiple times from then onwards. They reportedly used aliases and codes and frequently wiped computer data to avoid detection.[61]

In 2002, another al-Muhajiroun member, Mohammed Junaid Babar, entered the picture. An American of Pakistani descent, Babar grew up in Queens, New York, where he was preparing to become a taxi driver. He came to the FBI's attention after he appeared from Pakistan on a Canadian news program making remarks about his desire to kill Americans.[62] He subsequently attended a year of college at St. John's University but continued to serve as al-Muhajiroun's representative in New York.[63] In November 2001, the organization reassigned him to Pakistan.[64]

In late 2002, Babar traveled to London on a fundraising trip. It was at this point that he met members of what he called the "Crawley lot," including Khyam and Anthony Garcia, a British Muslim of Algerian descent, who had adopted the Islamic name Rahman Adam. Babar got along well with the group and before long his new home in Lahore, Pakistan, became the nerve center for the Crawley gang whenever they traveled there. He was not simply a spokesman or recruiter: he kept a supply of castor beans, allegedly for making the toxin ricin, in his bedroom cupboard and also had bomb-related equipment, including detonators, wiring, ammonium nitrate and aluminum powder, on hand so that he and his associates could test out various concoctions in his backyard.[65]

Amin reportedly maintained his own Jihadist connections at this time, too, staying in touch with Abu Munthir, who later turned out to be the deputy of senior al-Qaida leader Abdul Hadi al-Iraq.[66] By 2003, Amin was raising money and sourcing materials for fighters in Afghanistan and passing them to Abu Munthir. When Khyam made contact with Amin in Pakistan in 2003, hoping to train to fight in Afghanistan, Abu Munthir told them that the organization there was fully staffed but that they should consider doing something in Britain instead. In late 2003, Khyam and Amin took a two-day trip to a safe-house in Kohat, Pakistan, for training in bomb-making. Later, Khyam organized a session in the mountains around Malakand, near the Afghan border, in order to teach the others what he had learned. Posing as Western tourists visiting lakes and glaciers, Khyam, Babar, a Canadian computer engineer named Mohammed Momin Khawaja and another cell member began testing a variety of fertilizer-based explosives recipes, videoing everything in the hope of producing an instructional documentary. Khyam told the cell that al-Qaida wanted "multiple bombings," either "simultaneously or one after the other on the same day." According to Babar, he said that they needed to "hit certain spots like pubs, nightclubs and trains."[67]

The new member, Khawaja, was born and raised in Canada. His father was an outspoken proponent of fundamental Islam, and the author of several books on conflict resolution for Islamic fundamentalists living in the West.[68] Khawaja himself turned puritanical during his final year at college, growing a beard, praying five times daily, and refusing to date outside of his faith.[69] He made multiple trips to Pakistan between January 2002 and mid-2003. During the first of these, he stayed for two months with an uncle in a suburb of Islamabad, where he enrolled in advance computer courses. Another of the trips was to meet a prospective bride,[70] with whom he had previously spoken online. It was on this visit that the authorities tied Khawaja to Babar, who accompanied him to the girl's home.[71]

By August 2003, the group of men had coalesced into a determined, skilled terrorist cell. They had the will to kill and had honed their skills to do so. They decided to leave Pakistan—except for Amin, who had taken up residence there—and return to their respective homes in order to move the plot forward. In November, Garcia, calling himself "John Lewis," inquired about purchasing a large amount of ammonium nitrate fertilizer from an agricultural supply store in Burgess Hill, West Sussex. The cell decided to purchase 1,300 pounds of fertilizer and, using their own names, rented a public storage facility in order to house it. It took three of them to move the heavy containers into the storage unit.

Suspicious of the group, the manager called the police, who immediately inserted an undercover officer, "Amanda," as the new warehouse receptionist. They then secretly swapped the fertilizer with a benign substance and installed hidden cameras which recorded Khyam as he checked the contents of the containers. In February 2004, MI5 intercepted a phone call between Khyam, in Crawley, and Amin, in Pakistan, in which they discussed the quantities of ingredients needed to construct a fertilizer bomb. Police also planted audio-recording devices in the homes, apartments and cars of the cell members, gathering approximately 3,500 hours' worth of conversation, much of it incriminating. In March 2004, for instance, Khyam was recorded discussing simultaneous attacks on Britain's gas, electricity and water systems: "The electrics go off so it's a blackout, and then the gas lot move in and bang," he said. "Then something goes wrong with the water, a simultaneous attack."[72]

The Royal Canadian Mounted Police acted first, arresting Khawaja in his family's home in the Ottawa suburb of Orleans under Canada's 2001 Anti-terrorism Act. Officers found a half-built bomb detonator and an assortment of small arms. Over the next few days, the British arrested 18 others in a series of raids across southeast England. Amin surrendered to Pakistani intelligence. In the US, special agents from the FBI's New York office arrested Babar in Queens. In June 2004, he pleaded guilty to providing material support for terrorists and said in court that he had decided to testify against the other cell members in order to reduce his own sentence. He became the prosecution's star witness in the British trials against the cell.

July 7, 2005

Through a combination of luck, persistence and a robust international law enforcement and intelligence effort, the British authorities had thwarted what might have been a catastrophic terrorist attack. But, as soon became clear, this was not the only group of British Pakistani men plotting to attack the UK. In the course of the Crevice investigation, MI5 created a list of 55 suspects who had come into contact with the cell in some capacity. They prioritized 15 individuals as being "essential" for immediate follow-up. The other 40 were described as "desirable" subjects, whom they hoped to investigate when they had the necessary resources. These designations referred to probability of threat. The British government defines the categories in the following way:

- *Essential*—an individual who is likely to be directly involved in, or have knowledge of, plans for terrorist activity, or an individual who may have knowledge of terrorist activity;
- *Desirable*—an individual who is associated with individuals who are directly involved in, or have knowledge of, plans for terrorist activity or who is raising money for terrorism or who is in jail and would be an essential target if at large;
- *Other*—an individual who may be associated with individuals who are directly involved in, or have knowledge of, plans for terrorist activity.[73]

On the "desirable" list were two names—Muhammad Siddique Khan and Shehzad Tanweer—both of whom would become household names just over one year later. However, before the British police and security agencies could begin to follow these threads, they were forced to divert all available manpower into investigating another suspect, Dhiren Barot, a Hindu convert to Islam, who had proposed a series of attacks against the UK, including a radioactive "dirty bomb" and a plot to blow up limousines filled with gas cylinders in London. He had also planned attacks in America. By shifting their focus on to Barot, the authorities tragically allowed a similarly devastating plot the opportunity to come to fruition.

At 8:50 a.m. on July 7, 2005, three massive explosions ripped through the London Underground system: the first on the Circle Line between Aldgate and Liverpool Street, the next at Edgware Road station and the third on the Piccadilly Line between Russell Square and King's Cross. At 9:47 a.m. a fourth explosion occurred on the upper deck of a London bus in Tavistock Place. Fifty-two people were killed in the attacks and several hundred injured. The suicide bombers were later identified as Muhammad Siddique Khan, Hasib Hussain, Shehzad Tanweer, and Jermaine Lindsay, the first three British nationals of Pakistani origin and the fourth a Jamaican convert to Islam.

On the day of the attacks the group assembled at Luton train station and traveled together to King's Cross, from where they dispersed to conduct their explosions, all four of which were planned to be simultaneous. However, Hussain stopped to buy batteries and then a breakfast at McDonald's after his bomb had initially failed to detonate. Since the whole underground system had been closed down as a result of the first three bombs, he adapted his plans, boarded a double-decker bus and detonated his device. The explosions were caused by highly unstable but effective organic peroxide-based devices, packed into backpacks.

As the investigation into the attacks unfolded, it became clear that the cell had included precisely the type of individuals whom the British government knew they would have the most trouble identifying: British citizens with almost nothing exceptional about them; what counter-terrorism officials refer to as "clean skins." All four of these men were frighteningly mundane, which allowed them to exist just beneath the government's radar until they were ready to strike.

The cell leader, Muhammad Siddique Khan, was a secularly educated Muslim who in his youth had socialized with a diverse group of friends. He had seemed generally apathetic about political and social issues and was viewed as affable by those who knew him when he was growing up. After completing secondary school, he held a series of low-paying jobs, including one as an administrative assistant for the Department of Trade and Industry, where, as he was fluent in Urdu and Punjabi, he helped to promote British corporate activity abroad. He drank socially and may even have experimented with drugs for a time. Soon, though, he began to fall into a puritanical strand of Salafist Islam. Some reports attribute his desire to find religion to a particular incident at a nightclub. Others show a more gradual progression. What is clear, however, is that he began surrounding himself with similarly minded young men who stoked one another's conservative fires. But there is another layer to the story that is usually missed. Jonathan Hacker and Claudio Franco learned that Khan had once worked with Omar Sharif and Asif Hanif, the two British Muslims who attacked a nightclub in Israel in 2003, in order to recruit Muslim youth for training in Afghanistan.[74] One of his close friends, with whom he lectured and volunteered at a Salafist bookstore, was Shehzad Tanweer.

Tanweer was a bright student and an avid cricketer. He came from a well-regarded, hard-working family: his father was a respected entrepreneur in Leeds. Tanweer himself studied sports science at the city's Metropolitan University from 2001. He had always been serious about his faith but showed no inclination toward extremism: in fact, he was viewed by his peers as a nice, normal guy. He owned a red Mercedes, which his father had bought for him, wore designer clothing and took pride in looking good. Around the middle of 2002, though, his priorities shifted, and Islam became his world. In 2003, he dropped out of university and began devoting long periods to religious study while also working part-time at his father's fish and chip shop. This was when he became friends with Khan.

In January 2003, Khan and his wife performed the *Hajj*, or pilgrimage, to Mecca. Upon his return in February, those around him noticed a transformation in his perspective. He began slipping in his job working with children at a local community center, and when he did show up for work he seemed aggressive and was disconnected from the children whom he used to adore. Along with Tanweer and their small group of hardline friends he began to attract negative attention within the local Muslim community for his ultra-conservative Salafist opinions.

The group spent much of their time in Beeston, a suburb of Leeds with a large British Pakistani minority. It also had a pervasive drug problem. In a fascinating article, Shiv Malik explained how Khan got caught up with a group of self-righteous Pakistani youth vigilantes who sought to save their community from the drug epidemic:

> the older generation [of Pakistani Muslims] didn't know how to deal with the drug problem. They were largely illiterate and didn't know the system, so they would sooner move out than try to fight the dealers. The only people who seemed to do anything about the drug-taking were a group of second-generation Pakistanis called the "Mullah boys." This was a fluid group of 15

to 20 members that formed in the mid-1990s, initially as a response to the drugs issue. Muhammad Siddique Khan was a leading member . . . the group kidnapped young Pakistani drug addicts and, with the consent of their families, held them in a flat near the Wahabi-inclined mosque on Stratford Street—and forcibly cleansed them of their drug habits . . . [This was later] corroborated by an ex-drug user called Asim Suleman. He had been cold-turkeyed by the Mullah boys in 1996, and Siddique Khan, Khan's friend Naveed Fiaz and Tafazal Mohammed, Khan's line manager in his youth worker job, had asked Suleman back to help with another round in 2001. Following 9/11, the Mullah boys had become increasingly religious.[75]

Khan and Tanweer traveled to Islamist events outside the Leeds area to recruit Muslim youth in the North and the Midlands. They also spent countless hours viewing Jihadist websites together. One of their colleagues was Muhammad Quayyum Khan, a suspected al-Qaida contact who had also been fingered in the Operation Crevice investigation. In July 2003, Quayyum reportedly put Khan and Tanweer in touch with his contacts in Pakistan in order that they could receive training in bomb-making. Soon the two men were making multiple trips to Pakistan. In November 2004, they spent three months there. By this time, eight months before the London bombings, both seem already to have crossed the mental threshold for waging an attack in the UK. They then quickly moved one of their friends, Hasib Hussain, down the path of radicalization.

Hussain was the baby of the group, born in Leeds in September 1986. He was overweight, quiet in school and had few friends. In early 2002, he accompanied his family on pilgrimage to Saudi Arabia, where he seemed to find religion. Upon his return, he began wearing traditional Islamic clothing and white robes on Fridays. He also publicly supported al-Qaida in school, writing "Al Qaida No Limits" on the cover of one of his books. By 2003, he was actively searching out similarly dedicated young Muslim men in the area. It was through youth clubs that he became close to Tanweer and Khan. In 2004, he suddenly stopped dressing in traditional robes and returned to Western-style clothing, presumably to avoid attracting undue attention to himself or his associates as they became more committed to enacting violence against Britain.

The fourth member of the group, Jermaine Lindsay, was the only non-Pakistani: he was born in Jamaica in September 1985 to an unwed teenage mother. The following year they moved to Huddersfield with a man who reportedly treated Lindsay harshly as he was growing up. Nevertheless, he was a bright child, a good student and athletic: as a teenager, he was interested in martial arts and kickboxing. In 2000, his mother converted to Islam and Lindsay followed suit, hoping to find a community with which he could identify. Two years later, though, his mother moved with a new boyfriend to the United States, leaving the 17-year-old Lindsay living alone in the family home in Huddersfield. He began spending more time online, and met a white British convert to Islam on the internet whom he soon married. He also began to fall deeper into a more puritanical form of Islam. As many converts do, Lindsay felt the need to prove himself to other Muslims around him: he immersed himself in learning Arabic and memorizing long passages of the Quran; he began wearing traditional Islamic white robes; and he listened to the Jihadist preaching of another Jamaican, Abdullah al-Faisal, who is currently serving a prison sentence for soliciting murder, incitement to murder, incitement to racial hatred and distributing material of a racial hatred nature. In late 2004 Lindsay somehow came into contact with Khan and Tanweer.

In October of that year, Khan began fundraising for an attack. He took out a £10,000 personal loan and charged a variety of expenses to several credit cards. This surge of spending was probably mostly for travel to Pakistan. Around February 2005, Khan and Tanweer made their final trip there. It is now believed that Khan, at least, was taken to a remote tribal area of Pakistan or Afghanistan and put through a ten to 15-day intensive course on explosives construction. According to a Pakistani government official, "This new course dispenses with much physical and mental training and . . . they impart various methods in explosives and detonators . . . This includes how to make suicide jackets, how to convert readily available goods like fertiliser into explosives, how to make car bombs and certain other tips."[76] At some point during this course, Tanweer is believed to have joined Khan in the camp, and this was when they both filmed their "martyrdom" videotapes, which were later broadcast by al-Qaida's official propaganda outlet, as-Sahab.

The explosives construction phase of the plot began around March 2005, when Tanweer and Khan had returned to Britain. Khan and the others began liberally spending money, purchasing supplies for the attack. Khan defaulted on his personal loan repayments and was overdrawn on his bank accounts. Lindsay started making purchases by check, which bounced in June and July. Each device comprised several pounds of homemade explosives, which the cell concocted using readily available commercial ingredients.[77]

The creation of home-made explosives creates an almost paralyzing odor, which explains the facemasks that Tanweer and Lindsay purchased on the internet. Investigators also found that the tops of plants outside of the windows of their safe-house had been seared by toxic fumes, indicating that they had left the windows open to ventilate the room. Curiously, both Tanweer's and Hussain's families had noticed that their hair was growing lighter in June and July, which they explained as being the result of swimming-pool chlorine. The bleaching effect of the fumes also explains why the men purchased shower caps. By July 2005, the bombs had been assembled. They wasted little time and executed their attack on 7 July.

On September 1, 2005 a video message from Khan was aired on al-Jazirah television in which he said:

> I and thousands like me are forsaking everything for what we believe. Our driving motivation doesn't come from tangible commodities that this world has to offer. Our religion is Islam—obedience to the one true God, Allah, and following the footsteps of the final Prophet and messenger Muhammad . . . Your democratically elected governments continuously perpetuate atrocities against my people all over the world. And your support of them makes you directly responsible, just as I am directly responsible for protecting and

avenging my Muslim brothers and sisters. Until we feel security, you will be our targets. And until you stop the bombing, gassing, imprisonment and torture of my people we will not stop this fight. We are at war and I am a soldier.[78]

The British security services have come under intense criticism in the face of this seemingly bottomless pit of angry Muslim youth ready to kill themselves to make a point. In the review of intelligence records that it conducted, the British government found that it had on record a telephone number which it identified after the attacks as belonging to Lindsay. They also had on record a telephone number registered to a "Siddeque Khan" and details of contacts between that number and an individual who had been under investigation in 2003. A review of related surveillance data showed that Khan and Tanweer had met with others under secret service investigation in 2004. In relation to the meetings in 2003, the secret service said it was apparent that something was being planned but that there was no information about what it was. The individual under investigation was not himself an "essential" target, and there was no reason to believe that Khan was worthy of further investigation above other priorities.[79]

Further plots would later be uncovered, most notably an attempt by a cell of mostly British Pakistani Muslims to smuggle liquid explosives onto a plane and detonate them in mid-air. In June 2007, police found two vehicles packed with explosives and shrapnel outside London nightclubs. And soon after an attack was launched against Glasgow Airport using a car bomb loaded with propane tanks, fuel and shrapnel. Only the bombers themselves were seriously injured, with one of the two men dying from his wounds.

In response to the growing security threat Britain faces from within its own borders, MI5 has substantially expanded its staff, from 1,800 in 2001 to a projected 3,500 in 2008. But there is no doubt that the number of suspected terrorist networks continues to grow and adapt. In September 2006, a recently departed MI5 director, Dame Eliza Manningham-Buller, said that, under her watch, the service had been tracking more than 1,600 known active militants.[80] Given how entrenched global Jihadism has become over the past 20 years in the UK, however, it will likely take at least a generation of aggressive counter-radicalization initiatives before the ideology is truly marginalized there.

8 Toward a strategy

In the fifth century BC the ancient Chinese strategist of war Sun Tsu noted that "What is of supreme importance in war is to attack the enemy's strategy."[1] Without a deep knowledge of one's adversary, he argued, one cannot expect to wage an effective campaign. Every decision one makes with regard to that opponent, including their goals, their strengths and their vulnerabilities, would stem from a faulty premise. A war could therefore be lost before a single battle was fought if one failed to attack the enemy's strategy.

In order to defeat al-Qaida and its associated movements over the long term the world must craft and implement an integrated strategy that is built on a firm understanding of the Jihadist movement's own grand strategy. To date, no such counter-Jihadist strategy has been put in place. This is not to say that national governments have not formulated any counter-terrorism strategies. To the contrary, nearly every country has some sort of stated strategy to counter terrorist threats. These strategies, however, are almost entirely constructed on the basis of what the global Jihadist movement is *believed* to be, not what it actually *is*. In many ways, then, existing national strategies are built to fight an illusion of the real enemy.

Some argue that the lack of progress in developing an integrated global strategy that targets the Jihadist movement's strategy is due to the challenges of transforming large bureaucratic organizations. Others point to problems with information sharing within and across governments, stressing the need for further integration and coordination initiatives. But these are merely symptoms of a more serious malady: the Jihadist movement remains poorly understood within the policy community.

Strategies are invaluable for commanders as they provide a series of carefully crafted plans for achieving specific results. The most effective strategies are those that have been carefully calibrated to the context in which one is waging a campaign. This includes a mastery of one's own strengths and weaknesses as well as those of one's adversary. Ideally, strategies utilize all available, relevant and appropriate instruments at an individual's or organization's disposal in order to achieve objectives. There are few tasks that are more important for ensuring long-term global security than formulating a comprehensive strategy for suppressing the further promulgation of the global Jihadist ideology.

George Kennan argued in a landmark 1947 article that the United States should pursue "a policy of firm containment, designed to confront the Russians with unalterable counter-force at every point where they show signs of encroaching upon the interests of a peaceful and stable world."[2] The Western world today faces a strikingly similar contest of wills against global Jihadism. There is no doubt that global Jihadism is, at its core, incompatible with liberal democratic values. To be clear, its core doctrinal tenets reject the very basis upon which liberal democracies stand. The global Jihadist ideology must therefore at the least be held in check and at best eradicated.

Kennan's analysis ought to resound in the ears of policy-makers today: the world can fight an antagonistic ideology only through an integrated set of national policies aimed at limiting the scope and breadth of that ideology's spread. And as during the Cold War battle with the USSR, the global commitment to containing the spread of the global Jihadist movement must be persistent, aggressive, and enduring.

Behind the statements and white papers released by governments seeking to maintain domestic support for counter-terrorism initiatives, there remains a great state of confusion and discord with regard to the enemy's identity and its strategic goals. Most national-level counter-terrorism strategies share several basic elements, usually built around short-term and long-term functional tasks, including protecting the homeland, conducting military action and intelligence collection overseas and countering radicalization at home. These functional tasks, while critical for success, must still be guided by an overall strategic vision that is grounded in two very basic questions: "What specifically is the Jihadist movement trying to achieve?" and "How do its strategists plan to achieve it?" Without answers to these questions, no war ought to be fought, because it will be doomed to failure from the outset.

The global Jihadist movement must be contained in the short term and dismantled over the long term. Containment entails recognizing global Jihadism wherever and whenever it appears, something that is much more difficult to achieve in reality than on paper. Knowledge about the internal machinations, personalities and doctrine of the global Jihadist movement varies significantly from agency to agency, and even from office to office. Further complicating matters is that implementing this part of the strategy runs straight into the legal, national and political walls that have been built up to protect the rights of citizens.

Dismantling the global Jihadist movement requires promoting its implosion from within and attacking it from the outside, and both approaches must be pursued simultaneously. The challenge to catalyzing a self-induced implosion is that governments lack a firm sense of what fractures already exist within the global Jihadist movement that can be exacerbated or where potential insertion points exist for chipping away at the movement's internal architecture. As a result of these obstacles, governments have been more successful attacking the movement from the outside. Since 2001, law enforcement, military and intelligence agencies around the world have worked together in targeting the movement's senior leadership, facilitators, financiers and operatives. There is no doubt, however, that the movement is impressively resilient and continues to adapt to changing circumstances on the ground.

Because of their support for the military occupation of Iraq, most Western governments' popularity has plummeted across the Islamic world. There is little that the United States or the United Kingdom can say today that is perceived as anything other than self-interested propaganda by the Islamic world. Not engaging with the Islamic world, however, would be even worse—the foreign policy equivalent of ignoring an elephant in the room. So Western governments must continue to try to communicate their goals, successes, and failures in the likes of Iraq and Afghanistan in every way that they can.

Another conundrum is that Western governments can do nothing right in terms of describing their adversary and their fight against it. The variety of terms used to describe that adversary include "al-Qaida," "Jihadist," "militant Islamists," "radical Muslims," "Salafi-Jihadists," "Islamo-fascists," and more. These terms have been deemed objectionable by at least one major constituency, causing Western policy-makers to enter this discussion paralyzed. Because they will be criticized almost irrespective of which term they choose, the policy-makers have tended to avoid using any term that is too specific. So it has become difficult for them to define the adversary, and it is equally difficult to define the nature of the fight. Phrases like "global war on terrorism," "global struggle against violent extremism," "the long war" are all disliked by publics and leaders worldwide. No better slogan, however, has emerged to replace these stock phrases, meaning that Western policy-makers charged with communicating the nature of their efforts to their publics lack even the basic language to describe what they are trying to achieve.

Finally, it has proved very difficult to find qualified advisers on this topic. Fluent native Arabic speakers have often been turned away when trying to volunteer because of fears that they might be a security risk. The CIA and the Department of Homeland Security in the USA, according to some reports, have instead hired cadres of Western, school-trained Arabic speakers—people who are significantly less able to handle multiple dialects and idioms.[3] In 2006, for instance, the FBI was criticized by the *Washington Post* for having only 33 (out of a total of twelve thousand) special agents who were proficient in Arabic five years after 9/11.[4]

Making matters more difficult is that there is no shared lens through which policy-makers, military officials and intelligence analysts view Jihad. Understandings of the concept differ not just from agency to agency but from analyst to analyst. Attitudes across the US government, as one might expect, mirror the wide diversity of opinions and attitudes in the broader American public about the Islamic religion, Jihadism and the nature of the security threats posed by terrorist groups like al-Qaida.

Debates over the meaning of Jihad

The meaning of Jihad is a topic that causes both angst and contention among government officials. There are several reasons why non-Muslim policy-makers have been visibly awkward and vacillating in their discussions of issues relating to this term. First, there has been little incentive within Western bureaucracies for officials to develop a deep cultural and historical knowledge of Islam or to learn the Arabic language. Anecdotal evidence has shown that policy-makers in senior positions across governments do not understand even the basic concepts and dynamics of the global war on terror, the Middle East, or Islam.[5]

Government officials also operate in a highly charged and intensely scrutinized environment. In an era of generally heightened sensitivity to diversity, and an increased awareness that winning the hearts and minds of Muslims is key to defeating the spread of militant Salafism, government officials, most of whom seek readily understandable answers to their questions, are rewarded (or at least not punished) by taking the most politically neutral and non-offensive approach possible.[6] So, since the attacks of 9/11, non-Muslim policy-makers have taken extraordinary steps to demonstrate that they are both tolerant and progressive in their understanding of Islam. This has led to a number of senior policy officials speaking in overly simplistic terms about the nature of the religion. For example, former Secretary of State Colin Powell, the White House press secretary and the former Deputy Secretary for Public Diplomacy Karen Hughes, among others, have publicly and categorically asserted that "Islam is a religion of peace." Meanwhile, the National Aeronautics and Space Administration's Goddard Space Flight Center hosts an Islamic Study Group page on its website which features a presentation by the Council on American–Islamic Relations that clearly explains, "Jihad does not mean Holy War."[7]

An informed grand strategy

An effective grand strategy for defeating the global Jihadist movement must be multi-pronged in nature, global in scope and flexible in execution. It must draw on all sources of national power, including diplomatic, intelligence, military, economic, financial, information and law enforcement. And it needs to transcend conventional boundaries because, for the global Jihadist movement itself, such boundaries are increasingly irrelevant: the battlefield is now everywhere. But more than anything else, it must be grounded in a deep understanding of the global Jihadist movement.

In his book *The 33 Strategies of War*, Robert Greene provides an incisive study of the strategies crafted by some of history's greatest commanders, strategists and leaders.[8] Each of these strategies—including those of Sun Tsu, Clausewitz, and Bonaparte—relies on a particular combination of strength, seduction and deception. And many of them could be usefully applied by governments to combat and eradicate global Jihadism. The following strategies form a powerful grand strategic approach that could significantly enhance the coherence and effectiveness of global counter-terrorist initiatives.

The polarity strategy: declare war on the enemy

Al-Qaida and the Jihadist movement have repeatedly and openly declared war on most Western governments, all Islamic regimes not applying *Sharia* law, and a variety of other entities. They have purposefully sought to polarize the world into two camps: those with the Zionist–Crusader conspiracy and those against it. The movement's willingness specifically to identify its enemies has been a strategic success. It has established internal guidelines for action; what is referred to among military audiences as the "commander's intent." It informs Jihadists about whom they can trust and whom they must hate. The more specific the movement is about whom it stands against, the more protected it is from accusations of hypocrisy or duplicity, so long as its actions are in line with its rhetoric. Providing clear guidelines about whom Jihadists like and dislike is particularly important, given that the movement is physically disconnected and decentralized. Having an established commander's intent therefore empowers the movement's regional field commanders to take this general guidance and apply it in the best way for their local situation. This operational flexibility allows groups like al-Qaida to exist in a state of controlled chaos. It also helps the movement as a whole to inculcate an *esprit de corps* among its members, fostering a belief that they are standing unified against a group of aggressors.

There is no question that most of the world is currently waging war against the Jihadist movement. The enemy, as governments define it, however, might be "terrorists," "al-Qaida and its affiliated organizations," "religious extremists," "deviants," or any number of other derogatory terms. This continued inability to identify a specific enemy has left many governments open to criticism of inconsistency and hypocrisy from external audiences. Such criticism compounds the challenges facing governments seeking to compete with the Jihadist movement for hearts and minds. In contrast, by clearly identifying its enemy, the Jihadist movement has not only retained focus but has opened the door for collaboration with other enemies of its enemy. Jihadists can now readily tap into the grievances held by other groups or constituencies, even if they differ in methods or objectives. This expands their potential recruitment pool and support base. The United States, on the other hand, has framed its war in terms of "with us or against us," dividing the world into two camps and prioritizing exclusivity rather than the inclusivity of the Jihadist movement. This has made it more difficult for Western governments to capitalize on the long list of groups and influential individuals who view the Jihadist movement as a threat to them and their interests. Many of these parties are eager to join a fight *against* al-Qaida, but they could never countenance joining *with* the United States or the West in that fight.

Governments around the world must therefore recalibrate their national strategies to identify a specific and common enemy: the global Jihadist movement. They must also ensure that their public rhetoric centers on building a unified front against a shared enemy, concentrating on temporarily setting aside differences on other issues in order to deal with the greater threat.

The perfect economy strategy: choosing battles carefully

Every force has its limitations, be they manpower, ammunition, funding, morale or numerous other variables. No force is therefore able to execute every mission in exactly the way it desires. However, the Jihadist movement has been particularly effective in its allocation of scarce resources. Obviously outgunned and overpowered militarily, it has made several important decisions. First, it decided to make terrorism a core, although not an all-encompassing, part of its grand strategy. Terrorism allows a small number of people to have a disproportionate impact on a substantially larger enemy by targeting its non-combatants. It is also a relatively inexpensive way to pursue specific strategic objectives. Furthermore, it needs to be perpetrated only periodically in order to inflict long-term psychological trauma on the target population. The global Jihadist movement has therefore been able patiently to conduct reconnaissance, move assets into place, finance, implement training and execute attacks on its own schedule. Trading time —a resource that the Jihadist movement has in abundance—for the ability to calculate actions that will have the greatest effect, the movement has been highly effective in choosing its battles.

Western civilian populations generally do not appreciate that Jihadist terrorism is not focused on them as an end. Jihadists are not seeking to change people's ways of life or causing fear across populations just for the sake of it. Rather, they intend to use the fear they generate to bait Western military forces *into* the Middle East, drive Western business and investment *out* of the Middle East, and therefore bleed Western economies dry by forcing them to defend themselves against the threat of future terrorism.

Global Jihadists have also pursued classic guerrilla and insurgent strategies as a way of conserving energy. They employ these relatively inexpensive and low-tech approaches in order to keep Coalition and local security forces on the defensive with very few fighters. By eliminating static lines, embracing fluidity of operations and prioritizing mobility among their forces, global Jihadists have been able to maximize their limited resources. The Jihadist insurgent strategy fits closely with another important trend in the movement: transforming its single greatest weakness—its geographically dispersed structure—into its greatest strength. Its decentralized network has effectively allowed it to wage an insurgency on a global scale.

In contrast to the global Jihadists who have perfected the strategy of choosing their battles carefully, Western governments, particularly the United States, seem to be doing the opposite. A fortune in American counter-terrorism resources has been allocated to two enormous efforts: protecting the homeland and waging war in Iraq. The underlying assumption of American homeland security programs is that the global Jihadist movement is dedicated to wreaking havoc, mayhem and destruction against civilian targets internationally. By hardening potential targets, securitizing aviation, maritime and terrestrial transport systems and creating a robust network for monitoring the flows of money, information, goods, people and hazardous material within and across borders, governments worldwide have sought to make the terrorist's job more difficult.

Another critical aspect of defending against terrorist attack is communicating information across agencies. The need to gather and share terrorism-related intelligence and analysis internally and across national boundaries has not only been acknowledged but prioritized. Indeed, sharing this knowledge is critical if governments are to disrupt and disable would-be terrorist attacks, denying them entry to countries, hindering their movement if they are already inside, and establishing protective measures to reduce collective vulnerability to terrorist attack. Among the most important sectors for defense and first-response preparedness are: critical infrastructure and key resources, including energy, food and agriculture, water, telecommunications, public health, transportation, the defense industrial base, government facilities, postal and shipping, the chemical industry, emergency services, monuments and icons, information technology, dams, commercial facilities, banking and finance, and nuclear reactors, materials and waste.

The constant threat of terrorists acquiring weapons of mass destruction is a matter of chief concern for governments around the world. Therefore, there has been a unified global effort to deny terrorists access to the materials, expertise and other enabling capabilities required to develop such weapons through counter-proliferation and non-proliferation initiatives.

Divide and conquer: factionalizing the global Jihadist movement

For decades, Jihadism has exercised great fascination for the students of Egyptian intellectuals and the acolytes of charismatic Saudi shaikhs. Frustrated, discontented, hopeless of overthrowing the political system—or simply too impatient to attempt to do so legal means—Jihadists sought instead to change the face of society. Jihadist revolutionaries found in Salafist thought a highly convenient rationalization for their political desires, one that afforded religious justification for their impatience, for their categoric denial of any value in seeking reform from apostate leaders, for their yearning for political power and personal revenge.

It is not surprising that a small group of men came to believe and promote the undeniable truth of Salafist teaching in schools, universities, mosques, and now online. Edward Gibbon's words, used by Kennan to illustrate the process of self-delusion he saw among those in the Soviet Union, are equally apt in today's conflict:

> From enthusiasm to imposture the step is perilous and slippery; the demon of Socrates affords a memorable instance of how a wise man may deceive himself, how a good man may deceive others, how the conscience may slumber in a mixed and middle state between self-illusion and voluntary fraud.[9]

The global Jihadist movement would not exist today without its scholars, shaikhs and intellectuals. The power of these individuals to steer and guide the movement cannot be overstated. What is poorly understood today, however, is that massive fractures exist among these thinkers and their followers that could be widened in such a way to catalyze the self-destruction of the Salafist ideology.

Some of these fractures are visible in the debates over strategy and the future direction of the Jihadist movement. Consider, for instance, the debate that occurred between the emir of al-Qaida in Iraq, Abu Musab al-Zarqawi, and the organization's High Command in 2005. Zarqawi, the thug leader of al-Qaida's brutal operations in Iraq at the time, had been pursuing a strategy of turning everyone against everyone else. The logic was simple: by focusing effort on driving the American forces from Iraq, a virtually impossible task, Zarqawi would provide the Shia majority with the opportunity they needed to consolidate power, establish a functioning government, set up social infrastructure and build an effective national guard and police force. So by the time he was able to turn his focus on the Shia authorities, they would have entrenched themselves across the country and ingratiated themselves with the local population.

However, al-Qaida's senior leadership was highly displeased with Zarqawi for what they considered to be his overly violent methodology. Rather than conducting savage beheadings and massive explosions against other Muslims, Zarqawi should be concentrating on opening up security vacuums and establishing territorial footholds across Iraq. A stern letter-writing campaign was inaugurated by Ayman al-Zawahiri and his top deputies, including Atiyah abd al-Rahman and Abu Yahya Libi, all of whom scolded Zarqawi for his actions. The latter resisted their demands and the continuing dispute ripped apart the broader Jihadist community. The competition between supporters of Zarqawi and supporters of the High Command was played out in a very public way. If one media outlet released a propaganda video prominently featuring Zarqawi, it would be followed almost immediately by one from another media group highlighting Bin Laden and Zawahiri. The two sides were reconciled only with Zarqawi's death in June 2006.

Other splits have been more personal. Take the rift between the two founders of Egyptian Islamic Jihad, Zawahiri and Abd al-Qadir ibn Abd al-Aziz, that occurred in the early 1990s. The latter lost faith in his erstwhile friend and colleague because of Zawahiri's poor strategic judgement in waging war against the Egyptian government, his stubbornness and his decision to take sole credit for a book that they had co-authored. Or consider the feud between Abu Qatada and Abu Musab al-Suri over the former's continued support for Algerian terrorism in the mid-1990s, when the GIA's activities crossed the point of acceptability for most Muslims and even most Jihadists.

Jihadist thinkers often express sadness for and disappointment in any colleagues who recant, even when they know it may have been coerced. They commonly refer to these people as "turncoats" or "backbiters." Consider the fall from Jihadist grace of two Saudi shaikhs, Safar al-Hawali and Salman al-Awdah, who not only recanted but actively joined the Saudi government in fighting against the global Jihadist movement. The British-based thinker Abu Basir al-Tartusi similarly created a firestorm among some Jihadists when he spoke out against the use of suicide bombings in the United Kingdom. And the Kuwaiti Jihadist Shaikh Hamad al-Ali irritated a number of Jihadist scholars when he argued against the formation of the Islamic State of Iraq. Even the legendary scholar Abu Muhammad al-Maqdisi created rifts within the community when he castigated his former student and partner Abu Musab al-Zarqawi.

The center of gravity strategy: hit them where it hurts

The Jihadist movement's most important resources are its new recruits. If the amount of new blood entering the movement could be reduced, organizations like al-Qaida would inevitably become stale, out of touch and less active globally in the long term. By focusing on this "center of gravity," the point at which the entire movement draws its power and endurance, Western governments would be able to hinder the movement significantly.

Most discussions about public diplomacy and strategic communication efforts mention the audiences who should be targeted. Some argue that the target audience should be the Jihadists themselves, and there is indeed some evidence to show that committed participants in the movement can be swayed. A number of countries, most notably Saudi Arabia, have implemented re-education and de-radicalization programs to control the spread of Jihadist thought among the movement's foot soldiers. Others argue that, rather than focusing on the few who are already committed, resources might be better spent on the broader constituencies whom the Jihadists are trying to suck into their vortex. Thinking in terms of concentric circles, with al-Qaida in the center, the next ring out would include the uncommitted, albeit ultra-conservative and irate, Salafist youth. These people are fluent in the ideological doctrine and share the socio-economic and political grievances of the movement, but they have yet to cross the mental threshold of identifying themselves as "Jihadist." Nevertheless, they probably already possess several of the behavioral characteristics that are familiar among hardline Jihadists:

- *Social disillusionment*: Followers of Jihadism tend to emerge from populations who see themselves as disenfranchised by their own government and see no legitimate way to promote change in their country. Without a stake in the existing order, they are vulnerable to manipulation by those who advocate a perverse political vision based on violence and destruction. If they live in the West, they might also be angry with their immediate family for leaving what they tend to glamorize as a more religiously pure country.
- *Belief in conspiracies*: The global Jihadist message seems particularly resonant with people whose knowledge about the world is conditioned by conspiracy theorizing. Such theories keep grievances alive by filtering out or altering facts that would otherwise challenge prejudices and propaganda. Paranoia, obsession and mistrust of outsiders tend to be pervasive among Jihadist followers.
- *Need for simplification*: Those individuals who fall under the spell of the Jihadist ideology often share a need for black-and-white answers to problems. They need to know who they can trust and against whom they must defend themselves. Above all else, they look for guarantees that certain actions will guarantee them a place in Heaven.
- *Deference to leadership*: Although most discussions about the attraction of Jihadism for individuals center on peer networks, the role of charismatic leadership seems to be far more persuasive for Jihadist recruits. They desperately seek counsel from senior figures (both dead and alive) about all aspects of life, particularly in regard to their ideology.

If young Muslims exhibiting these characteristics can be identified before moving to violence, governments may succeed in weakening the global Jihadist movement.

Give Jihadists enough rope to hang themselves

Ultimately, the Jihadist movement's self-destructive tendencies will be its downfall. The only reason why the most recent manifestation of global Jihadism has not yet collapsed on itself is because it has consistently succeeded in redirecting criticism away from itself. This redirection campaign has been remarkably sophisticated and yet cunningly simple. In some cases, the global Jihadist leadership does little more than argue that it is the lesser of two evils. Usually in the aftermath of an unpopular attack, the leaders may deny their involvement or claim that an attack did not go as planned. Either way, they argue, the mistake can still be justified in the eyes of God because the enemy is so bad that Muslims must be willing to sacrifice themselves for the greater good. In other cases, the leadership might dismiss allegations made against it by its critics as nothing more than fabrication and falsities. Playing on popular conspiracy theories that pervade the Islamic world, the leaders are able to mitigate the damage of unfavorable characterizations by attacking the source's credibility, rather than responding to the substance of the charge.

One of the reasons why the Jihadist movement has become so good at conducting public relations damage-control operations is because it has had so much practice: most of its actions are unpopular among the broader Islamic world. Jihadism's fundamental weakness is that it offers no attractive end result to most people. This is why the movement has been so vocal about its motivations for fighting and its short-term objectives: its leaders are well aware that their terrorist methodology and their long-term strategic objectives are widely unpopular.

Those policy-makers around the world charged with defeating the Jihadist movement ought to pause momentarily and consider that sometimes less action can yield more fruit. As the great strategist Napoleon Bonaparte once said: "If your enemy is busy shooting himself in the foot, don't get in his way." Or, to put it another way, today's global fight against al-Qaida and its associated movements might be characterized as a failure by governments and societies around the world to let the enemy have enough rope to hang itself. Governments around the world should make a concerted effort to stop interrupting the Jihadist movement as it damages its own credibility within its core constituency and shatters the religious legitimacy in which it cloaks itself.

Forcing strategies: control the dynamic

Global Jihadists have spent decades learning how to dominate public discourse. As members of a generally unpopular and peripheral movement, Jihadist scholars have historically needed to defend themselves against vigorous smear campaigns waged by government-sponsored religious scholars. Jihadist scholars have also had to master the art of rhetorical manipulation in order to recruit new members into their movement. Governments across the Middle East have sought to make the movement as unattractive as possible. They have funded large-scale propaganda campaigns in the hope of ideologically immunizing their youth populations from being tempted by the movement. They have also engaged in highly public arrest and interrogation campaigns of Jihadists in order to intimidate those who might be ideologically committed to the movement from acting on their desires. Over time, though, Jihadists have learned how to navigate around these hurdles by seizing the offensive in the public debate. They realized that they could put governments and their religious advisers back on their heels by challenging their overall religiosity.

Governments looking to reclaim dominance in the court of public opinion ought to take the following steps:

- Aggressively assault the reputation of the global Jihadist movement by presenting the latter's most reprehensible words and actions. Prove that the movement has historically offered and continues to offer nothing but violence and bloodshed.
- Force mainstream Salafists to define their positions on specific issues as often and as publicly as possible. This will then be forced to discuss not only what they are for but what they are against, which will allow Muslims to see just how conservative much of their ideology is across multiple fronts.
- Steer conversations about terrorism away from religious issues and more toward common denominators (family, social justice, accountable leadership). Help people to find a theme on which they can unite, not an enemy against which they can unite. If Middle East audiences are told they must unite against an enemy, they will tend to pick the West, not Jihadism.
- Continue to promote the ideals of the Western liberal value system. There is no doubt that much of the world still looks to the West for hope. The values of respect for human dignity and protection of the minority voice are transcendental and hold sway over many of the audiences whom some have been eager to write off as lost causes.
- Move away from the inflexible "talking-points" that define (particularly American) public diplomacy initiatives and implement more process-driven campaigns through the realm of human-to-human exchanges and micro-level communication efforts. The goal must not be to communicate a specific point to an audience. Rather, it should be to catalyze discussion and inform that debate. Governments must empower a new cadre of young, smart professionals across the private, public and academic spheres, with the flexibility and resources to discuss hard issues candidly in a variety of public fora.

These initiatives ought to be paired with the hard-nosed counter-terrorism policies already in effect. The global Jihadist movement will not die easily, so stopping those operatives whose job it is to conduct attacks and the commanders who order them remains a critical piece of the overall counter-Jihadist strategy. Although the best methodology for stopping these individuals is open to debate, there is no doubt that success in this sphere requires an enormous amount of global cooperation on intelligence, military and law enforcement fronts.

Know your enemy: the intelligence strategy

Many followers of the global Jihadist movement have made studying the works of their adversary a chief priority. They read military strategy books, contemporary periodicals, and popular political commentary in order to target weaknesses and degrade strengths. In contrast, to date, the rest of the world has dedicated only a cursory amount of time toward really understanding the global Jihadist movement from the inside. One of the most effective ways to learn about the priorities, sensitivities and goals of Jihadist thinkers is simply to read their works. But as there are thousands of books, articles and blog postings in cyberspace, studying the enemy from their own side is a daunting task for anyone. However, thanks to Issa al-Awshan, the now dead Saudi Jihadist involved with al-Qaida's propaganda machine on the peninsula, there is a short cut. In *39 Ways to Serve and Participate in Jihad* (which has been translated into multiple languages and is one of the most widely read Jihadist books of the decade), Awshan provides readers with a road-map for learning about the movement.[10] There is no reason why those outside of the Jihadist Movement should not use his work in order to understand the enemy better.

Awshan explains that one of the best ways for Muslims not on the front line to support the movement is for them to learn the jurisprudence of Jihad and related legal issues. Doing this allows anyone to become a potential teacher, recruiter and religious adviser, he contends. Generally, Jihobbyists or those interested in the topic of Jihad should read works by Abdallah Azzam, Yousuf al-Ayiri, Abu Muhammad al-Maqdisi, Abu Qatada, and Abd al-Qadir ibn Abd al-Aziz. Awshan then references a multi-part Jihadist reading list compiled by an unnamed "virtuous scholar":

Beginner readings on Jihad

1 *Guidance of the Gentle Man in the Most Important Tasks of Ibrahim's Community* by Abu Muhammad al-Maqdisi.
2 *Mobilization*, a 2002/2003 sermon by Usama Bin Laden.
3 *Jihad and the Interpretation of Religious Texts* by Abu Qatada al-Filistini.
4 *The Basic Issue of Preparation* by Abd al-Qadir Abd al-Aziz.
5 *A Guide to Explain the Fine Points of Islam* by Sulaiman al-Ulwan.
6 *Defending Muslim Lands is the Most Important Individual Obligation* by Abdallah Azzam.

Intermediate readings on Jihad

1 *Unbelief and Tyranny* by Abu Basir al-Tartusi.
2 *Millat Ibrahim* by Abu Muhammad al-Maqdisi.
3 *Which of the Two Groups is More Deserving of Slaughter?* by Ahmad al-Dakhil.
4 *The New Crusader War* by Yosef al-Ayiri.
5 *A Warning against Excess in Accusations of Apostasy* by Abu Muhammad al-Maqdisi.
6 *Tendencies of the Savior* by Sulaiman al-Ulwan.

Advanced readings on Jihad

IDEOLOGY

1 *Facts about Monotheism* by Ali al-Khudayr.
2 *Hypocrisy* by Ali al-Khudayr.
3 *God's Triumph is Near* by Sulaiman al-Ulwan.
4 *Democracy is a Religion* by Abu Muhammad al-Maqdisi.
5 *Al-Wala wal-Bara: Inherited Ideology and Lost Reality* by Ayman al-Zawahiri.
6 *Garden of the Favored* by Abu Qatada al-Filistini.
7 *Beneficial Materials on the Apostasy of Those who Abandon Monotheism* by Muhammad Bin Abd-al-Wahab.

CALAMITY

1 *A Guide to the Apostasy of Those who Help the Americans* by Nasir al-Fahd.
2 *Articles on the Need for Jihad against the Crusaders and Jews* by Nasir al-Fahd.
3 *The Use of Weapons of Mass Destruction* by Nasir al-Fahd.
4 *Martyrdom Operations: Suicide or Martyrdom?* by Yosef al-Ayiri.
5 *Spies* by Abu Basir al-Tartusi.
6 *Ruling on the Obligation of Jihad against the Crusaders* by Sulaiman al-Ulwan.
7 *Selected Passages on Asking Infidels for Help* by Hamoud Bin Uqla as-Shuaybi.
8 *A Guide to the Tradition on Joining the Military* by Ahmad al-Khalidi.
9 *A Guide to the Condemnation of Opposition* by Abd al-Aziz al-Jarbu.
10 *The Need to Rescue the Oppressed from the Prisons of the Tyrants and Apostates* by Abu Jandal al-Azdi.

Awshan continues to list a variety of other biographies, books and articles related to Jihad. The authors in this bibliography are among the most prominent and revered within the global Jihadist movement; and, importantly, their works are increasingly being translated into and read in English.

The writings that Awshan highlights could be compared in their tone and scope to the works of other revolutionary zealots throughout history. Consider Adolf Hitler's *Mein Kampf*, for instance, a book that freely offered the world an advance outline of his hopes, dreams and fears. It was not read widely in the West; nor was it viewed as being serious by those who did read it. In exactly the same way, the Jihadist books that Awshan identifies are currently largely ignored by most governments. But thanks to his work, governments have a precious opportunity to read today's equivalents of *Mein Kampf*. If they seize that opportunity—and they must—they will be able to follow Sun Tzu's counsel about knowing one's enemy. Although the aforementioned writings are only a small fraction of the core readings for those Muslims who are considering waging violent Jihad, if the West continues to disregard them history will almost certainly repeat itself.

Hope for tomorrow

This book has sought to demonstrate that big ideas can have very big consequences. There can be little doubt that those individuals who are willing to engage in acts of Jihadist terrorism must be identified and neutralized before they can unleash their wrath upon the world. But an even greater issue is that no matter how many foot soldiers are killed or captured in the course of this fight against the global Jihadist movement, new generations of Jihobbyists will emerge. More young, angry men will offer themselves to God in exchange for an empty promise.

This reality will persist for as long as the Jihadist movement has a cadre of smart and motivated leaders and thinkers who are actively recruiting, training, educating and deploying their operatives globally. These leaders provide the vision that their followers strive to realize and emulate. They offer direction, discipline and inspiration for their subordinates to accomplish a given task. They take the reality of the world and simplify it in such a way that only two sides emerge: those who are willing to fight for *Sharia*, *Tawhid*, *Jihad* and their *Aqidah*; and those who are in the way.

If there is a bright side to this global war, it is that the Jihadist movement offers nothing more than empty rhetoric and wanton bloodshed. It is a bankrupt ideology that, like numerous historical precedents, will eventually collapse under its own internal contradictions. The world cannot simply wait for that to happen, however: it must, and it can, accelerate the process and triumph over the global Jihadist movement.

Notes

1 Introduction

1 "Meeting of Sawt al-Jihad with the Commander Abdul-Aziz Al-Muqrin." Translated by at-Tibyan Publications, October 2003.
2 Gilles Kepel, *Jihad: The Trail of Political Islam*. Cambridge, MA: Belknap Press, 2002.
3 This passage comes from a longer essay that appeared on a number of English-language Jihadist forums. The document from which this quotation was extracted came from: www.momeen.org/up/uploads/5e757ed9b5.doc.
4 Bin Laden wrote his 1996 "Declaration of War" in August of that year. It was published in *Al Quds Al Arabi*, a London-based newspaper. This translated excerpt comes from the full-text translation released by the Committee for the Defense of Legitimate Rights, which was posted on the internet in October 1996.
5 Anton LaGuardia, "Al-Qaida Places Recruiting Ads," *Daily Telegraph*, August 10, 2005.
6 "New al-Qaida Weekly Internet News Broadcast Celebrates US Hurricanes and Gaza Pullout, Reports on al-Zarqawi's Anti-Shiite Campaign and Chemical Mortar Shells in Iraq," *Middle East Media Research Institute Special Dispatch Series* 993, September 23, 2005. Available at: http://memri.org/bin/articles.cgi?Page=subjects&Area=jihad&ID=SP99305 (accessed March 27, 2006).
7 Stephen Ulph, "A Guide to Jihad on the Web," *Jamestown Foundation Terrorism Monitor* 2 (7) (March 31, 2005).
8 See "Bin Laden Allegedly Planned Turkey Attack," *Associated Press*, December 17, 2003 for a good discussion of al-Qaida's role in helping the cell plan and coordinate the attack.
9 Karl Vick, "Al-Qaida's Hand in Istanbul Plot," *Washington Post*, February 13, 2007, p. AO1.
10 This essay is widely available in English on multiple Jihadist bulletin boards. It is part of a larger compendium entitled *Edu-caution: Muslim Children and the Schools of the Tawghut*.

2 Doctrine and schools

1 Abu Muhammad al-Maqdisi, *Millat Ibrahim*. Available at: www.tawhed.ws/r?i=1.
2 Ayman al-Zawahiri, *Al-Wala wal-Bara*. Available at: www.tawhed.ws/r?i=523.
3 Available at: http://rapidshare.de/files/14101722/Shaykh_Faisal_-_al-Wala_wal-Bara.mp3.html.
4 Abu Umar al-Baghdadi, "Fourth Speech," April 17, 2007.
5 For further reading about the life of Hasan al-Banna, see Brynjar Lia's *The Society of the Muslim Brothers in Egypt: The Rise of an Islamic Mass Movement*. Reading:

Garnet, 1998; and Richard P. Mitchell's *The Society of the Muslim Brothers*. London: Oxford University Press, 1969.

6 Mahmud Sadiq, *Al-Watan al-'Arabi*, March 12, 1999, pp. 4–7. Translated by US Government Open Source Center.

7 Sayyid Qutb's most famous and expansive work, *In the Shade of the Quran*, spans the whole of the text of the Quran. The *tafsir*, or interpretation, was written and partly rewritten over a period of 15 years, most of which Qutb spent in Eygptian prisons, during the 1950s and 1960s.

8 "The Counterfeit Salafis: Deviation of the Counterfeit Salafis," in *Methodology of Ahlul Sunnah L/al Jama'a*. Dar Alargam, 2004.

9 For writings by a variety of "Establishment Salafist" scholars, see: http://salafidawah. tripod.com/.

10 Shaikh Bin Baz's official webpage is: www.binbaz.org.sa/. Other biographical information, with translations of his work, can be found at: http://www.allaahuakbar.net/ scholars/ibn_baaz/index.htm.

11 The issuing of this *fatwa* still generates significant discussion among Salafists of all stripes. See the thread hosted by the Islamic Awakening Salafist forum: http://forums. islamicawakening.com/showthread.php?p=17513.

12 See Douglas Jehl, "Sheik Abdelaziz bin Baz, Senior Saudi Cleric and Royal Ally," *New York Times*, May 14, 1999.

13 Shaikh Uthaymin's official webpage is: http://www.ibnothaimeen.com/index.shtml.

14 A sample of this debate can be found on the Salafist website Islamic Awakening at: http://forums.islamicawakening.com/showthread.php?t=491.

15 Madkhali's writings are available on a website dedicated to him: http://www.rabee.net.

16 A number of Madkhali's works are available in translation online at: http://www. salafitalk.net/st/printthread.cfm?Forum=6&Topic=3663.

17 *Summary of the Deviation of the Madkhalee 'Salafiyyah'*. At-Tibyan Publications. Available at: http://almuwahideen.blogspot.com/.

18 His students include: Shaikh Hamdi Abdul-Majeed, Shaikh Muhammad 'Eed Abbaasi, Dr. Umar Sulayman al-Ashqar, Shaikh Muhammad Ibrahim Shaqrah, Shaikh Muqbil ibn Haadi al-Waadi'i, Shaikh Ali Khushshaan, Shaikh Muhammad Bin Jameel Zainoo, Shaikh Abdur-Rahmaan Abdus-Samad, Shaikh Ali Hassan Abdul-Hameed al-Halabi, Shaikh Saleem al-Hilaali, and Shaikh Abdur-Rahman Abdul-Khaaliq.

19 http://tawhed.ws/r?i=150.

20 From the now-defunct Tibyan Publications website.

21 "A Decisive Refutation of www.salafipublications.com," www.geocities.com/ sprefutations/, March 13, 2001.

22 For more on al-Tabtaba'i, see N. Janardhan, "Kuwait Wakes up to the Militant Force of Islam," *Jamestown Foundation Terrorism Monitor* 3 (9) (May 2005).

23 US State Department, "Country Reports on Human Rights Practices, 2005." Released by the Bureau of Democracy, Human Rights, and Labor, March 8, 2006.

24 Moshari Alfaidi, "Sami al-Mutairi: Murderer of an American near Camp Doha," *al-Sharq al-Awsat*, February 1, 2005.

25 *Ibid.*

26 Nazim Fethi on Magharebia, December 22, 2006. The Magharebia website— www.magharebia.com—is sponsored by the United States Africa Command, the military command responsible for supporting and enhancing US efforts to promote stability, cooperation and prosperity in the region.

27 http://www.magharebia.com/cocoon/awi/xhtml1/en_GB/features/awi/reportage/2006/ 12/22/reportage-01.

28 Usama Bin Laden recommended this book by Muhammad Qutb in his January 4, 2004 videotaped statement. The book is available at: http://www.tawhed.ws/files/1587.zip.

29 Muhammad Abdallah Nab, "Disagreements between Jamis, Sururis in Saudi Arabia," *Ilaf*, May 20, 2005.

30 Surur supporters do not like to be in the public eye and prefer to work behind the scenes. A source requesting anonymity informed *Al-Sharq al-Awsat* in an article that "Al-Shaikh Surur has not given a single interview to the media for more than 15 years." The source stated that Surur supporters maintained such strict secrecy with the media that not one picture of the leader has ever appeared in any newspaper (Muhammad al-Shafi'i, "Al-Surur Organizational Leader Returns to Jordan," *Al-Sharq al-Awsat*, November 15, 2004, p. 6).

31 Mishari al-Dhayidi, "Muhammad Surur Left Syria after Brotherhood's Catastrophe, Settled, Taught in Baridah, Mixed Brotherhood Movement with Qutb's Revolutionariness, Ibn-Taymiyah's Salafism," *al-Sharq al-Awsat*, October 28, 2004, p. 4.

32 Muhammad al-Shafi'i, "Al-Surur Organizational Leader Returns to Jordan," *Al-Sharq al-Awsat*, November 15, 2004, p. 6.

33 George W. Bush, "Georgia Welcomes President Bush," *Atlanta Marriott Marquis*, January 31, 2002.

34 Ibn Taymiyyah, *Majmu' Fatawa Ibn Taimiyah*. Was available on the now-defunct www.islam.org.au.

35 Mirathul Anbia, "Conditions of Tawheed." Available at: http://www.unifiedummah.com/sections/books/books/MiraathulAnbiya(InheritanceOfTheProphets)_Part1-2_The-BookofTawheed(English).pdf.

36 Jihadists typically point to: Saheeh al-Bukhari, Chapter 24: The Book of Zakaat, Book 1, *Hadith* no. 1399 as proof.

37 Nasir bin Hamad al-Fahd, "Whoever Does Not Do *Takfir* of the Disbeliever is a Disbeliever." Available at: http://www.tawhed.ws/.

38 Yousef al-Ayiri in a book of his works that was posthumously compiled by Shawq Al-Mujahid entitled *The Orator of the Peninsula: The Great Yusuf Al-Ayiri, in the Age of Humiliation and Insult*. August 2003.

39 "This is our *Aqidah*." Available at: http://millatibraheem.muslimpad.com/2007/01/07/this-is-our-aqidah/.

40 For useful discussion of the Jihad concept, see David Cook's *Understanding Jihad*. Los Angeles: University of California Press, 2005; and Richard Bonney's *Jihad: From Qur'an to Bin Laden*. New York Palgrave Macmillan, 2004.

41 Abdullah Azzam, *Al-Jihaad: Linguistically and Legally*. Available in translation at: http://www.islamicawakening.com/viewarticle.php?articleID=685&.

42 For a comprehensive collection of Abdullah Azzam's works, see: www.tawhed.ws/a?i=477.

43 Fath al-Qadeer by Ibn Humaam, 5/187.

44 al-Kasaani said in al-Bada'i', 9/4299.

45 Hashiya al-'Adawi/as-Sa'edi, 2/2, and ash-Sharh as-Sagheer/Aqrab al-Masaalik by ad-Dardeer, 2/267.

46 al-Bajawari / Ibnul-Qasim, 2/261.

47 Ibn Hajr said in al-Fath, 6/2.

48 See Umdatul-Fiqh and Muntahal-Iraadaat, 1/302.

49 Yusuf al-Ayiri, *The Ruling on Jihad and its Divisions*. Available at: http://www.tawhed.ws/r?i=3660.

3 Ideologues

1 Although these sessions used to be held primarily in the form of written dialogue, they are increasingly moving to real-time audio conversations using the latest internet chat technology, like Paltalk.

2 Shaikh Khudair's biography and comprehensive list of works in Arabic are available at: www.tawhed.ws/c?i=57.

3 As recounted by the web forum user "Brother_Mujahid," a senior member at the

Islamic Awakenings forum in a posting entitled, "Shaykh Hamoud's Opinion of Abu Basir and Abu Qatadah," made on February 19, 2007. Brother_Mujahid joined the forum in May 2004. Bracketed clarifications of Arabic terms are my own, not Khudair's.

4 By deferring to his teacher, Shaikh Uqla as-Shuaybi, Khudair also shows that there is more to being part of the Jihadist elite than simply holding the right beliefs. Unlike Shia Islam, where there is a clearly established religious hierarchy structure, Sunni Muslims, including Jihadists, rely on a more informal authority structure. The problem is that such a structure is less useful for most Jihadist clerics, particularly with regards to recruitment and mobilization. Therefore, Jihadist clerics have worked diligently over the past two decades to clarify a pecking order. Khudair's public deference to his teacher in determining the Jihadist credentials of other clerics perfectly illustrates this point.

5 This has been well articulated in Thomas Hegghammer's *Saudi Islamist Backgrounder.* International Crisis Group Report, September 2004.

6 "Interview with Abu-Muhammad al-Maqdisi," *Al-Jazirah*, July 5, 2005. (Date and place of the interview were not given.)

7 Safar al-Hawali's official English website is at: http://www.alhawali.com/en/.

8 *The True Promise, the Bogus Promise*, is available in English and Arabic on the internet.

9 The Egyptian government at this time viewed al-Hawali as politically dangerous, given the increased availability of his cassettes in Egyptian markets.

10 "Message from Usama Bin-Muhammad Bin Laden to His Muslim Brothers in the Whole World and Especially in the Arabian Peninsula: Declaration of Jihad against the Americans Occupying the Land of the Two Holy Mosques; Expel the Heretics from the Arabian Peninsula," September 1996.

11 These publications are all currently available on the Arabic pages of www.islamtoday. net.

12 See his letter, "From behind Bars." Available at: http://www.geocities.com/saudhouse_ p/letter2.htm.

13 Other early reformist clerics included Nasir al-Omar, the prominent Saudi cleric; Sulayman al-Rushudi, a lawyer, former judge and co-founder of the Committee for the Defense of Legitimate Rights (CDLR); Dr. Sa'ud Mukhtar al-Hashimi, a professor at the King Abd-al-Aziz University; Abd-al-Aziz Bin-Sulayman al-Khurayji, a physician and businessman; Abd-al-Rahman al-Shumayri, a professor at Umm al-Qura University; Musa Bin-Muhammad al-Qarni, a professor of Islamic Law; Al-Sharif Sayf-al-Din Al Ghalib, a private Saudi businessman; Isam Bin-Hasan Basrawi, a Saudi lawyer; Shaikh 'Abd-al-'Aziz al-Qasim, who worked as a judge before being dismissed and arrested twice; Shaikh Salih al-Jarbu' who was a prominent imam at a mosque in Riyadh; Shaikh 'Uthman al-Huwayl, who was a prominent preacher in Riyadh and al-Ahsa; Abd-al-Aziz al-Umayri, who was a senior deputy to Salman al-Awdah's office, where he staged a sit-in until he was arrested and put in jail; Shaikh Khalid al-Rashid; Shaikh Jasir al-Qahtani; and Shaikh Dr. Sa'id al-Ghamidi.

14 Al-Firdaws English. Posted June 2, 2007, by Salafi_Jihaadi, moderator.

15 Thomas Hegghammer and Stephane Lacroix have written one of the most authoritative accounts of Juhayman al-Utaybi's life and thought in their article "Rejectionist Islamism in Saudi Arabia: The Story of Juhayman al-Utaybi Revisited." *International Journal of Middle East Studies*, 39, 1 (2007).

16 Hegghammer and Lacroix obtain remarkable insights from direct interviews with one of Juhayman's closest aids, Nasir al-Huzaymi.

17 Hammoud bin Uqla as-Shuaybi's followers host a website dedicated to his writings and teachings at: http://saaid.net/Warathah/hmood/.

18 Available, for instance, at: http://www.at-tawheed.com/forums/showthread.php?t=4078.

19 "The Day of Buraida—The Day of Good News; The Huge Success of the Second

Sit-in Protest." Communique No. 31 of the Committee for the Defense of Legitimate Rights of Saudi Arabia (CDLR), 31 March 1995.

20 *Fatwa on the Sharia Implementation of the Taliban Government in Afghanistan by His Excellency*, November 29, 2000.

21 http://www.ummah.net/forum/showthread.php?t=128660.

22 For a comprehensive list of Nasr al-Fahd's works in Arabic, see: www.almaqdese.net/a?i=12.

23 Some of Fahd's more popular (and militant) works include: *Letter from the Imprisoned Shaykh, Da'wah in the West, Clarification on the Apostasy of Those who Assist the Americans*, parts one and two (*At-Tibyaan Fee Kufri Man A'aan Al-Amrikaan*), *Speaking with Falsehood is Greater (in Evil) than Keeping Silent Regarding the Truth* (Taken from the book *At-Tankil bi ma fi Bayan Al-Muthaqafin min Al-Abaatil*), *The Use of Weapons of Mass Destruction, The Dangers of the Naturalization [of the Relations with Israel] for Muslims, Condemning the Lies of the Intellectuals, The Vanguard of Condemnation, Helping the Mujahidin When They Are Sought*, and a variety of other articles on the need to wage violent Jihad against Jews and Christians.

24 A comprehensive list of Shaikh al-Ulwan's works in Arabic is available at: www.tawhed.ws/c?i=54.

25 He also gave lessons in the classification and terminology of *Hadith* (*Mustalah al-Hadith*) as well as their defects (*Ilal*), jurisprudence (*Fiqh*), grammar and *Tafsir*. And from the lessons, which he gave from the books of belief (*Aqidah*), were: "Al-'Aqidah at-Tadmuriyyah," "Al-Aqidah al-Haawiyyah," and "Al-Aqidah al-Wasitiyyah" by Shaikh al-Islam Ibn Taymiyya; "Kitab at-Tawhid" by Muhammad Ibn Abd al-Wahab; "As-Sharia" by al-Ajuri; "As-Sunnah" by Abdullah Ibn Ahmad; "As-Sunnah" by Ibn Nasr; "Al-Ibanah" by Ibn Battah; and "As-Sawaiq" and "An-Nuniya" by Ibn al-Qayyim.

26 Nasr al-Fahd, *The Exposition Regarding the Disbelief of the One that Assists the Americans*. Available at: http://tawhed.ws/a?i=12.

27 "Address from the Shaikhs: Hammoud bin Uqla ash-Shuaibi, Ali al-Khudair and Sulaiman al-Alwaan to the Commander of the Believers (Amir-ul-Mumineen): Muhammad Umar and those Mujahideen with him," January 3, 2002. Available at: http://tawhed.ws/a?=12.

28 http://www.buraydahcity.net/vb/showthread.php?t=75279.

29 For a comprehensive list of Maqdisi's works in Arabic and his official biography, see: www.tawhed.ws/c?i=174.

30 Mshari al-Zaydi, "Abu Mohammed al Maqdisi: al-Zarqawi 'Spiritual Godfather.'" *Al-Sharq al-Awsat*, July 26, 2005.

31 *Ibid*.

32 *Ibid*.

33 Twenty-first issue of *Nidaa'ul Islam*. December–January 1997–1998.

34 Abu Muhammad al-Maqdisi, *Millat Ibrahim*. Available at: http://www.kalamullah.com/Books/MillatIbraheem.pdf.

35 Mary Anne Weaver, "The Short, Violent Life of Abu Musab al-Zarqawi," *Atlantic* 298(1), July/August 2006.

36 Luqman Iskandar, "Calling for Formation of Global Body of Sunni Ulemas, al-Zarqawi's Former Spiritual Guide Criticizes his Deeds in Iraq. Al-Maqdisi: 'I Reject the Killing of Civilians, Shiites in Iraq.'" *Al-Arab al-Yawm*, July 5, 2005, p. 3.

37 Maqdisi interview with Muaffaq Kamal. *Al-Ghadd*, July 5, 2005, p. 3.

38 "Jordanian Authorities Arrest al-Maqdisi Once Again after Trying to Contact Conference." *Al-Quds al-Arabi*, July 7, 2005, p. 8.

39 Nabil Sharaf-al-Din, "Abu-Qutadah, the New Repudiation Leader." *Cairo al-Ahram al-'Arabi*, June 12, 1999, pp. 40–42.

40 Shaikh Abu Qatadah, "Statements of the Scholars Regarding the Replacers of the Shareeah." In his *Limaadhal-Jihaad*. Available at: http://www.almaqdese.net/r?i=4329.

41 *BBC News*, March 23, 2004.

42 *BBC News*, February 26, 2007.
43 A comprehensive collection of Sayyid Imam's early books can be found in Arabic on www.tawhed.ws/a?i=6.
44 Abu Musab al-Suri, *A Call to Global Islamic Resistance*. Available at: http://www.mjotd.com/Library/books.rar.
45 *Ibid.*, p. 1147.
46 Available at: http://www.almasry-alyoum.com/.
47 Jailan Halawi, *al-Ahram Weekly* (English Edition), October 9–15, 2003.
48 Muhammad Shafey, *Asharq Alawsat* (English Edition), December 6, 2007.
49 Camille al-Tawil, "The Two Leaders, Dr. Fadl and Abd-al-Aziz al-Jamal," *al-Hayah*, March 22, 2007.
50 Ayman al-Zawahiri, "Advice of One Concerned," July 5, 2007.
51 Abu Yahya al-Libi video release, September 10, 2007.
52 Muhammad Khalil al-Hakaymah, "Statement about What Has Been Published of the Document Entitled 'Rationalization of Jihad Operations," *al-Fajr Media Center*, November 26, 2007.

4 Strategists

1 Issa bin Awshan recounts this and following incidents in his renowned biography of Yousef al-Ayiri, available on many global Jihadist websites.
2 Thomas Hegghammer and Brynjar Lia, "Jihadi Strategic Studies: The Alleged Al Qaida Policy Study Preceding the Madrid Bombings," *Studies in Conflict and Terrorism*, 27, 5 (September/October 2004), pp. 355–375.
3 Abu Ubayd al-Qurashi, "A Lesson in War," *Majallat al-Ansar*, December 19, 2002, pp. 10–16.
4 Abu Ubayd al-Qurashi, "Strategic Equations," *Majallat al-Ansar*, September 22, 2002, pp. 10–16.
5 *Ibid.*
6 Abu Ubayd al-Qurashi, "Al-Qaida and the Art of War." Posted on Alneda.com, June 13, 2002.
7 Abu Ubayd al-Qurashi, "America's Nightmares," *Majallat al-Ansar*, February 13, 2002, pp. 15–21.
8 Muhammad Khalil al-Hakaymah, *The Myth of Delusion Exposing the American Intelligence*. Originally available on the now-defunct Islamic Renewal Organization website.
9 Abu Bakr Naji, *Management of Savagery*, trans. William McCants. Available at: http://www.tawhed.ws/files/3372.zip.
10 This and subsequent quotes from Abu Ubayd al-Qurashi, "The War of the Ether," *Majallat al-Ansar*, November 20, 2002, pp. 9–15.
11 This and subsequent Abu Yahya al-Libi quotes from his video message, September 10, 2007.
12 See Michael Scheuer, "Al-Qaida's Theological Enforcer," *Terrorism Monitor*, 4, 25 (July 31, 2007), for an in-depth examination of Abu Yahya's recent statements.
13 *Rationalizations on Jihad in Egypt and the World*, serialized in *al-Masry al-Youm*, November–December 2007.
14 See Christopher Boucek, "Extremist Reeducation and Rehabilitation in Saudi Arabia," *Terrorism Monitor* 5 (16) (August 16, 2007).
15 For a more in-depth discussion of these dynamics, see http://ctc.usma.edu/atlas/.
16 Abu Ubayd al-Qurashi, "The Fourth Generation of Wars," *Majallat al-Ansar*, February 28, 2002, pp. 15–21.
17 Abu Ubayd al-Qurashi, "A Sniper: An Overlooked Weapon," *Majallat al-Ansar*, October 22, 2002, pp. 9–14.

18 *Ibid.*
19 Center for Islamic Studies and Research website: http://www.pages4free.bix/image 333.
20 Abu Ubayd al-Qurashi, "The Autumn of Iraqi Fury," *Majallat al-Ansar*, August 24, 2002, pp. 10–16.
21 Abu Ubayd al-Qurashi, "The Illusions of America." *Majallat al-Ansar*, August 10, 2002, pp. 10–14.
22 This and subsequent Atiyatallah quotes from "Slander from the Imperfect Evil is Testimony for the Righteous Heroes," posted on the now-defunct World News Network website. (Note: this is not Lewis Atiyatallah.)
23 Published in *Sawt al-Jihad*, February 2, 2007.
24 Ayman al-Zawahiri's letter to Abu Musab al-Zarqawi, July 9, 2005.
25 Ayman al-Zawahiri's reaction to the French headscarf ban, audio tape released to *al-Arabiya*, February 24, 2004.
26 *Ibid.*
27 *Ibid.*
28 Ayman al-Zawahiri's criticism of US Middle East plans, audio tape released to *al-Arabiya*, June 11, 2004.
29 Ayman al-Zawahiri, *The Emancipation of Mankind and Nations under the Banner of the Koran*, video produced by *as-Sahab*, January 30, 2005.
30 Abu Musab al-Suri, *A Call to Global Islamic Resistance*, published online, December 2004.

5 Propagandists

1 For a detailed description of this period in Banna's life, see Richard Paul Mitchell, *The Society of the Muslim Brothers*. Oxford: Oxford University Press, 1993.
2 See http://sunnah.org/history/Scholars/mashaykh_azhar.htm.
3 Barry Hooker, *Indonesian Islam*. Honolulu: University of Hawaii Press, 2003.
4 Brynjar Lia, *The Society of Muslim Brothers in Egypt*. London: Garnet and Ithaca Press, 1988.
5 Gilles Kepel, *Muslim Extremism in Egypt: The Prophet and Pharaoh*. Berkeley: University of California Press, 1993, p. 106.
6 *Ibid.*
7 Abu-al-Walid reportedly wrote his book while training at al-Qaida's Afghan camp, al-Faruq, in 1994 and signed it with his original name, Mustafa Hamid.
8 Part II of a series of articles by Muhammad al-Shafi'i: "Chatter on the World's Rooftop: Arab Afghans' Theorist Says the Caliph Held Those who Did Not Swear Allegiance to Him to be Infidels, Threatened to Take Women of Pakistani Arabs into Captivity; Abu-al-Walid: The Caliphate Organization Embodies Tragedy of Arab Community in Peshawar," *al-Sharq al-Awsat*, October 25, 2006.
9 Email correspondence with author.
10 Abdullah Azzam, *The Lofty Mountain*, trans. Umm Salamah al-Ansariyyah and Shaheed Suraqah al-Andalusi. UK: Azzam Publications, 2003.
11 Available at: http://darulislam.info.
12 Wadi al-Hage in the April 2001 trial transcript of the United States v. Usama Bin Laden, Day 6.
13 Al-Jazirah. July 1, 2004.
14 Mohammed Hafez, *Why Muslims Rebel: Repression and Resistance in the Islamic World*. Boulder, CO: Lynne Reiner, 2004, p. 132.
15 *Ibid.*
16 The biography that informs much of what follows was posted originally on Suri's home-page, www.fsboa.com/vw in March 2005. That site is currently unavailable and is now

located on al-Qaida's library site, http://tawhed.ws, which was also down at the time of writing (accessed March 30, 2006).

17 Suri's biography, as above.

18 "Fuel to Fire," *al-Ahram Weekly*, 763, October 6–12, 2005. Available at: http://weekly. ahram.org.eg/2005/763/in3.htm.

19 Suri's biography, as above.

20 "Interview with the Imprisoned Shaikh Abu Muhammad al-Maqdesi," *Nidaa'ul Islam*, December–January 1997–1998.

21 "Moroccan-Born Dane Gets Prison Term for Promoting Terrorism," *Agence-France Presse*, April 11, 2007.

22 Abu Hamza al-Masri, *Khawaarij and Jihad*. Birmingham: Maktabah al-Ansar, 2000, p. 90.

23 Peter Bergen, *The Osama Bin Laden I Know: An Oral History*. New York: Simon and Schuster, 2006, p. 184.

24 Suri's biography, as above.

25 Index of Suri's publications prepared on August 11, 2001 in Kabul by Salah Abu Nasr al-Halabi, who died on June 26, 2002.

26 Reposted to: http://alansar.hopto.org/vb/showthread.php?t=4676 (accessed November 15, 2006).

27 Craig Whitlock, "Briton Used Internet as his Bully Pulpit," *Washington Post*, August 8. 2005, p. A01.

28 United States of America vs. Babar Ahmad, Affidavit in Support of Request for Extradition (September 2004). Available at: http://www.usdoj.gov/usao/ct/Documents/AHMAD%20extradition%20affidavit.pdf.

29 The publication's now-defunct website was: http://www.islam.org.au. Some back copies can be retrieved via the internet archive's "Way-Back Machine" at: http://web.archive. org/web/*/http://www.islam.org.au.

30 Muhammad al-Shafi, "Repentant Confessions in Saudi Arabia Reveal Ignorance," *al-Sharq al-Awsat*, January 14, 2004.

31 Pino Buongiorno, "Bin Ladin's Latest Challenges," *Milan Panorama*, September 18, 2003, pp. 40–44.

32 Muhammad al-Shafi, "'Al-Qaida University' for Jihadist Sciences on the Internet," *al-Sharq al-Awsat*, November 20, 2003, p. 4.

33 Available at: http://www.tajdeed.org.uk/forums/showthread.php?s=950fcea4b8ab46 484c72bf7b4ae9dce8&threadid=26840.

34 Muhammad al-Shafi'i, "Fundamentalist Move toward Uniting Their Mouthpieces on the Internet under Cover of What They Call 'Islamic Media Front'," *al-Sharq al-Awsat*, October 6, 2004, p. 5.

35 Posted on www.mohajroon.com/vb on August 21, 2006.

36 "Combatant Status Review Tribunal Hearing for ISN #10024." Transcript avaiable on http://www.defenselink.mil/.

37 Raffi Khatchadourian, "The Making of an Al Qaida Homegrown," *New Yorker* January 22, 2007.

38 Carmen L. Gleason, "Security Forces, Citizens Decrease Violence in Iraq," *American Forces Press Service*, October 28, 2007.

39 Posted by al-Fajr Media at: http://www.almeer.net/vb, June 21, 2006.

6 Al-Qaida in Saudi Arabia

1 Nicholas Rufford and Nick Fielding, "Saudi Briton Was Killed by al-Qaida," *Sunday Times*, June 30, 2002.

2 Brian Whitaker, "Saudis Admit to al-Qaida Threat as 100 Are Held," *Guardian*, November 21, 2002.

3 In one raid of a suspected al-Qaida safe-house, police in the al-Shifa district of Riyadh found a number of armed operatives, all veterans of Afghanistan. Police were able to shoot and capture one operative, Mohammad al-Sahim, who would later be praised in al-Qaida's official Saudi magazine, *Sawt al-Jihad*.

4 Javid Hassan, "Shooting Incidents Not Targeted at BAE," *Jedda Arab News* February 23, 2003.

5 Mashari al-Dhayidi. "So as Not to Drink the Delusion: The US Consulate Operation," *al-Sharq al-Awsat*, December 7, 2004, p. 11.

6 It took until January 2004 for Saudi authorities to acknowledge officially that al-Qaida-run training camps littered the Saudi desert. The camps were set up to train militants to use weapons and prepare for terror operations, an official told the Associated Press on condition of anonymity. He did not specify the number of camps or say when they were found. He did, however, confirm that Dandani and Ayiri had commanded the camps.

7 Evan Kohlman, *Al-Qaida's Committee in Saudi Arabia 2002–2003*. NEFA Foundation, 2005. Available at: http://www.nefafoundation.org/miscellaneous/qaidasaudi02-03.pdf.

8 Global Islamic Media website, http://groups.yahoo.com/group/globalislamicmedia, 38-minute production *The Martyrs of the Confrontations in Bilad al-Haramayn*, produced by as-Sahab, December 5, 2003.

9 Attorney-General Ashcroft in news conference with FBI Director Mueller, January 17, 2002.

10 "The East Riyadh Operation and Our War with the United States and its Agents." Statement issued under the auspices of the Center for Islamic Studies and Research, 2003.

11 "Some 600 Arrested since Riyadh Bombings, Two-Thirds Still in Custody," *Agence France Presse*, October 23, 2003.

12 Ibrahim al-Amir, "Blood-Smeared Letter Signed by Bin Laden found on al-Ayiri's Body," *al-Watan*, June 3, 2003.

13 Saudi Press Agency, June 17, 2003.

14 "Four Demands Preceded al-Faq'asi's Surrender," *al-Hayat*, June 29, 2006.

15 "Terrorist Killed in Jizan on FBI Wanted List," *Arab News*, September 25, 2003.

16 Naji al-Hazimi and Sultan Asiri, "Security Services Raid Two Houses Rented by Sultan al-Qahtani in al-Qiyas and Asir," *al-Watan*, September 26, 2003.

17 "The Who and Why of the Saudi Bomb," *Financial Times*, November 14, 2003.

18 Tarek al-Issawi, "Purported al-Qaida Video Details Preparation, Execution of Riyadh Bombing," *Associated Press*, February 5, 2004.

19 Saudi Press Agency, December 1, 2003.

20 *Mideast Mirror*, November 20, 2003.

21 "Shaikh al-Khalidi Retracts Previous *Fatwa*," Saudi Press Agency, December 14, 2003.

22 "Interior Ministry Source," Saudi Press Agency, March 15, 2004.

23 Robin Gedye, "Blast Destroys Saudi Police HQ," *Daily Telegraph*, April 22, 2004.

24 Kingdom of Saudi Arabia Radio, Riyadh, April 23, 2004.

25 "Al-Qaida Reveals Identity of Second Perpetrator of Sinful Attack on Traffic Department. We Are Willing to Destroy the Cities and Desert Communities to Achieve Our Objectives," *al-Riyad*, July 20, 2004.

26 Layla al-Shayib telephone interview with Sàad al-Faqih, head of the Movement for Islamic Reform in Arabia," al-Jazirah, May 1, 2004.

27 Abd al-Aziz al-Muqrin, "To All Those Who Desire to Wage Jihad in the Arabian Peninsula," *Muaskar al-Battar*, 10 (May 2004).

28 Neil Macfarquhar, "After the Saudi Rampage, Questions and Few Answers," *New York Times*, June 1, 2004.

29 Suleiman Nimr, "Al-Qaida Killers Give Saudi Forces the Slip amid Fears of Worse Bloodshed to Come," *Agence France Presse*, May 31, 2004.

30 Michael Theodoulou and Daniel McGrory, "Disguised Gunmen Try to Free Terror Leader," *The Times*, June 9, 2004.
31 Abdallah al-Urayfaj, "Ukaz Discloses Details: A Tight Ambush Kills al-Muqrin and His Companions in Seconds," *Ukaz* June 20, 2004.
32 Brian Whitaker, "Sacked Sergeant is New al-Qaida Chief in Saudi Arabia," *Guardian*, June 22, 2004.
33 James C. Oberwetter, US Ambassador to Saudi Arabia, and Consul General Gina Abercrombie-Winstanley, on-the-record briefing, Jeddah, Saudi Arabia, December 7, 2004.
34 In April 2006, al-Qaida in Saudi Arabia published a 289-page book entitled *al-Athariyah Letters*, a compilation of Utaybi's writings.
35 Adnan Malik, "Deadly Three-Day Standoff between Saudi Police, Islamic Extremists Ends," *Associated Press*, April 5, 2005.
36 Al-Qaida in the Arabian Peninsula, *Blood that Will Not Be Wasted. A Special Series on the Martyrs of the Arabian Peninsula. The Will of Commander Fahd bin-Farraj al-Juwayr al-Farraj, One of the Leaders of al-Qaida Organization in the Arabian Peninsula*. Posted on the internet by the Global Islamic Media Front on March 16, 2006.

7 Global Jihadism in the UK

1 Kamran Khan, "Al Qaida Arrest in June Opened Valuable Leads," *Washington Post*, August 3, 2004, p. A01.
2 For more on Ramzi Youssef's involvement in the 1993 World Trade Center bomb plot, see the 9/11 Commission Report, Chapter 3, at *http://www.9-11Commission.gov*.
3 "Al-Qaida's Computer Expert," *BBC News*, August 6, 2004.
4 Richard W. Stevenson and Douglas Jehl, "US Opens Effort to Disrupt Plots by Terror Group," *New York Times*, August 5, 2004.
5 Douglas Farah, "Report Says Africans Harbored Al Qaida Terror Assets Hidden in Gem-Buying Spree," *Washington Post*, December 29, 2002, p. A01.
6 "US, London Banks Step up Security," *BBC News*, August 3, 2004.
7 Alan Cowell, "British Court Hears of Qaida Plans for 'Black Day,'" *New York Times*, November 7, 2006.
8 United States District Court Southern District of New York: United States of America v. Usama Bin Laden, S(9) 98 Cr. 1023.
9 See the FBI's "Most Wanted" information at: *http://www.fbi.gov/wanted/terrorists/teralliby.htm*.
10 The *Manchester Manual* is available on the United States Department of Justice website at: *http://www.usdoj.gov/ag/manualpart1_1.pdf*.
11 Richard Reid's indictment is available at: *www.usdoj.gov/ag/reidindictment.pdf*.
12 See United States v. Sajid Badat at: *http://news.findlaw.com/cnn/docs/reid/usbadat 904ind.pdf*.
13 "Profile Omar Saeed Shaikh," *BBC News*, July 16, 2002.
14 Martin Bright and Fareena Alam, "Making of a Martyr: From Pacifism to Jihad," *Guardian*, May 4, 2003.
15 "Real Spooks with New Role after 9/11," *BBC News*, December 4, 2007.
16 "UK Terror Suspect in Court," *BBC News*, September 28, 1998.
17 Abd-al-Latif al-Minawi and Muhammad al-Shafi'i, "Operation Challenge Provokes Sharp Disagreements among Fundamentalist Leaders in London," *al-Sharq al-Awsat*, September 25, 1998, p. 4.
18 *Ibid.*
19 Biographical information for Hani al-Sibai can be found at: *http://www.tawhed.ws/a?i=173*.
20 The al-Maqrizi Centre's website is: *http://www.almaqreze.net/*.

21 Ben Leapman, "Muslim Terror Suspect Allowed to Stay in UK, *Sunday Telegraph*, August 19, 2007.

22 Abd-al-Latif al-Minawi and Muhammad al-Shafi'i, "Operation Challenge Provokes Sharp Disagreements among Fundamentalist Leaders in London," *al-Sharq al-Awsat*, September 25, 1998, p. 4.

23 Peter Ford, "A Radical Vows to Fight Britain's Expulsion Plan," *Christian Science Monitor*, September 13, 2005.

24 For more details about Yassir al-Sirri's involvement with supporting Egyptian Islamism, see: United States of America v. Ahmed Abdel Sattar, Yassir al-Sirri, Lynne Stewart and Mohammad Yousry, April 9, 2002.

25 Ahmad Mussa, "Scotland Yard Arrests Yasir al-Sirri," *al-Ahram*, October 27, 2001, pp. 30–31.

26 *Ibid.*

27 Ahmad Mussa, "Uncovering Escape Attempt by Jihad Leader from Tora Prison: Have Terrorists Become Britain's National Wealth?," *al-Ahram*, November 30, 2002, p. 28.

28 Ahmad Mussa, "Scotland Yard Arrests Yasir al-Sirri," *al-Ahram*, October 27, 2001, pp. 30–31.

29 Muhammad Barakat, "Egyptian Terrorism," *al-Watan al-'Arabi*, January 22, 1999, pp. 4–8.

30 Ahmad Mussa, "Scotland Yard Arrests Yasir al-Sirri," *al-Ahram*, October 27, 2001, pp. 30–31.

31 Sayyid Gharib, "Interview with Abu-Hamzah al-Masri, Leader of the Supporters of the *Sharia* Organization in London," *al-Majallah*, March 21, 1999, pp. 58–64.

32 *Ibid.*

33 Sean O'Neill, "You Can Preach What You Like, But No Bloodshed, MI5 Told Me," *The Times*, January 20, 2006.

34 Sayyid Gharib, "Interview with Abu-Hamzah al-Masri, Leader of the Supporters of the *Sharia* Organization in London," *al-Majallah*, March 21, 1999, pp. 58–64.

35 *Ibid.*

36 *Ibid.*

37 For a good discussion of Abu Hamza's work with the Supporters of Sharia organization, see Quintan Wiktorowicz's *Radical Islam Rising: Muslim Extremism in the West*. Lanham, MD: Rowman and Littlefield, 2005.

38 *Ibid.*

39 Chris Hastings and Jessica Berry, "Bin Ladin Fighters Train in Britain," *Sunday Telegraph*, November 7, 1999.

40 A list of Abu Qatada's written works and his biography can be found at: http://www.almaqdese.net/r?i=3877.

41 Jason Burke and Martin Bright, "Cleric Hits Back over Bomb 'Plot' Claims," *Observer*, December 19, 1999.

42 Gavin Cordon, "Palestinian Refugee on US List Denies Terror Links," *Press Association*, October 19, 2001.

43 "Statement on Stay in Afghanistan of Suspected Terrorist Mzoudi Verified by Visa for Pakistan," *Hamburg Spiegel Online*, October 12, 2002.

44 "Muslim Cleric Denies Terror Link," *BBC News*, October 19, 2001.

45 see *http://www.almaqdese.net/r?i=3877*.

46 A variety of news stories began to break in 2002 referring to Abu Qatada as Usama Bin Laden's "European Ambassador." See, for instance, Magdi Allam, "Usamah's Network Laying Siege to Italy's Mosques," *La Repubblica*, July 9, 2002, pp. 112–113.

47 "UK: 'Senior' Al-Qaida Figure Detained Under Anti-Terror Laws," *BBC News*, October 25, 2002.

48 Alan Cowell, "Threats and Responses: The Investigation; Fugitive Muslim Cleric, an

Outspoken Supporter of Al Qaida, is Arrested in London," *New York Times*, October 26, 2002.

49   Jamal Khashuqji and Muhammad Salah, "'Umar Bakri Tells *al-Hayah*: The Uproar Surrounding the London Conference is a Victory for Muslims," *al-Hayah*, September 5, 1996.

50   *Ibid.*

51   Quintan Wiktorowicz, *Radical Islam Rising: Muslim Extremism in the West*. Lanham, MD: Rowman and Littlefield, 2005.

52   Mahan Abedin, "The Dangers of Silencing Saudi Dissent," *Asia Times*, January 21, 2005.

53   Uriya Shavit, "Al-Qaida's Saudi Origins Islamist Ideology," *Middle East Quarterly*, Fall 2006.

54   For further reading on this episode in Saudi political history, see Mamoun Fandy, *Saudi Arabia and the Politics of Dissent*, New York: St. Martin's Press, 1999.

55   Mahan Abedin interview with Saàd al-Faqih, *Middle East Intelligence Bulletin*, November 2003.

56   See press releases on the matter at the United States Department of Treasury website: *http://www.treasury.gov/press/releases/js2632.htm and js2164.htm.*

57   "Profile: Salahuddin Amin," *BBC News*, April 30, 2007.

58   Jeevan Vasagar, "The Five Who Planned to Bomb UK Targets," *Guardian*, April 30, 2007.

59   Peter Bergen and Paul Cruickshank, "Al Qaida-on-Thames: UK Plotters Connected," *Washington Post*, April 30, 2007.

60   *Ibid.*

61   *Ibid.*

62   Josh Meyer, "Quiet Investigation Centers on Al Qaida Aide in New York," *New York Times*, September 3, 2004.

63   *Ibid.*

64   Anne Barnard, "Call to Fight," *Boston Globe*, November 2, 2001.

65   Elaine Sciolino and Stephen Grey, "British Terror Trial Traces a Path to Militant Islam," *New York Times*, November 26, 2006.

66   *Ibid.*

67   Duncan Gardham, "Fertiliser Bombers Linked to 7/7 Attacks," *Daily Telegraph*, January 5, 2007.

68   Fred Sherwin, "Target of RCMP Raid Claims His Family is Innocent," *Orleans Online* (*Ottawa*), March 30, 2004.

69   "Momin Khawaja," CBC Television, January 12, 2005.

70   James Tapsfield, "Security Sources Dismiss Claims of Suspects' Family," *Scotsman*, March 31, 2004.

71   "Momin Khawaja," CBC Television, January 12, 2005.

72   Elaine Sciolino and Stephen Grey, "British Terror Trial Traces a Path to Militant Islam," *New York Times*, November 26, 2006.

73   Gordon Corera, "Analysis: MI5 and the Bomber," *BBC News*, April 30, 2007.

74   As quoted in Shiv Malik's "My Brother the Bomber," *London Prospect*, June 1, 2007.

75   *Ibid.*

76   Massoud Ansari, "British Afghan Hunted as the Link between Tube Bombers and Al-Qaida," *Sunday Telegraph*, July 9, 2006.

77   "Report of the Official Account of the Bombings in London on 7th July 2005," House of Commons, May 11, 2006.

78   "British Bomber Video Text in Full," *BBC News*, September 1, 2005.

79   "Report of the Official Account of the Bombings in London on 7th July 2005." House of Commons, May 11, 2006.

80   "MI5 Tracking 'Thirty Terror Plots,'" *BBC News*, September 10, 2006.

8 Toward a strategy

1 Sun Tzu, *The Art of War*, trans. Lionel Giles: El Paso, TX: Norte Press, 2005, ch. 3.
2 "The Sources of Soviet Conduct," *Foreign Affairs*, 25, July 1947.
3 Dan Ephron, "Smart, Skilled, Shut Out: Intel Agencies Are Desperate for Arabic Speakers. So Why Do They Reject Some of the Best and Brightest?," *Newsweek*, June 26, 2006.
4 Dan Eggen, "FBI Agents Still Lacking Arabic Skills. 33 of 12,000 Have Some Proficiency," *Washington Post*, October 11, 2006.
5 See Jeffrey Stein, "Democrats' New Intelligence Chairman Needs a Crash Course on al Qaida," www.CQ.com, and "Can You Tell the Difference between a Sunni and Shia?," *New York Times*, October 17, 2006.
6 European policy officials are currently facing pressures of political correctness regarding the nature of Islam. See Cal Thomas, "Charting Disloyal Tides," *Washington Times*, December 12, 2006.
7 See *http://islamic.gsfc.nasa.gov/masjids.html* (accessed December 18, 2006).
8 Robert Greene, *The 33 Strategies of War*. New York: Penguin Press, 2006.
9 Gibbon, *The History of the Decline and Fall of the Roman Empire*. New York: J. and J. Harper: 1831 (5th US from the last London edn), III, p. 346. Kennan, writing as "X", "The Sources of Soviet Conduct," *Foreign Affairs*, 25, July 1947.
10 Issa Ibn-Sad Ibn-Muhammad al-Awshan, *39 Ways to Serve and Participate in Jihad*, available at: *www.tawhed.ws/c?i=57*.

Index